2

PATHWAYS

SECOND
EDITION

Listening, Speaking, and Critical Thinking

BECKY TARVER CHASE

**NATIONAL
GEOGRAPHIC**
L E A R N I N G

Australia • Brazil • Mexico • Singapore • United Kingdom • United States

NATIONAL GEOGRAPHIC
L E A R N I N G

Pathways 2: Listening, Speaking, and Critical Thinking, 2nd Edition

Becky Tarver Chase

Publisher: Sherrise Roehr

Executive Editor: Laura Le Dréan

Managing Editor: Jennifer Monaghan

Senior Development Editor:
Mary Whittemore

Associate Development Editors:
Lisl Bove and Jennifer Williams-Rapa

Director of Global and U.S. Marketing: Ian Martin

Product Marketing Manager: Tracy Bailie

Media Research: Leila Hishmeh

Senior Director, Production: Michael Burggren

Manager, Production: Daisy Sosa

Content Project Manager: Mark Rzeszutek

Senior Digital Product Manager: Scott Rule

Manufacturing Planner: Mary Beth Hennebury

Interior and Cover Design: Brenda Carmichael

Art Director: Brenda Carmichael

Composition: MPS North America LLC

Cover photo: A road winds through the Dades Gorge and into the valley, Boumalne Dades, Morocco. ©Angiolo Manetti

For product information and technology assistance, contact us at
Cengage Learning Customer & Sales Support, cengage.com/contact

For permission to use material from this text or product,
submit all requests online at **cengage.com/permissions**
Further permissions questions can be emailed to
permissionrequest@cengage.com

Student Edition: 978-1-337-40772-4
SE + Online Workbook: 978-1-337-56252-2

National Geographic Learning
20 Channel Center Street
Boston, MA 02210
USA

National Geographic Learning, a Cengage Learning Company, has a mission to bring the world to the classroom and the classroom to life. With our English language programs, students learn about their world by experiencing it. Through our partnerships with National Geographic and TED Talks, they develop the language and skills they need to be successful global citizens and leaders.

Locate your local office at **international.cengage.com/region**

Visit National Geographic Learning online at **NGL.Cengage.com/ELT**
Visit our corporate website at **www.cengage.com**

Printed in China

Print Number: 03   Print Year: 2018

Contents

Scope and Sequence

Speaking & Presentation	Vocabulary	Grammar & Pronunciation	Critical Thinking
• Keeping a Conversation Going • Practicing Your Presentation **Lesson Task** Presenting Healthy Habits **Final Task** Participating in a Discussion about Health	Understanding Meaning from Context	• Expressions of Frequency • Final -s sounds	**Focus** Interpreting Visuals Analyzing, Applying, Organizing Ideas, Personalizing, Predicting, Prior Knowledge, Reflecting
• Giving Reasons • Making Eye Contact **Lesson Task** Discussing Self-Driving Cars **Final Task** Presenting a New Technology Product	Using Collocations	• Action and Nonaction Verbs • Stressed Content Words	**Focus** Synthesizing Analyzing, Brainstorming, Evaluating, Interpreting a Bar Graph, Organizing Ideas, Personalizing, Prior Knowledge, Reflecting
• Asking for and Giving Clarification • Using Good Posture **Lesson Task** Exchanging Information about Cowboys **Final Task** Presenting a Kind of Music	Keeping a Vocabulary Journal	• The Past Continuous • Reduced Function Words	**Focus** Activating Prior Knowledge Analyzing, Brainstorming, Making Inferences, Organizing Ideas, Personalizing, Reflecting
• Asking for and Giving Opinions • Speaking at the Right Volume **Lesson Task** Presenting a Clean Water Device **Final Task** Role-Playing a Meeting	Recognizing Suffixes	• Active and Passive Voice • Suffixes and Syllable Stress	**Focus** Prioritizing Analyzing, Applying, Evaluating, Interpreting a Map, Organizing Ideas, Personalizing, Predicting, Prior Knowledge
• Making Suggestions • Pausing to Check Understanding **Lesson Task** Discussing Problems and Solutions **Final Task** Planning a Presentation about the Human Brain	Using Context Clues	• Infinitives after Verbs • Linking	**Focus** Identifying Solutions Analyzing, Applying, Evaluating, Organizing Ideas, Personalizing, Predicting, Reflecting

Scope and Sequence

Speaking & Presentation	Vocabulary	Grammar & Pronunciation	Critical Thinking
• Interrupting and Returning to a Topic • Starting Strong **Lesson Task** Participating in a Group Discussion **Final Task** Presenting a Marketing Plan	Recognizing Parts of Speech	• The Real Conditional: Present and Future • Intonation: Finished and Unfinished Sentences	**Focus** Evaluating Analyzing, Brainstorming, Evaluating, Organizing Ideas, Personalizing, Predicting, Prior Knowledge
• Using Transitions • Speaking at the Right Pace **Lesson Task** Interviewing a Partner about an Experience **Final Task** Giving a Presentation about a Natural Disaster	Using *Affect* and *Effect*	• Gerunds as Subjects and Objects • Syllable Number and Syllable Stress Review	**Focus** Predicting Exam Questions Analyzing, Applying, Evaluating, Interpreting a Diagram, Interpreting a Map, Making Inferences, Organizing Ideas, Prior Knowledge, Reflecting
• Summarizing • Using Index Cards **Lesson Task** Presenting Ancient Artifacts **Final Task** Giving a Presentation about a Historical Site	Using Antonyms	• The Passive Voice with the Past • Question Intonation	**Focus** Applying Knowledge Analyzing, Applying, Brainstorming, Evaluating, Making Inferences, Organizing Ideas, Prior Knowledge, Reflecting
• Talking about Causes and Effects • Timing Your Presentation **Lesson Task** Presenting a Life Lesson **Final Task** Presenting a Research Proposal	Identifying the Correct Definition	• Phrasal Verbs • Stress in Multi-Syllable Words	**Focus** Personalizing Analyzing, Organizing Ideas, Prior Knowledge
• Rephrasing • Thinking about Your Audience **Lesson Task** Interpreting Quotations **Final Task** Presenting a New Product	Recognizing Adjectives and Adverbs	• The Present Perfect and Signal Words • Infinitives to Show Purpose • Thought Groups	**Focus** Interpreting Data Analyzing, Brainstorming, Interpreting Quotations, Organizing Ideas, Personalizing, Prior Knowledge, Ranking, Reflecting

Pathways Listening, Speaking, and Critical Thinking, Second Edition

uses compelling National Geographic stories, photos, video, and infographics to bring the world to the classroom. Authentic, relevant content and carefully sequenced lessons engage learners while equipping them with the skills needed for academic success.

Explore the Theme provides a visual introduction to the unit, engaging learners academically and encouraging them to share ideas about the unit theme.

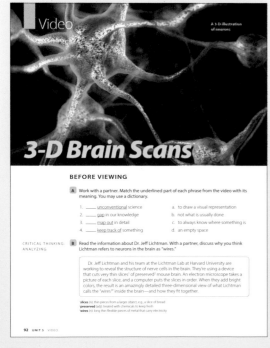

C ▶ 3.18 Listen to the conversation again. Which of these points do the speakers make? Choose Y for *Yes* or N for *No* for each statement.   LISTENING FOR DETAILS

1. Sartore is publishing more photos now than he used to.   Y   N
2. Sartore's photographic techniques require natural light.   Y   N
3. Sartore can't possibly photograph every animal species.   Y   N
4. Sartore's photo of a bird helped wildlife groups get more money from the government.   Y   N

NEW Integrated listening and speaking activities help **prepare students for standardized tests** such as IELTS and TOEFL.

UPDATED *Video* sections use relevant National Geographic **video clips** to give learners another perspective on the unit theme and further practice of listening and critical thinking skills.

Listening Skills

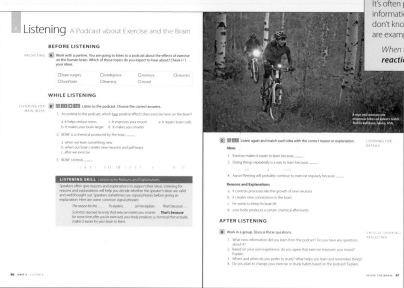

NEW *Vocabulary Skills* help students develop essential word building tools such as understanding collocations, word forms, and connotation.

Listening passages incorporate a variety of listening types such as podcasts, lectures, interviews, and conversations.

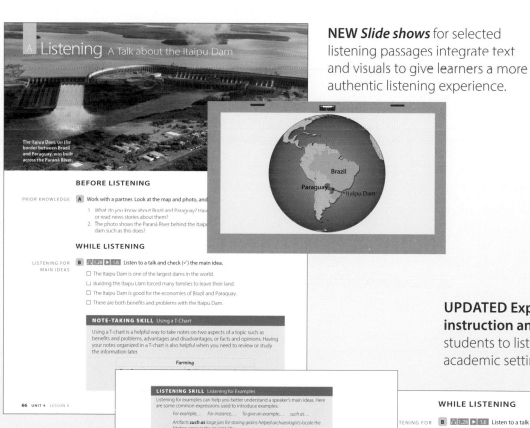

NEW *Slide shows* for selected listening passages integrate text and visuals to give learners a more authentic listening experience.

UPDATED Explicit listening skill instruction and practice prepares students to listen and take notes in academic settings.

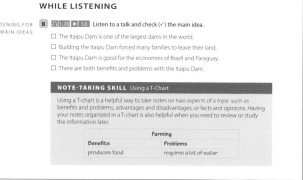

WHILE LISTENING

LISTENING FOR MAIN IDEAS **B** 🎧 1.28 ▶ 1.6 **Listen to a talk and check (✓) the main idea.**

☐ The Itaipu Dam is one of the largest dams in the world.

☐ Building the Itaipu Dam forced many families to leave their land.

☐ The Itaipu Dam is good for the economies of Brazil and Paraguay.

☐ There are both benefits and problems with the Itaipu Dam.

NOTE-TAKING SKILL Using a T-Chart

Using a T-chart is a helpful way to take notes on two aspects of a topic such as benefits and problems, advantages and disadvantages, or facts and opinions. Having your notes organized in a T-chart is also helpful when you need to review or study the information later.

Farming	
Benefits	**Problems**
produces food	requires a lot of water

Speaking lessons guide learners from controlled practice to a final speaking task while reinforcing speaking skills, grammar for speaking, and key pronunciation points.

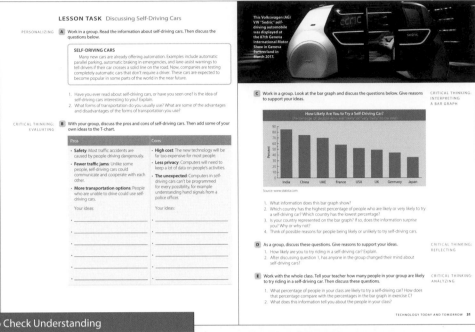

PRESENTATION SKILL Pausing to Check Understanding

When you present ideas, it's important to check to make sure your audience understands you. You can do this by pausing occasionally and looking at your audience. If they look confused, ask them if they need you to repeat any information or give clarification. Stop occasionally and ask your audience if they have any questions. Here are some questions you can ask:

Are there any questions at this point?   *Is there anything that needs clarification?*

Presentation skills such as starting strong, using specific details, making eye contact, pausing, and summarizing, help learners develop confidence and fluency in communicating ideas.

A **Final Task** allows learners to consolidate their understanding of content, language and skills as they collaborate on an academic presentation.

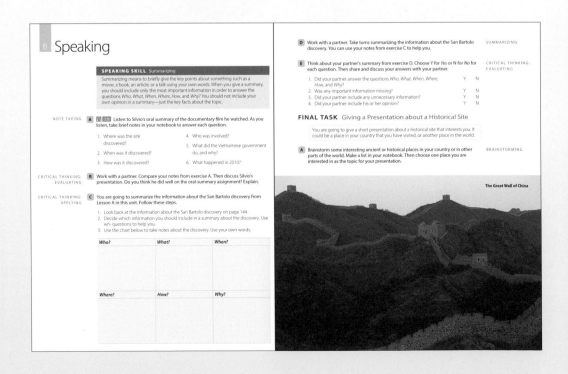

HEALTHY LIVES 1

A woman runs up stadium stairs.

THINK AND DISCUSS

1 What is the woman in the photo doing? Why do you think she's doing this?

2 Do you consider yourself healthy? Why or why not?

Look at the photos and read the information. Then discuss these questions.

1. Which Tip(s) for Living a Long, Healthy Life is the person or people in each photo practicing?

2. Which of these tips do you practice now? Which tip(s) do you want to start practicing?

3. What are some other things people can do to live long, healthy lives?

4. Would you like to live to be 100 years old or older? Why or why not?

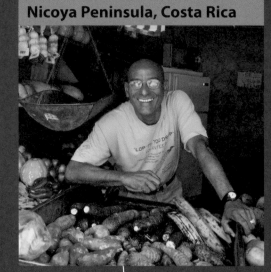

Nicoya Peninsula, Costa Rica

◀ A man sells fresh fruits and vegetables in Nicoya, Guanacaste, Costa Rica.

LIVING A LONG, HEALTHY LIFE

TIPS FOR LIVING A LONG, HEALTHY LIFE

This map shows some places around the world where an unusually high percentage of the population is 100 years old or older. The people in these places share some healthy lifestyle habits such as eating well and getting daily exercise. Here are some tips that can help you live a long, healthy life, too.

- Eat a healthy diet that includes a lot of fruits and vegetables.
- Exercise for at least 30 minutes a day, five days a week.
- Get enough sleep. Try to sleep at least seven hours a night.
- Spend time with friends and family.
- Think positive and be grateful for the people and things in your life that make you happy.
- Manage stress. Find ways to relax and have fun.
- Don't smoke.

Sardinia, Italy

Elvira Ibba and Dario Loi have a lively conversation in Sardinia, Italy.

Okinawa, Japan

An 87-year-old fisherman shows his muscles, in Okinawa, Japan.

Ikaria, Greece

A 98-year-old man and his wife on Ikaria Island, Greece

A Vocabulary

A woman cooks a healthy meal in Okinawa, Japan.

A Read the information in the T-chart. Notice each word or phrase in **blue** and think about its meaning.

Sardinia, Italy	Okinawa, Japan
• Men **are** as **likely** as women to live to be 100 years old or older.	• People have low rates of cancer and other serious **diseases**.
• Men don't have a lot of **stress** in their lives, and stress can **cause** high blood pressure.[1]	• A positive **attitude** leads to a healthier life.
	• Their **diet** is very healthy. It **consists of** a lot of vegetables.
• Working outdoors **provides** daily exercise.	• Healthy **habits** help **prevent** health problems.

[1] **blood pressure** (n): The force with which your blood flows around your body. Blood pressure can be normal, low, or high.

B 🎧 1.2 Listen to the information. Check (✓) the words and phrases in **blue** in the T-chart as you hear them.

C Write each word or phrase in **blue** from exercise A next to its definition.

1. _____ (n) difficulty in life that makes you worried

2. _____ (phrasal v) is made up of

3. _____ (v) are probably going to

4. _____ (n) things that you do often or regularly

5. _____ (n) illnesses

6. _____ (v) to make something happen

7. _____ (v) gives something or makes it available

8. _____ (v) to stop something from happening

9. _____ (n) the foods you eat regularly

10. _____ (n) a feeling about someone or something

D Complete each sentence with the correct form of a word or phrase from exercise C.

1. In Okinawa, good food and healthy habits may _____ health problems.

2. My father always thinks he's going to get sick, but I have a more positive _____. I tell myself I'm going to stay healthy!

3. My grandmother is 90 and very healthy. I think she _____ to live to 100.

4. Ed has a lot of _____ in his life right now. I think he needs to relax more.

5. A healthy lifestyle _____ good food, regular exercise, plenty of sleep, and time with family and friends.

6. The typical Sardinian _____ includes a lot of fish and fresh vegetables.

7. Eating too many burgers can _____ health problems.

8. Smoking is a very bad _____. You should quit.

9. Today a lot of people in the United States suffer from heart _____. It's a very common illness.

10. Grandchildren can _____ comfort and happiness to their grandparents.

E Work in a group. Discuss these questions.

CRITICAL THINKING: REFLECTING

1. What other cultures do you know of that have a very healthy diet?
2. What are some ways that people can prevent health problems such as heart disease and cancer?
3. Why do you think women are more likely to live to 100 than men?
4. What habits do you think can help you live a long, healthy life?

F Find out how likely you are to live to be 100. Check (✓) *Yes* or *No* for each question. Then work with a partner and take turns asking and answering the questions. Explain your answers. Then look at the information at the bottom of the page.

PERSONALIZING

QUESTIONNAIRE: HOW LIKELY ARE YOU TO LIVE TO BE 100?

	Yes	No
1. Do you have only a little stress in your life?	☐	☐
2. Does your diet include a lot of fruits and vegetables?	☐	☐
3. Do you exercise for 30 minutes a day or more?	☐	☐
4. Has anyone in your family lived to be 90 or older?	☐	☐
5. In general, do you have a positive attitude toward life?	☐	☐

Answer: The more questions you answered with "yes," the more likely you are to live to be 100!

A Listening A Talk about Preventing Heart Disease

BEFORE LISTENING

A 🎧 **1.3** Read the statements and the information below. Then listen to the beginning of a talk by a public health nurse. Choose T for *True* or F for *False*. Correct the false statements.

> **PUBLIC HEALTH NURSES**
>
> The World Health Organization encourages employers to support healthy lifestyles for their employees. Inviting public health nurses to speak at companies is one way of doing this.
>
> 1. Public health nurses take care of one person at a time.   T   F
> 2. Public health nurses take care of whole communities of people.   T   F
> 3. Public health nurses sometimes do their job by visiting companies.   T   F
> 4. Tonight's talk will mostly be about the work of public health nurses.   T   F

PREDICTING **B** Work with a partner. Discuss this question: Which of these topics do you expect to hear about in the talk about preventing heart disease? Check (✓) your ideas.

> ☐ attitude   ☐ diet   ☐ smoking   ☐ stress
> ☐ blood pressure   ☐ exercise   ☐ social life

WHILE LISTENING

CHECKING PREDICTIONS **C** 🎧 **1.4** Listen to the complete talk and check your predictions from exercise B. Which of the topics does the nurse include in her talk?

> **LISTENING SKILL** Listening for Main Ideas
>
> When listening to a talk, you need to be able to identify the main ideas. The main ideas are the speaker's most important ideas, or what the talk is about. Here are some techniques you can use to help you identify main ideas:
>
> • Listen carefully to the beginning of a talk. Most speakers will mention the main idea in their introduction.
> • Listen for repetition. Speakers often repeat key words and phrases to emphasize their main ideas.

D 🎧 1.4 ▶ 1.1 Read the questions below. Then listen again and check (✓) the correct LISTENING FOR
answers for each question.   MAIN IDEAS

1. What advice does the nurse give for preventing heart disease?

   ☐ Get your blood pressure checked.   ☐ Eat a healthy diet.
   ☐ Get enough exercise.   ☐ Quit smoking.
   ☐ Drink a lot of water.   ☐ Read about heart disease.
   ☐ Deal with stress in healthy ways.   ☐ Don't work too much.

2. What does the nurse say are some common causes of heart disease?

   ☐ high blood pressure   ☐ smoking   ☐ living alone   ☐ high blood sugar

E 🎧 1.4 Listen again and choose the correct word or phrase to complete each sentence. LISTENING FOR
   DETAILS

1. According to the nurse, if you have high blood pressure, you might need

   to _____ .

   a. lose some weight   b. get more sleep

2. According to _____, healthy eating habits can keep your weight and your blood
   pressure down.

   a. medical journals   b. government reports

3. To deal with stress, the nurse suggests going for a walk or _____ .

   a. practicing yoga   b. listening to music

AFTER LISTENING

F Work with a partner. Discuss these questions.   CRITICAL THINKING:
   REFLECTING

1. What new information did you learn from the talk?
2. Do you plan to take any of the nurse's advice? Explain.

Boys practice yoga along the
Ganges River in Rishikesh, India.

Speaking

PRONUNCIATION Final -s Sounds

🎧 **1.5** Pronouncing the final -s sound correctly is important in communicating clearly. For most words, an -s or -es ending does not add a syllable to the word.

hour → hours   *like → likes*   *provide → provides*   *habit → habits*

If a word ends in an /s/, /ʃ/, /z/, /ʤ/, or /ʧ/ sound, an -s or -es ending is pronounced /əz/ (or /ɪz/) and adds a syllable to the word.

bus → buses   *wash → washes*   *exercise → exercises*

A 🎧 **1.6** Read the sentences below. Underline the words that end in -s or -es. Write the number of syllables above each word. Then listen and check your answers.

1. Frank <u>exercises </u>every day. He plays sports and lifts weights.
   <small>4</small>

2. There are 16 doctors and 37 nurses at the hospital.

3. I eat pears, peaches, and other kinds of fruit almost every day.

4. Stress causes a lot of health problems.

5. The yoga class begins when the teacher closes the door.

B Work with a partner. Take turns reading the sentences from exercise A. Pay attention to the pronunciation of the underlined words.

GRAMMAR FOR SPEAKING Expressions of Frequency

There are many expressions to talk about frequency. Here are some:

> *once*
> *twice*   +   *a(n) hour / day / week / month / year*
> *three times*

Frequency expressions can come at the beginning or end of a sentence.

> *I exercise **three times a week**.*
> ***Twice a year**, Anita takes a vacation with her family.*

We also use *every* to talk about frequency.

> *every*   +   *hour / day / week / month / year / Monday / six months / five years*
> ***Every Saturday**, we play tennis.*
> *I go to the dentist **every six months**.*

We use questions with *How often . . . ?* to ask about frequency.

> A: ***How often** do you visit your grandparents?*
> B: *Twice a year.*
> A: ***How often** does Michael go to the gym?*
> B: *Three times a week.*

C Work with a partner. Take turns asking and answering these questions. Use expressions of frequency in your answers.

PERSONALIZING

1. How often do we have this class?
2. How often do you see your best friend?
3. How often do you go to the doctor?
4. How often do you exercise?
5. How often do you speak to your parents?

D Work with a partner. Look at the photo and read the information about Dr. Levine's *treadmill desks*. Then discuss the questions that follow.

CRITICAL THINKING: ANALYZING

> Dr. James Levine of the Mayo Clinic says that most people do far too much sitting in the course of their day. He invented the *treadmill desk* so that more people can exercise while they work. In the photo above, an office worker uses a treadmill desk to walk while he works on a computer.

1. What is the man in the photo doing?
2. What effect might this have on his health?
3. How often do you take a break and move around when you are studying or working at a computer?
4. What advice might Dr. Levine give? Write a list of things you think he might tell people. Use expressions of frequency.

Everyone should exercise at least three times a week.

_____

_____

_____

A kayaker paddles on Lake Manapouri, New Zealand.

CRITICAL THINKING:
APPLYING

E Work in a group. Take turns interviewing each other about your exercise routines. Use questions with *How often* and expressions of frequency. Take notes in the chart.

Name	Type of Exercise	Frequency
Alberto	kayaking	once a week/summer

A: *What do you do to stay fit?*
B: *Not much, but I like kayaking.*
C: *Really, how often do you go kayaking?*
B: *About once a week in the summer.*

F With your group, report your findings from exercise E to the class. Use expressions of frequency and pay attention to your pronunciation of words that end in -*s* and -*es*.

> *Alberto doesn't exercise much, but he likes kayaking. He goes about once a week in the summer.*

LESSON TASK Presenting Healthy Habits

A 🎧 **1.7** You are going to give a presentation about your healthy habits. Listen to the example. Check (✓) the four parts of the presentation as you hear them.

1. ☐ An introduction
2. ☐ Information about personal health and exercise habits
3. ☐ Plans for staying healthy in the future
4. ☐ A conclusion and a *thank you* to the audience for listening

B Plan your presentation. Write notes to answer these questions. Remember to include the four parts listed in exercise A.

ORGANIZING IDEAS

1. What do you do every day to stay healthy? _____

2. How often do you exercise? _____

3. What kinds of exercise do you do (e.g., yoga, walking, jogging, and so on)?

   _____

4. How do you plan to stay healthy in the future? _____

> **PRESENTATION SKILL** Practicing Your Presentation
>
> Before giving a presentation, it's important to practice it. This will help you with timing, pronunciation, and confidence. If possible, practice it a few times. Ask a classmate, friend, or family member to listen to your presentation and provide feedback. Practicing in front of a mirror is also helpful.

C Work with a partner. Take turns giving your presentations to each other for practice. Make sure your presentation includes the four parts listed in exercise A.

D Give your presentation to the class.

PRESENTING

People ride bicycles in Stanley Park, Vancouver, Canada.

A honeybee coming
out of the hive

Bee Therapy

BEFORE VIEWING

PERSONALIZING **A** You are going to watch a video about using bees to help people with certain kinds of illnesses. Discuss these questions with a partner.

1. When you are sick, do you turn to modern medicine for help? Explain.
2. Have you ever tried traditional medicine such as acupuncture? Explain.
3. Which kind of medicine works better, modern or traditional? Explain.

B Work with a partner and match each word with its definition. You may use a dictionary. You will hear these words in the video.

1. _____ nerve (n)   a. an unpleasant feeling caused by an injury or illness

2. _____ sting (v)   b. to put a liquid into a person's blood or under the skin with a needle

3. _____ therapy (n)   c. a part of the body that carries messages between the brain and other parts of the body

4. _____ inject (v)   d. to cut into the skin, usually with venom (poison)

5. _____ pain (n)   e. treatment of an illness over time

C Work with a partner. Read about two illnesses. Then discuss these questions: What do you know about these illnesses? Do you know anyone who has them?

PRIOR KNOWLEDGE

> **Illness:** Multiple sclerosis (MS)
>
> **Symptoms:** It affects the nervous system (brain and spinal cord), so people with MS may not be able to walk, or may be in a lot of pain.
>
> **Illness:** Arthritis
>
> **Symptoms:** It affects the joints in the hands, knees, and other parts of the body. It causes pain and is common in older adults.

WHILE VIEWING

D ▶ 1.2 Watch the video. Match each person with the correct information below.

UNDERSTANDING MAIN IDEAS

1. Mr. Chen   2. Hso-rong Chen   3. Mr. Chen's wife

a. _____ had arthritic pain; could not cook

b. _____ has multiple sclerosis; couldn't move for six months

c. _____ bee-sting therapy master; used to be afraid of bees

E ▶ 1.2 Watch the video again and complete the sentences below with the numbers you hear.

UNDERSTANDING DETAILS

1. Every week, Mr. Chen and his assistants treat _____ patients and sacrifice _____ honeybees.

2. After _____ bees, you will look _____ years younger than your contemporaries.

3. Many think it is based on the _____ -year-old practice of acupuncture.

4. After _____ months, Mr. Chen's wife's red blood cell count increased. Her headache disappeared.

5. After _____ months of bee-sting therapy, Hso-rong Chen has seen a dramatic change.

AFTER VIEWING

F Work in a group. Discuss these questions.

CRITICAL THINKING: REFLECTING

1. What information from the video did you find most surprising? Explain.
2. What other kinds of traditional or natural medicine do you know about? What kinds of illnesses do they cure?

Vocabulary

MEANING FROM
CONTEXT

A 🎧 **1.8** Look at the diagram. Then read and listen to the information. Notice each word in **blue** and think about its meaning.

ALLERGIES

What are allergies? If you have an *allergy* to something, you become sick, or have an *allergic reaction*, when you eat, smell, or touch it. Many people are allergic to pollen[1]. The diagram below shows what happens when there is an allergic reaction to pollen.

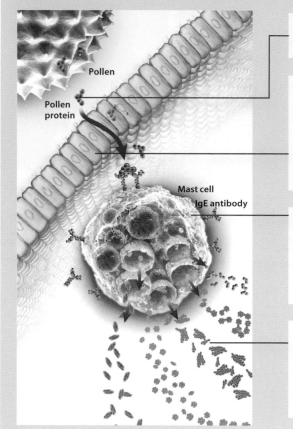

Pollen

Pollen protein

Mast cell
IgE antibody

1. First, pollen enters the body through the nose or mouth.

2. Second, the body's immune system **responds** to the pollen with IgE antibodies[2]. These antibodies **attach** to a mast **cell**. A mast cell is a cell that usually **defends** your body against health problems.

3. The next time the same pollen enters the body, the IgE antibodies "tell" the mast cell. The mast cell "thinks" there is a problem and tries to defend the body.

4. When this **occurs**, the mast cell **produces** substances in the body that cause allergic reactions such as sneezing, itching, and breathing problems.

[1]**pollen** (n): a powder produced by flowers to fertilize other flowers
[2]**antibodies** (n): substances your body produces to fight disease

B Write each word in **blue** from exercise A next to its definition.

1. _____ (n) the smallest part of an animal or plant

2. _____ (v) to join or connect to something

3. _____ (v) makes or creates

4. _____ (v) reacts by doing something

5. _____ (v) protects

6. _____ (v) happens

It's often possible to guess the meaning of a new word by paying attention to the other information around it, or the context. For example, in this excerpt from exercise A, if you don't know the word *reaction*, knowing that *sneezing, itching, and breathing problems* are examples of reactions can help you guess its meaning.

When this occurs, the mast cell produces substances in the body that cause allergic **reactions** *such as* **sneezing, itching, and breathing problems**.

C 🎧 **1.9** Read and listen to the information. Notice each word in **blue** and think about its meaning. Use the context to help you. Then write each word in **blue** next to its definition below.

MEANING FROM CONTEXT

ALLERGIES AND THE HYGIENE HYPOTHESIS

Many people work very hard to keep their houses clean. But can too much cleanliness cause health problems?

One **theory** is that dirt is good for us. Dirt on farms, for example, **contains** substances that exercise our immune systems when we're very young. **Research** shows that allergies are not **common** among people who live with farm animals.

Of course, there are many causes of allergies. For example, if your parents have allergies, you're more likely to have them, too. The stress of modern life could be another cause. But if the hygiene hypothesis is correct, it might be a good idea to have a cow at your house—or at least not to worry so much about cleanliness.

---

1. _____ (v) has something inside

2. _____ (adj) usual

3. _____ (n) work that involves studying something

4. _____ (n) an idea used to explain something

Listening A Conversation about Allergies

BEFORE LISTENING

A Read part of a conversation. Then discuss the questions below with a partner.

> **Raymond:** I've been hearing a lot more about allergies lately. I had no idea they were so serious and so common!
>
> **Elena:** Right, and I was surprised to learn that when allergic reactions occur, the physical process is pretty much the same—whether it's a reaction to pollen or to peanuts.

1. What is Elena surprised about?
2. Why might a food allergy, for example an allergy to peanuts, be a serious problem?

WHILE LISTENING

LISTENING FOR MAIN IDEAS

B 🎧 1.10 Listen to the conversation. What two things are the speakers most concerned about? Check (✓) your answers.

☐ air pollution   ☐ asthma   ☐ cats   ☐ chocolate   ☐ food allergies

---

NOTE-TAKING SKILL Writing Key Words and Phrases

When you take notes, you won't have enough time to write down every word that you hear. Don't try to write full sentences. Instead, listen carefully in order to understand and write down only key words and phrases that will help you remember the most important ideas.

> You hear: *Fortunately, I respond well to my asthma medication. It works really quickly, and I always take it with me.*
> You write: asthma medication, works quickly

NOTE TAKING

C 🎧 1.10 Listen again. Take notes using only key words and phrases to answer each question.

1. When are Elena's seasonal allergies a problem for her? _spring + early summer_

2. Which things are bad for Elena's asthma? _____

3. What kind of food policy does the speakers' campus have? _____

4. When did the number of people with food allergies grow quickly?

   _____

5. What percentage of children have food allergies nowadays? _____

AFTER LISTENING

> **CRITICAL THINKING**   Interpreting Visuals
>
> Visuals, such as graphs, maps, charts, and infographics, are used to show information in a clear way. To interpret a visual, first look at the title. Then use the legend or key to understand what the different colors, symbols, and other elements mean. For line graphs and bar graphs, look at the labels on the horizontal axis and vertical axis.

D Look at the bar graph and discuss the questions below with a partner.

CRITICAL THINKING: INTERPRETING A BAR GRAPH

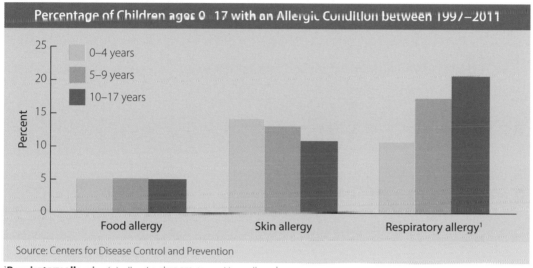

Percentage of Children ages 0–17 with an Allergic Condition between 1997–2011

Source: Centers for Disease Control and Prevention

¹**Respiratory allergies** (n). allergies that are caused by pollen, dust, pets, etc.

1. What does this bar graph show?
2. What does the vertical axis show? What does the horizontal axis show?
3. What information does the yellow bar show?
4. Which is the most common type of allergy among children 0–4 years old?
5. Which age group suffers the most from respiratory allergies?
6. Which type of allergy is more common among children 5–9 years old: skin allergies or respiratory allergies?
7. Which type of allergy shows the smallest difference between age groups?
8. What percentage of children between 10–17 years old have a food allergy?

E Discuss these questions with your partner.

PERSONALIZING

1. Do you or people you know have any allergies? Explain.
2. What information from the bar graph surprises you?
3. The speakers from the conversation mentioned a campus food policy. Do you think it's important for organizations to have policies like this? Explain.
4. Do you think this information about food allergies will affect your life? For example, will you think or do anything differently? Explain.

B Speaking

SPEAKING SKILL Keeping a Conversation Going

Keeping a conversation going is considered polite and is an important skill in social and business situations. Here are some ways to help keep a conversation going:

- Show the speaker that you are listening and are interested in what they are saying.

  A: *I'm going to Australia this summer.*
  B: *Oh, really? That's interesting!*

- Ask a follow-up question about something the speaker said.

  What are you going to do there?
  How's the weather there in July?

- Avoid *yes/no* questions. Use *wh-* questions instead. *Wh-* questions require speakers to give more information in their answers.

  What do you think about that?
  How often do you take a vacation?

EVERYDAY LANGUAGE Asking about Personal Experience

Do you know anything about...?
Have you ever...?
What about you?
Does anyone in your family...?

A Read the conversation. Then practice it with a partner.

A: *I really enjoy listening to live music.*
B: *Really? Where do you go for live music?*
A: *Sometimes I go to concerts. My brother played in a school concert last Saturday.*
B: *That sounds nice. What instrument does he play?*
A: *He plays two—guitar and mandolin.*
B: *Wow. That's great! What about you? Do you play any instruments?*

KEEPING A CONVERSATION GOING

B With your partner, take turns suggesting topics from the box below, or choose your own ideas. Practice keeping the conversation going. Use the information and questions from the Speaking Skill and Everyday Language boxes to help you.

education	friendship	interesting places/travel	music	sports
exercise	healthy food	jobs/careers	phone apps	your idea

A: *Let's talk about interesting places.*
B: *OK. What interesting places have you visited?*
A: *Well, I went to Costa Rica with my sister last summer. It was amazing!*
B: *Really? What did you do there?*

FINAL TASK Participating in a Discussion about Health

You are going to participate in a group discussion about health. You will choose a topic to discuss and practice keeping the conversation going.

A Work in a small group. Read the information about participating in a group discussion. Then choose one of the topics from the chart below for your group to discuss.

Group discussions are common in academic and professional settings. Here are some tips for participating in a group discussion:
- Participate. Everyone in the group is responsible for contributing ideas and keeping the discussion going.
- Speak clearly so others can hear you and understand your ideas.
- Pay attention and show interest when other people are speaking.
- Make sure everyone in the group has an opportunity to speak.
- Take notes, or choose someone to be the "secretary," or note taker, for the group.

Heart Health	Traditional Medicine	Allergies
What are some things people can do in their daily lives to prevent heart disease?	Why do people turn to bee therapy and other types of traditional medicine?	What are your experiences with allergies? (e.g., Do you or someone you know have them?)

B Take a few minutes to think about your group's topic and what you would like to say about it during the discussion. Write down key words and phrases in your notebook to help you remember your ideas.

ORGANIZING IDEAS

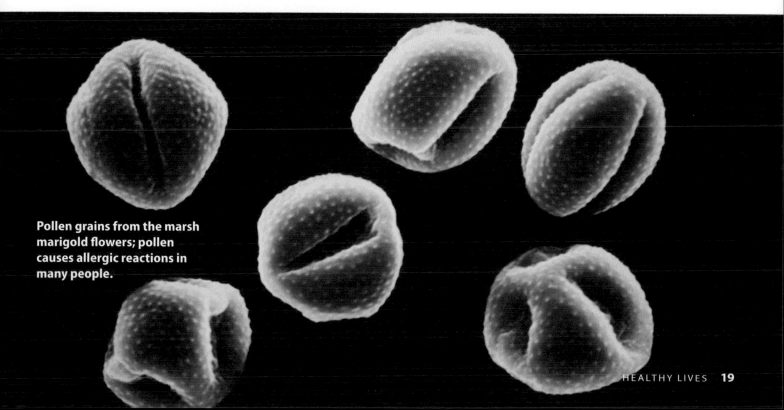

Pollen grains from the marsh marigold flowers; pollen causes allergic reactions in many people.

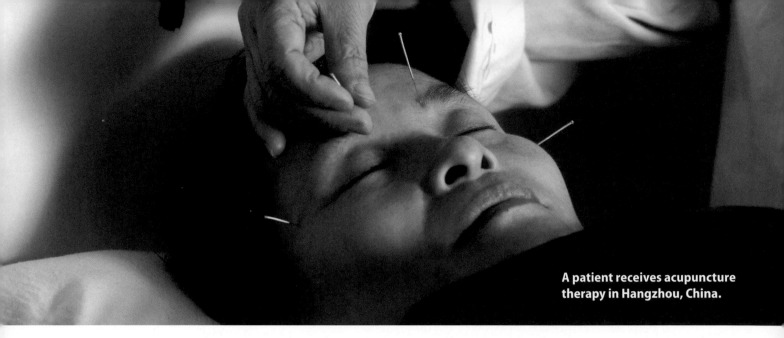

A patient receives acupuncture therapy in Hangzhou, China.

CRITICAL THINKING:
APPLYING

C Discuss your topic with your group for 4–5 minutes. Try to keep the discussion going. Remember to:

1. Show your group members that you are listening and are interested.
2. Ask questions to follow up on your group members' statements.
3. Use *wh-* questions to encourage discussion.

A: *I think people turn to traditional medicine because it seems more natural than modern medicine.*

B: *That's interesting. How do you feel about traditional medicine?*

A: *I think it can be helpful in some cases, but I've never tried it. What about you?*

C: *My cousin has had acupuncture and says it works ...*

CRITICAL THINKING:
REFLECTING

D Discuss these questions with your group.

1. Was your group able to discuss the topic completely in 4–5 minutes? Did you have more to say, or not enough to say in that amount of time?
2. Did all of the members of your group have a chance to share their ideas?
3. Did everyone show interest and use follow-up expressions to encourage discussion?
4. Was this discussion activity easy or difficult for you? Explain.

REFLECTION

1. Which skill in this unit was most useful for you? Why?

_____

_____

2. What information about health from this unit will you apply to your own life? How?

_____

_____

3. Here are the vocabulary words and phrases from the unit. Check (✓) the ones you can use.

☐ attach AWL	☐ contain	☐ produce
☐ attitude AWL	☐ defend	☐ provide
☐ be likely	☐ diet	☐ research AWL
☐ cause	☐ disease	☐ respond AWL
☐ cell	☐ habit	☐ stress AWL
☐ common	☐ occur AWL	☐ theory AWL
☐ consist of AWL	☐ prevent	

TECHNOLOGY TODAY AND TOMORROW 2

People play the game Pokémon
Go on their mobile phones in
La Villette Park in Paris, France.

THINK AND DISCUSS

1 What are the people in the photo doing? Have you ever tried this game or other games for mobile phones?

2 What's the title of this unit? What are some things you think you will learn about in this unit?

Look at the photos and read the information. Then discuss these questions.

1. Have you ever heard or read about any of the topics on these pages? Explain.

2. In 1968, how did movie audiences feel about AI? How do you feel about it? Why?

3. Do you know of any ways that you use AI in your daily life? Explain.

4. How do you think AI might impact our future?

MOMENTS IN AI HISTORY

Artificial Intelligence, or AI, is a machine's ability to "think" and perform tasks that are typically done by human beings. Although AI may seem like a very modern concept, it has been around for much longer than many people realize.

▶ **2011:** IBM's Watson computer beats its human competitors at the popular TV quiz show *Jeopardy!*

▶ 2016: The Mercedes Benz F 015 self-driving car stands at Dam Square in Amsterdam, the Netherlands.

▶ 1968: Movie audiences decide that AI Is dangerous when HAL, the computer in *2001: A Space Odyssey*, decides that keeping itself "alive" is more important than the lives of the astronauts.

▶ 1950: British mathematician, computer scientist, and codebreaker Alan Turing (far left) proposes the Turing test to determine a computer's ability to "think."

A Vocabulary

A **1.11** Read and listen to the information. Notice each word in **blue** and think about its meaning.

Timeline of AI History

1950: In *I, Robot*, a book of fictional[1] short stories by Isaac Asimov, the makers of robots **command** them not to harm humans. The robots, however, sometimes create their own rules depending on the **circumstances**.

1950s: Computers become a **practical** tool for doing calculations quickly, and since they don't make any mistakes, they are more **reliable** than humans.

1956: Researchers at Dartmouth College say they **intend** to study "**artificial** intelligence" during a two-month summer conference.

1997: A computer called Deep Blue wins a chess match against world champion Garry Kasparov, and it's clear that computers can go **beyond** just following instructions and can actually "think" for themselves. In the past, programmers had to **instruct** computers in great detail and tell them exactly what to do.

2011: A computer called Watson **replaces** one of the humans competing on the TV quiz show *Jeopardy!*—and wins! Watson is **capable** of understanding spoken questions.

2016: Google puts together a group of engineers in Switzerland to research "machine learning," an important part of artificial intelligence.

1950
1960
1970
1980
1990
2000
2010
2020

$3,400 $3,400

[1] **fictional** (adj): not real; from the author's imagination

B Complete each question with a word from the box. Use each word only once.

> capable (adj)   instruct (v)   intend (v)   reliable (adj)   replace (v)

1. Do you think computers are usually _____, or do they often not work?

2. What are some of the things most computers are _____ of doing?

3. In what kinds of jobs do you think robots might _____ human beings?

4. What does your English teacher often _____ the class to do?

5. What do you _____ to do after class?

C Work with a partner. Take turns asking and answering the questions from exercise D.

D Match each word with its definition.

1. _____ command (v)   a. to tell someone or something what they must do
2. _____ circumstances (n)   b. useful or sensible
3. _____ practical (adj)   c. farther than
4. _____ artificial (adj)   d. conditions which affect what happens in a
                                  situation
5. _____ beyond (prep)   e. created by human beings, not by nature

---

VOCABULARY SKILL Using Collocations

Collocations are words that are frequently used together. Knowing which words to collocate, or combine, will help you use new words correctly and make your English sound more fluent.

be capable of	Intelligent machines **are capable of** making decisions.
intend to	Do you **intend to** register for the history course?
under (the, any, etc.) circumstances	I'm afraid of robots. I wouldn't get one **under** any **circumstances**!

E Underline the collocations in the questions below. Then discuss the questions in a group.

CRITICAL THINKING: ANALYZING

A: *I'm not sure whether computers are capable of thinking.*
B: *The timeline information makes me think they're not that smart yet.*

1. Do you think computers are (or will be) capable of thinking in the same way that human beings do? Explain.
2. Can you imagine life now without computers or the Internet? How would life be different under those circumstances?
3. What homework or assignments do you need to do? When do you intend to do them?

Listening A Radio Show about AI

BEFORE LISTENING

PRIOR KNOWLEDGE   **A**   Work with a partner. Discuss these questions.

1. Which Internet search engines do you use? Why?
2. Do you do much shopping online? If so, what kinds of things do you buy?
3. How do doctors or hospitals use computers?

WHILE LISTENING

LISTENING FOR
MAIN IDEAS   **B**   🎧 **1.12** Listen to the radio show and choose the answer that best completes each statement.

1. Artificial intelligence plays a role when you are _____.

   a. sending an email message   b. searching the Internet

2. Machine learning could enable computers to _____.

   a. follow our instructions   b. discover something new

3. Intelligent computers could help doctors by _____.

   a. reading a lot of information   b. communicating with patients

▼ **Tourists communicate with guidance robot "Kaiba" at Haneda Airport in Tokyo, Japan. The airport aims to put these robots into use in 2019.**

C 🎧 1.12 Listen again. Take notes on the one or two details you think are the most important for each main idea. Use abbreviations.

NOTE TAKING

1. Main idea: Artificial intelligence limits Internet search engine results.

   _____

2. Main idea: Search engines are capable of a kind of thinking.

   _____

3. Main idea: Intelligent computers could help in the medical field, for example with cancer.

   _____

AFTER LISTENING

D Work with a partner. Compare and discuss your notes from exercise C. How did you decide which detail or details were the most important? Which words did you abbreviate and how?

E Discuss these questions with your partner.

CRITICAL THINKING: REFLECTING

1. Have you experienced the kind of intelligent search engine the radio-show guest describes?
2. How do you feel about computers that can possibly think and make decisions?

Speaking

GRAMMAR FOR SPEAKING Action and Nonaction Verbs

Action Verbs

Action verbs show physical or mental activities.

bring	compare	eat	increase	replace	respond	work
build	decide	happen	occur	run	speak	worry

Nonaction Verbs

Nonaction verbs describe states and conditions. Most nonaction verbs tell us about states of mind, emotions, the senses, or possession. We usually do not use nonaction verbs with the present continuous.

Here are some common nonaction verbs:

be	hear	love	need	remember	think
believe	know	matter	own	see	understand
have	like	mean	prefer	seem	want

Action Verbs	Nonaction Verbs
We **are learning** about computer science.	We **know** how to program computers.
Rita **is watching** people in the coffee shop.	She **sees** one person she knows.
I **am listening** to one of my favorite songs.	I **hear** a violin.

Some verbs can be both action verbs and nonaction verbs, but the meanings are different. Use the grammar and context clues to understand the meaning.

> I **am thinking** about my sister. She **thinks** homework is a waste of time.
> We **have** a lot of food in the house. We**'re having** a dinner party tonight.

A Read each sentence and look at the underlined verb form. Is it correct? Write C for *correct* and I for *incorrect* on the line after each sentence. Then make any necessary corrections.

1. My professor <u>thinks</u> that AI will benefit the medical field. _____

2. Many people <u>are believing</u> that AI is dangerous. _____

3. They <u>are working</u> on a new app this month. It will help children learn math. _____

4. These days, more scientists <u>are researching</u> cancer and diabetes. _____

5. How many pairs of shoes <u>are you owning</u>? _____

6. If the food is good, it <u>isn't mattering</u> if the restaurant is far away. _____

7. I can't talk right now. We <u>have</u> dinner. _____

8. Are you OK? You <u>seem</u> upset. _____

A woman takes a photo
with her smartphone
at sunrise.

B Work with a partner. Discuss these questions. Use the correct verb forms.

PERSONALIZING

1. What kind(s) of "smart" devices are you using these days? How are you using them?
2. Do you think it's a good idea for young children to use smartphones and computers?
3. What are some things you understand and don't understand about computers and AI?
4. What do you want from a smartphone? From a computer?
5. What are you reading in the news about computers and robots these days?
6. How do you feel about AI? Does it make you worried or optimistic? Explain.

SPEAKING SKILL Giving Reasons

It's important to give reasons when you want to support your opinions or explain a set of circumstances. Here are some words and phrases you can use to give reasons. Notice how *because* and *since* can connect clauses and show the relationship between ideas.

> Cancer is a problem for doctors **because** it's really many diseases—not just one.
> **Since** computers can read a lot of information very quickly, they might be able to discover new things.

Here are some other phrases that introduce reasons:

> **For this reason**, I'm worried about programs that track my behavior online.
> **Another reason** for my concern is the lack of privacy online.

C Complete each sentence so it is true for you. Then read and discuss your sentences with a partner.

PERSONALIZING

1. Because I am studying English, _____.

2. _____ since all of my friends are using cell phones.

3. I enjoy spending time with my best friend because _____.

4. Since I'm a(n) _____ person, I usually _____.

5. My family lives in _____. For this reason, _____.

LESSON TASK Discussing Self-Driving Cars

A Work in a group. Read the information about self-driving cars. Then discuss the questions below.

> **SELF-DRIVING CARS**
>
> Many new cars are already offering automation. Examples include automatic parallel parking, automatic braking in emergencies, and lane-assist warnings to tell drivers if their car crosses a solid line on the road. Now, companies are testing completely automatic cars that don't require a driver. These cars are expected to become popular in some parts of the world in the near future.

1. Have you ever read about self-driving cars, or have you seen one? Is the idea of self-driving cars interesting to you? Explain.
2. What forms of transportation do you usually use? What are some of the advantages and disadvantages of the forms of transportation you use?

B With your group, discuss the pros and cons of self-driving cars. Then add some of your own ideas to the T-chart.

Pros	Cons
• **Safety**: Most traffic accidents are caused by people driving dangerously.	• **High cost**: The new technology will be far too expensive for most people.
• **Fewer traffic jams**: Unlike some people, self-driving cars could communicate and cooperate with each other.	• **Less privacy**: Computers will need to keep a lot of data on people's activities.
• **More transportation options**: People who are unable to drive could use self-driving cars.	• **The unexpected**: Computers in self-driving cars can't be programmed for every possibility, for example understanding hand signals from a police officer.
Your ideas:	Your ideas:
• _____	• _____
• _____	• _____
• _____	• _____
• _____	• _____
• _____	• _____
• _____	• _____

This Volkswagen "Sedric" self-driving automobile was displayed at the 87th Geneva International Motor Show in Geneva, Switzerland in March 2017.

C Work in a group. Look at the bar graph and discuss the questions below. Give reasons to support your ideas.

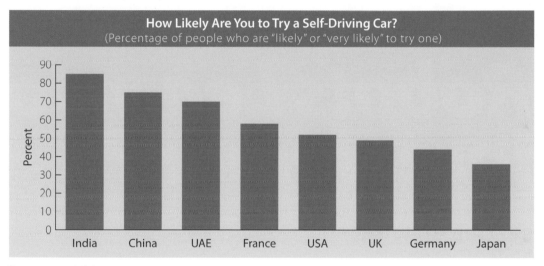

How Likely Are You to Try a Self-Driving Car?
(Percentage of people who are "likely" or "very likely" to try one)

Source: www.statista.com

1. What information does this bar graph show?
2. Which country has the highest percentage of people who are likely or very likely to try a self-driving car? Which country has the lowest percentage?
3. Is your country represented on the bar graph? If so, does the information surprise you? Why or why not?
4. Think of possible reasons for people being likely or unlikely to try self-driving cars.

D As a group, discuss these questions. Give reasons to support your ideas.

1. How likely are you to try riding in a self-driving car? Explain.
2. After discussing question 1, has anyone in the group changed their mind about self-driving cars?

E Work with the whole class. Tell your teacher how many people in your group are likely to try riding in a self-driving car. Then discuss these questions.

1. What percentage of people in your class are likely to try a self-driving car? How does that percentage compare with the percentages in the bar graph in exercise C?
2. What does this information tell you about the people in your class?

Video

A robot soccer referee gives a player a red penalty card. The robot soccer players are able to sense their surroundings and respond to other players' movements.

Can Robots Learn to Be More Human?

BEFORE VIEWING

CRITICAL THINKING:
ANALYZING

A Work with a partner. Look at the photo and read the caption. Then discuss these questions.

1. Describe what you see. What is happening in the photo?
2. Do you think that robots can learn to be more human? Explain.

B Match each word or phrase with its meaning. You may use a dictionary. You will hear these words and phrases in the video.

1. _____ human features (n)
2. _____ compelling (adj)
3. _____ barriers to entry (n)
4. _____ accessibility (n)
5. _____ natural language commands (n)
6. _____ remote presence device (n)

a. how easy something is for people to use
b. spoken words that tell machines what to do
c. a machine that can be somewhere that a person can't be
d. body parts that people have, such as eyes, ears, and arms
e. things that prevent people from using something
f. convincing

C Read the information about Chad Jenkins. With a partner, discuss ways that robots could help human beings. If you had a robot, what would you ask it to do for you?

CRITICAL THINKING: ANALYZING

> **MEET CHAD JENKINS.** He's a National Geographic Explorer, a computer scientist, and roboticist. His research group at Brown University in the U.S. is looking for ways that robots can help human beings and improve their lives. One aspect of Jenkins's research involves teaching robots though demonstration. This means that instead of using computer codes to program robots, people simply show the robot a behavior, and the robot learns it. Jenkins appreciates the progress that's been made in computer science, but he thinks the progress in robotics will be even more impressive in the future. When it comes to robotics, he says, "We have more wisdom about the technology to do it better."

WHILE VIEWING

D ▶ 1.3 Read the statements. Then watch the video and choose T for *True* or F for *False*. Correct the false statements.

UNDERSTANDING DETAILS

1. The human features that Jenkins mentions are eyes and ears.   T   F

2. Jenkins says that robots might be able to help elderly (very old) people. T   F

3. One of the barriers to entry that Jenkins mentions is cost.   T   F

4. In order to control a robot, you need to be a computer programmer.   T   F

5. The video shows the remote presence device inside Jenkins's home.   T   F

E ▶ 1.3 Read the quotes from the video. Then watch the video again and fill in the blanks with the information you hear.

UNDERSTANDING DETAILS

1. "Traditionally I've worked in the area of robot _____ from demonstration…"

2. "There's many different ways you can actually _____ a robot."

3. "A much _____ approach is to just take the robot's arm and guide the robot's arm…"

4. "Another approach is to treat the robot as a remote-control _____."

5. "We'd love to make it based on what we call natural language _____…"

6. "Robotics is really an extension of the _____ Technology Revolution…"

AFTER VIEWING

F Discuss these questions in a group.

CRITICAL THINKING: ANALYZING

1. What are three ways robots could help elderly or disabled people (e.g., people who are not able to see or walk)?
2. What are three ways robots could help other people in their daily lives?
3. If you had a robot, how do you think it could improve your life?

B Vocabulary

MEANING FROM CONTEXT

A 🎧 **1.13** Read and listen to the information. Notice each word or phrase in **blue** and think about its meaning.

SAVING THE ENVIRONMENT IN GERMANY

Germany has a history of caring about the environment, but it's a country with a lot of industry that **consumes** enormous amounts of coal. When coal and other **fossil fuels** such as petroleum are burned, they send **carbon** into the air, and carbon is the main cause of climate change. In order to fight air pollution and climate change, Germans have **cut back on** the amount of coal they use. As part of this effort, they are also using cleaner energy sources such as solar and wind power.

Innovative forms of technology, including enormous wind turbines and huge numbers of solar panels, are helping Germany reach its goal of having only 20 percent of its energy come from fossil fuels by the year 2050. The change has been **gradual**—beginning in the 1970s—and it hasn't been easy. Many environmental groups as well as **individual** people in Germany have spent a lot of time and money on clean energy.

CHANGING LIVES IN INDIA

Around 1.1 billion people **worldwide** live without electricity, and about 25 percent of those people live in India. Solar energy—in the form of small lights that get their power from the sun—is now solving problems for many of them. This innovative technology lets small businesses stay open at night, so people in India are earning more money. In addition to the positive economic **impact**, the air inside homes is cleaner since people are not burning wood or kerosene[1] for light. Solar power is also a good **alternative** to expensive batteries[2] that need to be replaced. With the help of innovative technology, people in rural villages can live more like people in large cities.

---

[1]**kerosene** (n): a liquid fuel made from petroleum
[2]**batteries** (n): small devices that provide electrical power

A couple in India holds a solar powered lamp during their wedding ceremony.

B Write each word or phrase in **blue** from exercise A next to its definition.

1. _____ (n) something that can be used instead of another thing
2. _____ (n) coal, petroleum, and natural gas
3. _____ (adv) existing or happening throughout the world
4. _____ (adj) relating to just one person or thing
5. _____ (adj) new and original
6. _____ (n) a chemical element that coal and diamonds are made of
7. _____ (phrasal v) to reduce
8. _____ (n) effect
9. _____ (adj) happening slowly over time
10. _____ (v) uses something up

C Work with a partner. Take the quiz. Then check your answers below.

CRITICAL THINKING: ANALYZING

QUIZ: WHAT'S YOUR SOLAR-POWER I.Q.?

1. Which system consumes the most energy in most homes?

   a. electronics   b. heating and cooling rooms   c. water heating   d. refrigeration

2. Which energy source sends the most carbon into the air?

   a. oil (petroleum)   b. coal   c. natural gas   d. solar power

3. Which alternative to fossil fuels produces the most power in the United States?

   a. wind   b. solar   c. geothermal[1]   d. wood

4. How much does the addition of solar equipment increase the value of a home in the United States?

   a. $1,000   b. $2,000   c. $7,000   d. $17,000

5. When was the innovative technology that makes solar panels work invented?

   a. 1940s   b. 1950s   c. 1970s   d. 1980s

Source: worldwildlife.org

[1]**geothermal** (adj): related to heat found deep inside the earth

D Work in a group. Discuss these questions.

CRITICAL THINKING: EVALUATING

1. What are some ways people can cut back on the amount of energy they use?
2. Who do you think has a more significant impact when it comes to using less energy or using alternative forms of energy: individual people or groups (e.g., companies or governments)? Explain.
3. Germany wants 80 percent of its power to come from innovative technology such as solar, wind, and biofuels by the year 2050. Do you think that goal is realistic for your country? Explain.

Answers: 1. b, 2. b, 3. a, 4. d, 5. d

Listening A Conversation about Technology

BEFORE LISTENING

A 🎧 **1.14** Read and listen to information about an innovative solution to a problem in Baltimore, USA.

BALTIMORE'S MR. TRASH WHEEL

With innovative technology, we can solve old problems in new ways. One old problem was the trash from the city of Baltimore, Maryland, that ended up in the Jones Falls River. The river flows into Baltimore's Inner Harbor—a popular tourist destination—and from there into the Chesapeake Bay and the Atlantic Ocean.

Meet Mr. Trash Wheel, a device that uses the motion of river water and energy from solar panels to collect plastic bottles, cigarette butts, carry-out food containers, and other garbage from the river. Baltimore's Inner Harbor is now a more attractive place for visitors. Hundreds of tons of trash have been removed from the water system, and other communities are thinking about building their own trash wheels.

CRITICAL THINKING:
INTERPRETING
A GRAPHIC

B Look at the graphic below. Then match each part of Mr. Trash Wheel with its function.

1. _____ floating booms
2. _____ rotating forks
3. _____ waterwheel
4. _____ solar panels
5. _____ Dumpsters

a. turn the wheel when the water is moving slowly
b. direct floating trash toward the forks
c. collect and hold the trash from the conveyor belt
d. pick up trash from the water, put it on the conveyor belt
e. uses movement of river water to move the conveyor belt

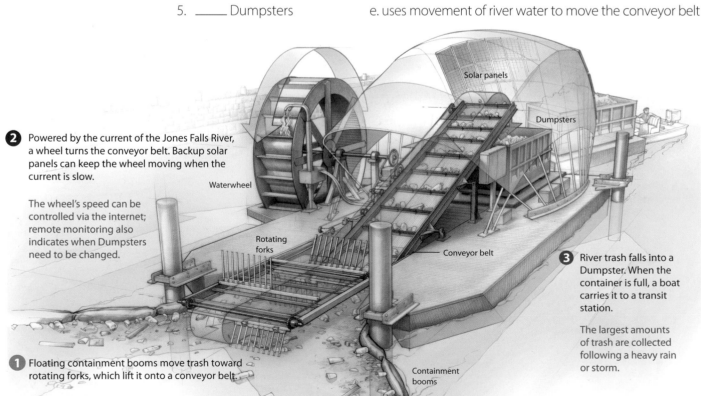

2 Powered by the current of the Jones Falls River, a wheel turns the conveyor belt. Backup solar panels can keep the wheel moving when the current is slow.

The wheel's speed can be controlled via the internet; remote monitoring also indicates when Dumpsters need to be changed.

Waterwheel

Rotating forks

Solar panels

Dumpsters

Conveyor belt

3 River trash falls into a Dumpster. When the container is full, a boat carries it to a transit station.

The largest amounts of trash are collected following a heavy rain or storm.

1 Floating containment booms move trash toward rotating forks, which lift it onto a conveyor belt.

Containment booms

WHILE LISTENING

C 🎧 **1.15** Listen to the conversation. Then answer the questions.

LISTENING FOR
MAIN IDEAS

1. What two kinds of energy does the trash wheel use? _____

2. Which part of Mr. Trash Wheel is a very old kind of technology?

   _____

3. What kind of new technology is making people like Mr. Trash Wheel?

   _____

D 🎧 **1.15** Listen again. Choose the correct word or phrase to complete each sentence.

LISTENING FOR
DETAILS

1. The (city / boat) takes away the Dumpsters when they are full of trash.
2. Mr. Trash Wheel catches (50 / 90) percent of the trash from the river.
3. One kind of trash that is mentioned is (soda / garbage) cans.
4. People online suggested adding (eyes / ears) to the trash wheel.
5. Several other communities (are building / might build) trash wheels.

AFTER LISTENING

> **CRITICAL THINKING** Synthesizing
>
> When you synthesize, you combine, or put together, information from two or
> more sources in order to understand a topic in a new way. This can also involve
> combining new information with your own ideas and knowledge about a topic.
> Synthesizing can help you find a solution to a problem or think of new ways of
> doing or improving something.

E Work with a partner. Discuss this question: What are three ways the Internet is used to operate or promote Mr. Trash Wheel? Use information from the conversation and the graphic on page 36. Write your ideas in the chart.

CRITICAL THINKING:
SYNTHESIZING

Mr. Trash Wheel's Success: Three Ways the Internet Is Used		
1.	2.	3.

F Form a group with another pair of students. Compare your answers from exercise E. Then discuss this question: How could the Internet and other new kinds of technology be used to help Mr. Trash Wheel have an even bigger impact on the environment?

CRITICAL THINKING:
SYNTHESIZING

B Speaking

CRITICAL THINKING:
ANALYZING

A With your partner, look at the types of technology listed in the box, and ask and answer the questions below.

A: *What's changing with TV or movies?*
B: *People are watching them on their phones, but they're still going to the movie theater, too.*

> apps/programs   cameras   computers   the Internet   phones   TV/movies   other

1. What is happening or changing with each kind of technology these days?
2. How do people use each kind of technology to solve problems in their daily lives?
3. In your country, what impact are cell phones or other devices having on your culture? For example, are these devices changing education, or the ways people make money or make new friends?

EVERYDAY LANGUAGE Giving Advice

*You **should** create a stronger password for your wi-fi.*

*You **shouldn't** work so hard.*

*We **had better** get back to work.*

*Luisa **had better not** forget to set her alarm. She has an early exam.*

CRITICAL THINKING:
EVALUATING

B Read each statement and choose A for *Agree* or D for *Disagree*.

1. People shouldn't check their phones when they're doing things with their friends or family.   A   D

2. Governments should make sure everyone in their country has access to the Internet.   A   D

3. People had better not share their personal information online.   A   D

4. Engineers should invent some inexpensive devices so that everyone can afford them.   A   D

5. App designers should focus on helping to solve people's problems, rather than entertaining them with games.   A   D

▶ **Men using their cell phones, Bali Island, Indonesia**

38 UNIT 2 LESSON B

C Work in a group. Take turns saying the statements in exercise B aloud and whether you agree or disagree. Give reasons for your opinions.

PRONUNCIATION Stressed Content Words

[🎧 1.16] In English, not every word in a sentence gets the same amount of stress or emphasis. Content words receive more stress because they have more meaning or give more information than other words. This means the stressed syllable in content words is a bit louder, longer, and higher in pitch. Content words include:

nouns	main verbs	adjectives
adverbs	question words	

*The **book** is on the **table** in the **back** of the **room**.*
*My **friend took** a **chemistry course** in **college**.*

D Underline the content words in each sentence.

1. Nabila is taking a course in computer programming.
2. Samir wants to become a software designer.
3. All of my friends have cell phones.
4. Large televisions consume a lot of electricity.
5. I'm trying to cut back on the time I spend online.
6. Kenji wants to buy a phone with a better camera.

E [🎧 1.17] Listen to the sentences from exercise D and check your answers. Then practice saying the sentences with a partner. Remember to stress the content words.

FINAL TASK Presenting a New Technology Product

> You are going to give a short pair presentation. You and a partner will think of a real problem and a new kind of technology product that could help solve that problem. Your job is to convince your audience that the idea is good and the product is worth buying.

A Work with a partner. Brainstorm a list of problems that you care about. The problems could be major issues that your community or the world is dealing with (e.g., pollution, crime, or traffic), or they could be smaller everyday problems (e.g., oversleeping, forgetting vocabulary words, or being late). Write the list in your notebook.

B Look at your list of problems and choose one that you both want to focus on.

C Brainstorm ideas for new technology products that could help solve the problem you chose in exercise B.

D Choose one of your ideas from exercise C and create a proposal for a new kind of technology product. It should be for a product that doesn't exist yet. Think about what the product will do, its name, who will want to buy it (e.g., children, doctors, governments), and any other important details. Complete the proposal outline below with brief notes as you plan your presentation.

Proposal Outline

a. Description of problem: _____

b. Product description (name of product; How does it solve the problem?):

_____

c. Target market (Who will buy it? Who is it for?): _____

d. Other details (price, location, etc.): _____

e. Conclusion (Summarize the product's benefits.): _____

E Decide who will present which information. Write brief notes to use during your presentation. Use the information from your proposal to help you. Then practice your presentation. Give reasons to support your ideas, and remember to stress content words.

PRESENTATION SKILL Making Eye Contact

When you are giving a presentation, it's important to look up from your notes often and speak directly to your audience. If it's a small group, try to make brief eye contact with each person. If it's a large group, be sure to look toward every part of the room at least once. This will make people want to listen to you and will help you connect with your audience.

F Give your presentation to the class. Remember to make eye contact with your audience.

REFLECTION

1. What are some useful vocabulary collocations you learned in this unit?

_____

_____

2. What do you think is the most innovative kind of technology discussed in this unit?

_____

_____

3. Here are the vocabulary words and phrases from the unit. Check (✓) the ones you can use.

☐ alternative AWL   ☐ consume AWL   ☐ instruct AWL

☐ artificial   ☐ cut back on   ☐ intend

☐ beyond   ☐ fossil fuel   ☐ practical

☐ capable AWL   ☐ gradual   ☐ reliable AWL

☐ carbon   ☐ impact AWL   ☐ replace

☐ circumstance AWL   ☐ individual AWL   ☐ worldwide

☐ command   ☐ innovative AWL

CULTURE AND TRADITION 3

A cowboy in Montana's
Judith Basin, USA

ACADEMIC SKILLS

LISTENING Asking Questions While Listening
Using a Numbered List
SPEAKING Asking for and Giving Clarification
Reduced Function Words
CRITICAL THINKING Activating Prior Knowledge

THINK AND DISCUSS

1 Who is the man in the photo? What do you think he is doing?

2 What do you know about cowboys?

3 In which countries do cowboys live and work?

Look at the photos and read the information. Then discuss these questions.

1. Why are the people in the photos receiving gifts?

2. When do people typically give gifts in your country?

3. When you receive a gift in your country, do you open it in front of the person who gave it to you, or do you wait until later? Explain.

4. In your country, what kinds of things do people typically give as wedding gifts?

GIFT GIVING AROUND THE WORLD

Giving gifts is an important part of nearly every culture in the world. People give gifts to celebrate holidays, special occasions, and to say "thank you," "congratulations," or "welcome." Gift-giving customs, such as what to give as a gift, when to open a gift, and how to wrap, or cover, a gift differ from culture to culture.

A girl opens a gift at her *fiesta de quinceañera* (15th birthday celebration) in Miami, Florida, USA.

A young woman unwraps gifts during a baby shower in Las Vegas, Nevada, USA.

Elderly residents receive Angpao and food during Chinese New Year or Lunar 2567 in Semarang, Indonesia.

A Vocabulary

A 🎧 1.18 Read the sentences. Notice each word in **blue** and think about its meaning. Choose the correct word or phrase in parentheses to complete each sentence. Then listen and check your answers.

1. In my country, we have a **custom** of giving money to children on their birthdays. Parents (usually / never) give their children money as a gift.

2. The **actual** cost of a big holiday celebration can be higher than people expect. People often end up spending (more / less) money on food and gifts than they plan to.

3. Culture is a **factor** in gift giving. People from some cultures feel that if they receive a gift, they must give a gift in return. Their culture is a (reason for / result of) that feeling.

4. Women in Japan **still** wear a kimono for their wedding. They (have / haven't) stopped wearing these beautiful clothes.

5. In Korea, people eat **traditional** foods such as rice cakes on New Year's Day. They have done this for a (short / long) time.

6. We are **developing** a program to teach foreigners about our culture. We are now (making plans / selling tickets) for this program.

7. In the future, many languages will probably **disappear**. Someday (many people / no one) will speak these languages.

8. A group of people called the Inuit live in the Arctic **regions** of the world. They live in cold (cities / areas).

9. Many cultures use storytelling to help **preserve** their language and traditions. They tell stories to help (keep / change) them.

10. Scientists **estimate** that there are over 7,000 languages in the world. They (know / don't know) the exact number.

B Work with a partner. Match each word in **blue** from exercise A with its definition.

1. _____ custom (n)   a. an action or practice that is common to a person or group

2. _____ actual (adj)   b. areas of a country or of the world

3. _____ factor (n)   c. up to and including the present

4. _____ still (adv)   d. to keep or protect

5. _____ traditional (adj)   e. an issue in, a cause of

6. _____ developing (v)   f. real

7. _____ disappear (v)   g. to make a guess based on available information

8. _____ regions (n)   h. making into something bigger or more complete

9. _____ preserve (v)   i. to no longer exist or be visible

10. _____ estimate (v)   j. customary or normal in a certain culture

C 🎧 1.19 Fill in each blank with the correct form of a word from exercise B. Use each word only once. Then listen and check your answers.

Cowboy Life and Culture

In the 1800s, cowboys worked with cattle all across the Western _____1_____ of the United States. An important _____2_____ in the cowboys' work was the long distance from cattle ranches[1] to the nearest railroad. Cowboys moved cattle in huge cattle drives. It was hard work. Experts _____3_____ that in a cattle drive, only about 10 cowboys would be involved in moving over 3,000 cattle.

Over time, cowboys _____4_____ some very interesting _____5_____ . For example, some cowboys would sing to their cattle at night to keep them quiet. Some _____6_____ American songs were originally cowboy songs, and people _____7_____ sing them today.

Cowboys have not _____8_____ completely; however, there are not nearly as many as there were in the past. And even though there are fewer _____9_____ cowboys now, many people in parts of the United States wear cowboy hats and boots. Rodeos[2] are also very popular in some parts of the United States and help _____10_____ some aspects of the cowboy culture.

[1]**ranches** (n): large farms where animals are raised
[2]**rodeos** (n): public events where cowboys show their skills

D Work with a partner. Take turns completing the sentences with your own ideas.

PERSONALIZING

1. A traditional food from my country that I like is …

2. Some people in my country still …

3. A holiday custom that I enjoy is …

4. In my country, … has/have disappeared.

5. I think it's really important to preserve …

▶ **A cowboy on a cattle drive in Castle Valley, Utah, USA**

Listening A Lecture about Cowboys

BEFORE LISTENING

> **CRITICAL THINKING** Activating Prior Knowledge
>
> Before you listen to a talk, think about the topic and what you already know about it. This will help you make connections between the new information in the talk and your prior knowledge, which will help you better understand what you hear.

PRIOR KNOWLEDGE **A** You are going to listen to a lecture about cowboys in North America. Discuss these questions with a partner.

1. What do you know about the work that cowboys do?
2. Besides North America, do you know of any other regions that have cowboys?
3. What else would you like to learn about cowboys?

WHILE LISTENING

LISTENING FOR
MAIN IDEAS

B 🎧 1.20 ▶ 1.4 Listen to the lecture. Choose the correct answers.

1. Which two countries are mentioned in the lecture?

   a. Canada   b. the United States   c. Mexico   d. Spain

2. Which two aspects of Robb Kendrick's book does the lecturer mention?

   a. photos   b. number of pages   c. information about modern cowboys
   d. how old the book is

▶ **Left: A portrait of Tyrel Tucker taken by Robb Kendrick, Powell, Wyoming, USA**

▶ **Right: A portrait of Manuel Rodriguez taken by Robb Kendrick, Muzquiz, Mexico**

▸ **A Mexican charro roping a horse**

C 🎧 1.20 Listen again. Complete the notes about the two cowboys.

LISTENING FOR DETAILS

Tyrel Tucker

- got his first horse when he was _____
- one winter, he and his brother took care of _____ cattle
- lived in a shack with no _____

Manuel Rodriguez

- started working with his father when he was

  _____
- got _____ and moved to the city
- planned to _____ to the countryside and work as a vaquero again

D 🎧 1.20 Read the statements below. Listen again and choose T for *True* or F for *False* for each statement. The professor does not say the answers directly. You will need to think about what you hear. Correct the false statements.

CRITICAL THINKING: MAKING INFERENCES

1. Tyrel liked school.   T   F

2. Tyrel and his brother ate a healthy diet.   T   F

3. Both of these cowboys would be unhappy living in a big city.   T   F

4. The two men want to get better jobs.   T   F

E Work with a partner. Compare your answers from exercise D and discuss this question: What information from the lecture helped you choose your answers?

AFTER LISTENING

F Work with a partner. Discuss these questions.

CRITICAL THINKING: REFLECTING

1. What ideas did you have about cowboys before you listened to the lecture? Have your ideas changed at all? Explain.
2. Why do you think Robb Kendrick used an old kind of camera to take photos of cowboys?
3. Why do you think some people still want to be cowboys today?
4. Would you like the cowboy way of life? Explain.

Speaking

SPEAKING SKILL Asking for and Giving Clarification

When participating in a conversation, you often need to ask for or give clarification. Here are some expressions you can use:

Asking for Clarification	Giving Clarification
I'm sorry, did you say ... ?	*No, I said that ...*
Excuse me, I have a question.	*Let me explain.*
Could you please explain that?	*Yes, I mean that ...*
Do you mean that ... ?	*To put it another way, ...*
I'm afraid I don't understand.	*In other words, ...*

A 🎧 1.21 Read and listen to the conversation. Write the missing phrases you hear.

Emily: During the lecture, you said that the cowboy tradition in Mexico began in the 1600s. _____₁ the situation there today?

Professor Diaz: Certainly. Some cowboys in Mexico are workers who live with the cattle and take care of them. The ranches there can be very large, and cattle need to be moved from place to place, so there are still cowboys working in Mexico today.

Liam: You talked about *two* kinds of cowboys in Mexico. _____₂ them again?

Professor Diaz: Sure. The most famous cowboys in Mexico are the *charros*. They ride their horses in contests called *charreadas*. The other kind of cowboys are the *vaqueros*—the ones who work with cattle every day.

Liam: _____₃ . What kind of work do *charros* do, exactly?

Professor Diaz: I'll _____₄ . For *charros*, riding horses and roping cattle is mostly a sport, or a hobby. *Charros* have many of the same skills as any cowboy, and they perform those skills for an audience in the *charreada* events. But for the *vaqueros*, this is their job. It's how they make a living.

Liam: OK. So, Manuel Rodriguez ... the cowboy in the book ... is a *vaquero*, not a *charro*, right?

Professor Diaz: Exactly!

Emily: Just to clarify, _____ *charros* aren't real cowboys?
₅

Professor Diaz: No, _____ *charros are* a part of the cowboy tradition,
₆

but many of them don't do it as actual work.

B Complete the sentences with your own ideas. Then with a partner, take turns reading your sentences. Practice asking for and giving clarification.

ASKING FOR AND GIVING CLARIFICATION

A: *In my opinion, the cowboy way of life is difficult.*
B: *Do you mean that cowboys' work is difficult or the way they live?*

1. In my opinion, the cowboy way of life is _____ .

2. A tradition that is now disappearing is _____ .

3. I think one of the main reasons why traditions disappear is _____ .

4. An example of traditional clothing is _____ .

5. When you receive a gift in my country, the custom is to _____ .

GRAMMAR FOR SPEAKING The Past Continuous

We form the past continuous with *was/were* plus the *-ing* form of a verb.

We use the past continuous:

1. to talk about actions that were in progress at a certain time in the past.

   > Tyrel **was riding** horses <u>at the age of two</u>.

   > Sumi **wasn't living** in New York <u>in 2014</u>.

2. with the simple past to show that one action was in progress when another action happened.

   > He **was working** as a vaquero in Coahuila, Mexico, when Kendrick <u>met</u> him.

   > We <u>saw</u> a beautiful bird while we **were walking** home.

3. to talk about two actions that were in progress at the same time.

   > He **was working** outside while his classmates **were** indoors **playing** computer games.

   > **Were** you **listening** to music while you **were studying**?

C Read the sentences and underline the verbs in the past continuous. Then with a partner, discuss why each sentence uses the past continuous.

CRITICAL THINKING: ANALYZING

1. His grandfather was still running the ranch when Manuel was born.
2. Tyrel was working on a ranch in 2007.
3. He was singing to the cattle while his brother was making dinner.

D Complete each sentence with the past continuous form of the verb(s) in parentheses.

1. When I saw Ricardo yesterday, he _____*was studying*_____ (study) in the library.

2. In 2010, I _____ (live) with my parents in Mexico City.

3. On Saturday afternoon, I _____ (clean) the house while my children _____ (watch) TV.

4. I _____ (do) my homework at eight o'clock last night.

5. I _____ (drive) to work when you called this morning, so I didn't answer.

6. It _____ (not/rain) when the soccer game started.

7. Some students _____ (talk) while Tim _____ (give) his presentation. They were very rude!

8. What _____ you _____ (laugh) about in class this morning?

PERSONALIZING **E** Complete sentences 2, 3, and 4 from exercise D with true information about yourself. Use the past continuous. Then with a partner, take turns reading your sentences. Ask your partner follow-up questions for more information.

A: *In 2010, I was living in Toronto, Canada.*
B: *That's interesting. Why were you living there?*

CRITICAL THINKING:
REFLECTING **F** Take turns discussing these topics with your partner. Use the past continuous.

1. Where were your parents living when they met? How did they meet? What were they doing?
2. How did you meet your best friend? Where were you living and what were you doing?
3. Think of a funny, scary, or surprising experience you've had recently. What happened?

LESSON TASK Exchanging Information about Cowboys

A Work with a partner. Student A will read about *paniolos*. Student B will read about *gauchos*. As you read your paragraph, take brief notes to answer these questions.

1. What kind of cowboy is the paragraph about? Where do these cowboys live?
2. What kind of work does/did this kind of cowboy do? What other interesting details does the paragraph include?
3. How is life for these cowboys different now than in the past?

Student A

Paniolos

Hawaii has traditional cowboys called *paniolos*. The first cattle in Hawaii were a gift to the king in 1793. Many years later, the first three cowboys came to Hawaii. They were Mexican men who were living in California at the time. The king invited them to the island to control the cattle that were growing in number there, and also to teach cattle-handling skills to the local people. Because those first cowboys spoke Spanish (*español*), Hawaiians gave them the name *paniolo*. Now there are only a few large ranches in Hawaii, and the last *paniolos* are very old, but people still enjoy learning about Hawaiian cowboy culture.

Student B

Gauchos

Gauchos are the cowboys of Brazil, Argentina, and Uruguay. *Gauchos* were working in those countries as early as the 1700s. Today, people still admire *gauchos* for their independence, bravery, and skills—especially their horseback riding. *Gauchos* are the subject of many stories and legends, but in real life, most *gauchos* were very poor. Usually, the only things they owned were their clothing and their horses. Today *gauchos* still work in South America, but their lives are better than they were in the past. Now most of them receive a steady salary, and they no longer have to move from place to place to find work.

B Close your books and take turns telling each other about the kind of cowboy you read about. Use your notes to help you. Ask for and give clarification as needed.

Gauchos relax at the end of the day in Pantanal, Brazil

Men at the Holi Festival, Rajasthan, India

Faces of India

BEFORE VIEWING

A Read the information about Rajasthan, India. Notice each underlined word and think about its meaning. You will hear these words in the video.

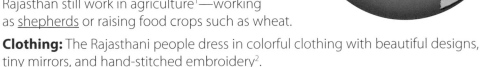

Rajasthan, India

TRADITIONAL RAJASTHAN

Occupations: Although city people attend universities and have professional <u>careers</u>, most people in the large Indian state of Rajasthan still work in agriculture[1]—working as <u>shepherds</u> or raising food crops such as wheat.

Clothing: The Rajasthani people dress in colorful clothing with beautiful designs, tiny mirrors, and hand-stitched embroidery[2].

Music and Dance: The region is famous for a kind of dance called *ghoomar* as well as several types of music played on traditional instruments.

Way of Life: Many people in Rajasthan are <u>nomads</u>. Moving from place to place across the dry <u>landscape</u> allows shepherds to find grass for their sheep, and allows <u>entertainers</u> to find new audiences who have not seen them perform.

People: It's a custom for people in Rajasthan to be <u>hospitable</u>, so visitors always feel comfortable and welcome there.

[1]**agriculture** (n): farming and ranching
[2]**hand-stitched embroidery** (n): decoration made by sewing designs with colored thread

B Work with a partner. Write each underlined word from exercise A next to its definition. Use context clues to help you.

1. _____ (n) people without permanent homes
2. _____ (n) people who take care of sheep in the fields
3. _____ (n) life's work, especially in business or a profession
4. _____ (adj) friendly and welcoming
5. _____ (n) a large area of land
6. _____ (n) people such as singers or dancers who provide enjoyment

C Read the information about Steve McCurry. With a partner, discuss things that visitors from other countries appreciate about your culture.

PERSONALIZING

> **MEET STEVE MCCURRY.** He's a National Geographic Contributing Photographer, and he loves to travel the world. For over 30 years, McCurry has taken pictures of people and places on every continent. In India, however, McCurry feels a special appreciation for the culture. According to him, "There's no place in the world that has the depth of culture like India."

WHILE VIEWING

D ▶ 1.5 Read the statements. Then watch the video and choose T for *True* or F for *False*. Correct the false statements.

UNDERSTANDING MAIN IDEAS

1. After college, McCurry's first job was working as a travel agent. T F
2. Rajasthan is on the border with Bangladesh. T F
3. McCurry says going to Rajasthan is like going to another planet. T F
4. Some of the entertainers in Rajasthan are having to find new ways to make a living. T F
5. McCurry is immediately comfortable talking to the people he meets in Rajasthan. T F

E ▶ 1.5 Watch the video again and check the examples of traditional culture that you see.

UNDERSTANDING DETAILS

☐ moving animals from place to place ☐ traditional clothing
☐ cooking traditional food ☐ singing and dancing
☐ entertainers working with snakes ☐ traditional houses

AFTER VIEWING

F Discuss this question with a partner: What do you think daily life is like for the people you saw in the video? Discuss your ideas about their work, their free time, and their education.

CRITICAL THINKING: ANALYZING

B Vocabulary

MEANING FROM
CONTEXT **A**   🎧 1.22   Read and listen to the assignment. Notice each word in **blue** and think about its meaning.

Anthropology 106: Culture and Music

Assignment: Oral Presentation

For this assignment, you will **select** a kind of music from another country and teach your classmates about it. Your presentation should be at least two minutes.

- **Describe** how the music sounds. Does it have a nice melody[1]? Is the **rhythm** fast or slow? What kinds of instruments do the musicians play? Are there typically singers and **lyrics**? Play an example of the music so your audience can hear it.

- **Explain** where and when people typically listen to this kind of music. Do they listen to it on special occasions, such as weddings or holidays?

- **Compare** this kind of music to another kind of music you know about. How are they similar? Then **contrast** the two kinds of music. How are they different?

- **Define** any words you think your classmates may not know.

- In your conclusion, **summarize** the different **aspects** of the music that you discussed, and remind your audience of the most important ideas of your presentation.

[1]**melody** (n): a series of musical notes, or the tune of a song

B   Match each word in **blue** from exercise A with its definition.

1. _____ select (v)   a. to tell the meaning of a word
2. _____ describe (v)   b. to give details that help someone understand your idea
3. _____ rhythm (n)   c. to discover the similarities between two things
4. _____ lyrics (n)   d. the words of a song
5. _____ explain (v)   e. to choose
6. _____ compare (v)   f. to show the difference between two things
7. _____ contrast (v)   g. a series of sounds that repeats
8. _____ define (v)   h. to briefly tell the most important points about something
9. _____ summarize (v)   i. one part of a topic or situation
10. _____ aspect (n)   j. to tell what something is like

A member of the Between Music band plays the drums in an underwater tank during a rehearsal for the Aquasonic underwater concert in Aarhus, Denmark.

Keeping a vocabulary journal can help you learn new words and build your vocabulary. When you hear or see a new word, write it along with its definition, its part of speech (e.g., noun, verb), and the context (where you heard or saw it). It is also helpful to write a sentence that includes the new word.

> rhythm (noun): a series of sounds
>
> context: an exercise about music
>
> "Salsa music has a quick, lively rhythm."

C Work with a partner. Take turns talking about the topics below. Try to talk about each topic for at least 30 seconds. Your partner will time you.　　PERSONALIZING

> *I like to listen to Reggae music because it has a good rhythm and it's fun to dance to . . .*

1. Describe a kind of music you like to listen to.
2. Explain how you learn new vocabulary words.
3. Summarize a book or movie you enjoyed.
4. Compare and contrast two kinds of food.
5. Select one aspect of your life to tell your partner about.

Listening An Assignment about Music

BEFORE LISTENING

PRIOR KNOWLEDGE **A** You are going to listen to an assignment and then to a student's presentation about the music of the Roma people. Read the information and look at the photo. Then discuss the questions that follow with a partner.

Roma musicians in Budapest, Hungary

THE ROMA

The Roma people were living in India before they moved into Europe about 1,000 years ago. Now they live in many different countries, but they have kept their own culture and language. There are many Roma people in Bulgaria, Hungary, and Romania, but they also live in other parts of the world. The Roma are known for their music and dancing, and they have been very important to jazz, classical, and flamenco music.

1. What did you already know about the Roma people before you read the paragraph?
2. Are you familiar with Roma music? What do you know about it?
3. What else would you like to know about the Roma people?

WHILE LISTENING

NOTE-TAKING SKILL Using a Numbered List

Using a numbered list is a simple way to record and organize the main points of a lecture, parts of an assignment, or the steps in a process. Also, having your notes organized in a clear list is helpful when you need to review or study them later.

B 1.23 Listen to the professor as he explains the assignment, and complete the notes in the numbered list below. NOTE TAKING

Assignment: A Presentation

1. ______________ a kind of ______________ from another ______________
2. talk about the ______________ the music comes from
3. ______________ the music, and ______________ which aspects are ______________ and which aspects are new, or ______________
4. compare and ______________ it with another kind of ______________
5. ______________ a sample of the music if you can
6. summarize the ______________ ideas, and allow a few minutes at the end for ______________

LISTENING SKILL Asking Questions While Listening

You will understand more of what you hear if you are an active listener. One way to be an active listener is to ask yourself questions while you are listening. You can ask yourself *yes/no* or *wh-* questions to prepare for the kind of information that will probably come next or to evaluate information you hear.

For example, if you hear: *Bossa Nova comes from samba music, so these two kinds of music are similar in some ways . . .*

you could ask yourself: *How are they similar?*

C 1.24 Listen to a student's presentation. As you listen, ask yourself these questions: Does this information complete part of the assignment in exercise B? If so, which part? Circle the numbers of the parts of the assignment in exercise B that the student includes in his presentation. LISTENING FOR MAIN IDEAS

AFTER LISTENING

D Work with a partner. Compare your answers from exercise C.

E Discuss these questions with your partner. PERSONALIZING

1. Do you know about any other kinds of traditional music that people are playing in new ways? If so, what kinds?
2. What kind of music is traditional in your country? Is it still popular? Do people still play it the same way, or is it changing?
3. Do you think it's OK to change traditional music, or should we try to keep it the same? Explain.

B Speaking

A Work with a partner. Discuss these questions.

1. What musical instruments do you like to listen to? Why?
2. Do you play (or want to learn to play) any musical instruments? Explain.
3. Do you feel comfortable describing things in English? Explain.

EVERYDAY LANGUAGE   Checking Understanding

Is that clear?   *Do you want/need me to repeat that?*

Do you have any questions?   *Does that make sense?*

B Work with a partner. Student A will read about bagpipes. Student B will read about steel drums. As you read your information, take brief notes to answer these questions.

1. How is the instrument described? Where is it played?
2. How does the instrument work?
3. What is special or interesting about the instrument?

Student A

Bagpipes

Bagpipes are a very old musical instrument. They have a large bag that holds air, and one or more small pipes that make the notes of the music. The player blows air into the bag, and then the air comes out slowly through the pipes to make a very loud sound.

Bagpipes have a long history. Musicians in ancient Rome played a similar instrument with an airbag and pipes. Today, the most famous bagpipes are in Scotland and Ireland, but there are many different instruments like this in different regions of Europe, North Africa, and the Middle East.

A bagpiper plays in the ruins of Urquhart Castle beside Loch Ness in Scotland.

Student B

Steel Drums

Steel drums are from the island of Trinidad, in the Caribbean. They are made from old steel oil barrels. Steel drums are not very old instruments, however—the first steel drums were made in about 1947. But musicians in Trinidad loved the sound and quickly started using them in their traditional music.

The sound of a steel drum is very light and happy. The top of the drum has different sections, and each section makes a different musical note. Steel drums are usually played by groups of musicians called a *steel band*. Steel bands play all kinds of music at the popular *Carnival* festival in Trinidad every spring.

◄ **A man plays steel drums.**

C Close your books. With your partner, take turns telling each other about the instrument you read about. Use your notes to help you. Ask for and give clarification, and check understanding when necessary.

PRONUNCIATION Reduced Function Words

🎧 **1.25** In English, not every word in a sentence gets the same amount of stress or emphasis. Some words are *reduced*, which means that they are usually said quickly, and the vowel sound is shortened. Reduced words include:

articles   conjunctions   pronouns
auxiliary verbs   prepositions

The sound of a steel drum is light and happy.
We bought a birthday gift for Molly.
What are you reading? Can I see it?

D 🎧 **1.26** Underline the function words in each sentence. Then listen and check your answers.

1. The violin is my favorite instrument.
2. Our friends are waiting outside.
3. Only a few people play this kind of guitar.
4. You can probably hear it on the radio.
5. The group is playing in a small theater.
6. Tell Maria about the class assignment.

E Work with a partner. Practice saying the sentences from exercise D. Remember to reduce the function words.

FINAL TASK Presenting a Kind of Music

> You are going to prepare and give an individual presentation on a kind of music.

BRAINSTORMING **A** Work in a group. Brainstorm a list of the kinds of music you are familiar with. Use the ideas below to help you get started. Write your ideas in your notebook.

classical	hip-hop	K-pop	reggaetón	rock

ORGANIZING IDEAS **B** Work on your own. Read the instructions for your assignment. In your notebook, write notes to help you remember what you will say for each part of your presentation.

Presentation Assignment:
1. Select a kind of music from the brainstorming list you made in exercise A.
2. Tell the class what kind of music you selected and explain why.
3. Describe the music you selected. Explain where it is from, what instruments it uses, and what it sounds like (e.g., rhythm, melody, lyrics).
4. Play a sample of the music (if possible).
5. Compare and contrast it with another kind of music you know.
6. Summarize the most important ideas from your presentation, and answer any questions your classmates have.

PRESENTATION SKILL Using Good Posture

Posture means how you hold your body. When you speak in front of the class, you should stand up straight on both feet. If you aren't holding notes, use your hands for simple gestures as you speak. This shows that you are confident and well-prepared.

PRESENTING **C** Give your presentation to the class. Remember to use good posture. Check understanding and give clarification if necessary.

REFLECTION

1. What is the most useful skill you learned in this unit?

_____

_____

2. Which culture or place from this unit would you like to learn more about? Why?

_____

_____

3. Here are the vocabulary words from the unit. Check (✓) the ones you can use.

☐ actual
☐ aspect AWL
☐ compare
☐ contrast AWL
☐ custom
☐ define AWL
☐ describe
☐ develop

☐ disappear
☐ estimate AWL
☐ explain
☐ factor AWL
☐ lyrics
☐ preserve
☐ region AWL

☐ rhythm
☐ select AWL
☐ still
☐ summarize AWL
☐ traditional AWL

A THIRSTY WORLD

4

Three million black plastic balls help turn away the sun's UV rays and protect the drinking water in the Ivanhoe Reservoir in Los Angeles California, USA.

THINK AND DISCUSS

1   Look at the photo. What do you think these people are doing?

2   Which do you think is a bigger problem—too much water, or not enough water?

**Look at the infographic and read the information.
Then discuss the questions.**

1. What is *Hidden Water*, or *virtual water*?
2. How many gallons of water are required to produce a cup of tea? A pair of jeans? A T-shirt? A pound of figs?
3. Which kind of diet requires more water: a mostly vegetarian diet or a diet that includes meat? Why?
4. Does any of the information from the infographic surprise you? Will it cause you to change any of your everyday habits?

HIDDEN WATER

The world consumes trillions of virtual gallons of water. When you serve a pound of beef, you are also serving 1,857 gallons[1] of water. A cup of coffee? That's 37 gallons, enough water to fill the average bathtub. When you wear a pair of jeans, you're wearing 2,900 gallons. This is the amount of fresh water that we consume but don't actually see. It's called *virtual water:* the amount of water used to create a product.

[1]one gallon = 3.785 liters

ANIMAL PRODUCTS
Virtual-water totals include the amount of water used to raise the animals and make the product into food (e.g., making milk into cheese).

589
PROCESSED
CHEESE

400
EGGS

371
FRESH
CHEESE

138
YOGURT

MEAT
The virtual water for meat is the water the animals drink and the water used to grow their food and clean their living areas.

1,857
GALLONS OF WATER
USED TO PRODUCE ONE
POUND OF BEEF

469
CHICKEN

FRUITS AND VEGETABLES

Both rainwater and irrigation water are included in the virtual-water totals for fruits and vegetables.

EVERYDAY ITEMS

Cotton is used to make many items that we wear and use every day, such as T-shirts, jeans, and bedsheets, and it requires a lot of water.

2,900
GALLONS TO PRODUCE ONE PAIR OF BLUE JEANS

379 GALLONS FOR A POUND OF FIGS

154 AVOCADOS

109 CORN

193 PLUMS

43 BEANS

31 POTATOES

25 EGGPLANTS

185 CHERRIES

103 BANANAS

84 APPLES

78 GRAPES

55 ORANGES

33 STRAWBERRIES

2,800 ONE COTTON BEDSHEET

766 ONE COTTON T-SHIRT

634 ONE BURGER

9 ONE CUP OF TEA

37 ONE CUP OF COFFEE

53 ONE GLASS OF MILK

WHY MEAT USES MORE WATER

A human diet that regularly includes meat requires 60 percent more water than a mostly vegetarian diet. This is due to the amount of water needed to raise cattle. The graphic on the right shows the amount of water needed to raise an average cow (approximately 3 years).

88,400 GALLONS FOR 18,700 POUNDS OF FEED

+

6,300 GALLONS FOR DRINKING

+

1,900 GALLONS FOR CLEANING

=

816,600 GALLONS USED DURING THE LIFE OF THE ANIMAL

A Vocabulary

MEANING FROM CONTEXT

A 🎧 **1.27** Read and listen to the statements in the quiz below. Notice each word in **blue** and think about its meaning.

QUIZ: HOW MUCH DO YOU KNOW ABOUT WATER?

1. The Amazon River **supplies** about 20% of the fresh water that enters the world's oceans. T F

2. Farmers **require** 911 gallons (3,450 liters) of water to produce 2.2 pounds (1 kilogram) of rice. T F

3. The **risk** of disease is high if the water you drink is not clean. About 1 million people die each year from drinking dirty water. T F

4. Farming uses a **significant** amount of water—up to 40 percent of the fresh water used worldwide. T F

5. The United States has built more than 80,000 dams[1] to **manage** water for different uses such as producing electricity. T F

6. Scientists say that 13 gallons (50 liters) of water per day is **adequate** for one person. T F

7. You can **collect** water in a desert with just a sheet of plastic and an empty can. T F

8. Water is a renewable **resource**, so we can use the same water again and again. T F

9. The Nile River in Africa (the longest river in the world) **flows** through four different countries. T F

10. People in Australia use the smallest **amount** of water of any country in the world. T F

---

[1]**dam** (n): a wall built across a river to stop the water from flowing, often to make electricity

B Match each word in **blue** from exercise A with its definition.

1. _____ supplies (v)	a. material people can use
2. _____ require (v)	b. how much there is of something
3. _____ risk (n)	c. possibility that something bad will happen
4. _____ significant (adj)	d. enough
5. _____ manage (v)	e. moves slowly without stopping
6. _____ adequate (adj)	f. to bring together
7. _____ collect (v)	g. gives or provides something
8. _____ resource (n)	h. to need
9. _____ flows	i. important, meaningful
10. _____ amount (n)	j. to use carefully

A hiker filters water in the Talkeetna Mountains near Palmer, Alaska, USA.

C Take the quiz from exercise A. Choose T for *True* or F for *False* for each statement.

D Work with a partner. Compare and discuss your answers from the quiz. Then check your answers at the bottom of this page.

VOCABULARY SKILL Recognizing Suffixes

Adding a suffix to a word changes its part of speech, or grammatical function. For example, the suffixes *-ion /-tion/-ation*, *-ance/-ence,* and *-ment* change verbs to nouns. Recognizing suffixes and parts of speech can help you build your vocabulary.

Verb	Noun
preserve	preservation
govern	government
occur	occurrence

E Choose the correct form of the word to complete each sentence. Then compare your answers with a partner's.

1. Chemistry 101 is a (require / requirement) for my major, so I have to take the course.
2. I have an interesting (collect / collection) of stamps from different countries.
3. Where I live, rainstorms (occur / occurrence) frequently in summer.
4. We (depend / dependence) on fresh water for many things in our daily lives.
5. Good water (manage / management) can help our city during the dry season.
6. Desert plants (require / requirement) very little water to grow.

F Work in a group. Discuss these questions.

CRITICAL THINKING: ANALYZING

1. What are the risks of not having enough water? Of having too much water? Do you know of any places that have experienced these problems recently?
2. Besides water, what are some things you require each day?
3. How is the water supply in your country? Is it difficult to get an adequate amount of clean water where you live?
4. Good management of natural resources can make them last longer. Besides water, what are some natural resources that people need to manage well?

Answers: The false statements are 3. (about 6 to 8 million people die each year), 4. (around 70 percent of fresh water is used for farming), 9. (11 different countries), and 10. (Mozambique, in Africa).

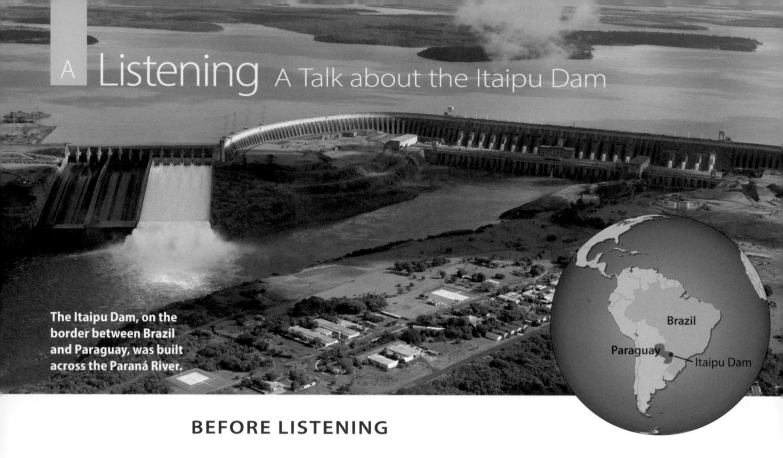

Listening A Talk about the Itaipu Dam

The Itaipu Dam, on the
border between Brazil
and Paraguay, was built
across the Paraná River.

Brazil

Paraguay • ┌ Itaipu Dam

BEFORE LISTENING

PRIOR KNOWLEDGE

A Work with a partner. Look at the map and photo, and discuss these questions.

1. What do you know about Brazil and Paraguay? Have you ever been to those countries or read news stories about them?
2. The photo shows the Paraná River behind the Itaipu Dam. Can you explain what a dam such as this does?

WHILE LISTENING

LISTENING FOR
MAIN IDEAS

B 🎧 1.28 ▶ 1.6 Listen to a talk and check (✓) the main idea.

☐ The Itaipu Dam is one of the largest dams in the world.

☐ Building the Itaipu Dam forced many families to leave their land.

☐ The Itaipu Dam is good for the economies of Brazil and Paraguay.

☐ There are both benefits and problems with the Itaipu Dam.

NOTE-TAKING SKILL Using a T-Chart

Using a T-chart is a helpful way to take notes on two aspects of a topic such as benefits and problems, advantages and disadvantages, or facts and opinions. Having your notes organized in a T-chart is also helpful when you need to review or study the information later.

Farming	
Benefits	Problems
produces food	requires a lot of water

C 🎧 1.28 Listen to the talk again, and complete the notes in the T-chart with the information you hear.

Itaipu Dam (Paraná River, Paraguay and Brazil)	
Benefits	Problems

– Building the dam created jobs: about _____ workers were required.
 1
 	
 – Good for economy:
 	
   1. Provides about _____ %
      2
     of the electricity used in Brazil and
     about _____ % in Paraguay.
        3
 	
   2. Tourist attraction: _____ can
                4
     go on free tours and go _____
                        5
     in natural areas.
 	
 – Supplies water that _____ can
                            6
   use during times of drought.
	– Reservoir covered _____ square
	                   7
	   miles of _____ with water.
	          8
	
	 – Around _____ families lost their
	         9
	   _____ and had to leave the area.
	     10
	
	 – Some _____ and
	         11
	   _____ sites now underwater.
	     12
	
	 – Farmers say reservoir may be raising
	   _____ temperatures by as much
	     13
	   as 4°C.
	
	 – Not everyone thinks the _____
	                           14
	   between the two countries is
	
	   _____ .
	     15

AFTER LISTENING

D Work with a partner. Decide which person (or people) would agree with each of the statements below. Then discuss the statements and give reasons for the ones you agree with.

1. _____ The problems with the dam are more significant than the benefits it provides.

2. _____ It might be necessary for some families to lose their land if the result is electricity for many people.

3. _____ The benefits of the dam are more significant than the problems.

4. _____ More countries should build very large dams to manage their water.

a. The guest speaker

b. A family who lost their land

c. The owner of a tourism company near the dam

d. A farmer who grows food crops near the dam

e. You

A Speaking

GRAMMAR FOR SPEAKING Active and Passive Voice

In the active voice, the subject performs or does the action.
> The dam **provides** electricity for many people.

In the passive voice, the subject receives the action.
> Electricity **is provided** by the dam.

We form the passive voice with the verb *be* plus the past participle of a verb.
> The water in our city **is managed** carefully.
> How **is** this word **pronounced**?

We often use the passive voice to talk about processes.
> Water **is collected** in containers and **used** for washing clothes.

We use *by* with the passive when we want to specify *who* or *what* did the action.
> These books were given to us **by the school**.

A Underline the verb form in each sentence. Choose P for *Passive Voice* or A for *Active Voice*. Then complete each sentence to make it true.

1. Rice <u>is grown</u> in countries such as _____   P   A
   and _____ .

2. In my country, a lot of electricity is provided by _____ .   P   A

3. Nowadays, many people study online instead of in _____ .   P   A

4. At my house, we use a significant amount of water   P   A
   for _____ .

5. In my country, children are taught to _____ .   P   A

6. My favorite dish is made with _____ .   P   A

B Work with a partner. Take turns saying and explaining your sentences from exercise A.

> *Rice is grown in countries such as India and Thailand.*

C Take turns asking and answering these questions with a partner. Use the passive voice in your answers.

> *Coffee is grown in Brazil, Colombia, …*

1. Where does coffee grow?
2. Who owns or rents the house or apartment next to yours?
3. Who manages the money in your household?
4. What are some of the ways people use smartphones?
5. What kind of people collect coins?
6. Who corrects the homework in this class?

PRONUNCIATION Suffixes and Syllable Stress

🎧 1.29 When the suffixes *-tion*, *-ity*, *-ial*, and *-ical* are added to words, the stress changes.
The syllable just before each of these suffixes receives the main stress, or primary stress.

Paying attention to suffixes and syllable stress can help you improve your listening
comprehension and pronunciation skills.

-tion	*-ity*
educate → edu**ca**tion	a**vai**lable → availa**bi**lity
-ial	*ical*
industry → in**dus**trial	**hi**story → his**tor**ical

D 🎧 1.30 Underline the syllable with the main stress in each **bold** word. Then listen and
check your answers.

1. **po**litics   It was a significant **po**li<u>ti</u>cal event.
2. **resident**   This is a **residential** apartment building.
3. **apply**   We turned in our **application** before the due date.
4. **possible**   There is a **possibility** of finding water on other planets.
5. **inform**   We need more **information** before we make a decision.
6. **theory**   This is only a **theoretical** situation. It's not real.

E Work with a partner. Take turns reading the sentences from exercise D aloud.
Pay attention to the suffixes and syllable stress.

F Take turns asking and answering these questions with a partner. Pay attention to
suffixes and syllable stress.

PERSONALIZING

1. Many people enjoy being active. What are some of the activities you like to do in
   your free time?
2. People define the word *busy* in different ways. What is your definition of *busy*?
3. Parents influence their children in important ways. Who else has been influential
   in your life?
4. Many people want to conserve electricity. What are some devices you use that
   consume a significant amount of electrical power?

LESSON TASK Presenting a Clean Water Device

A Work in a group. Read the situation below and the information about three clean water devices on this and the next page. Use the information to say sentences about each device. Use the passive voice. Then discuss the questions that follow.

> *The drum is used to bring clean water to houses.*

Situation: You work for an organization called Safe Water Now. Your organization wants to spend $1 million for a new device that will help provide clean water for people. You have to give a presentation to the directors of your organization that explains which device is best and why.

1. What problem does each device try to solve?
2. Who could benefit from each device?
3. How easy or difficult do you think it is to make each device and get it to people?

Device 1 The **Q Drum** carries 13 gallons (50 liters) of water easily.

- drum/use to bring clean water to houses
- rope/put through a hole
- drum/pull/not carry
- drums/make/in South Africa
- drums/sell for $70

Device 2 The **KickStart Pump** helps farmers provide more water for their crops.

- pump/sell to farmers in Africa
- pump/operate with your feet
- more crops/grow with the water
- money from crops/use for family's health and education
- pumps/make in Kenya/sell for $70

Device 3   The **LifeStraw** provides clean water for one person for a year.

- LifeStraw/use with any kind of dirty water
- one end/put in a person's mouth/the other end/put into water
- LifeStraw/use in emergency situations and for camping
- no electrical power/require to use the LifeStraw
- LifeStraw/make by a Swiss company/sell for about $20

A man uses a LifeStraw in Yosemite National Park, California, USA.

B With your group, follow the steps below to plan your presentation.   ORGANIZING IDEAS

1. Decide which device you will present to the directors.
2. Plan what you will say. Use the passive voice when appropriate. Your presentation should answer these questions:

- Which device did your group choose?
- How does the device work?
- Who will this device help? How will it help them?
- Why do you think this is the best device?

   > *It's easier to use because the drum is pulled, not carried.*
   > *More crops can be grown with the water from the pump, which helps farmers.*

3. Decide which information each member of your group will present.
4. Write notes to help you with your part of the presentation.
5. Practice your presentation.

PRESENTATION SKILL Speaking at the Right Volume
When you are giving a presentation, you need to speak a little louder than normal so your audience can hear and understand you. This also shows that you are confident. At the beginning of your presentation, check your volume with your audience. Here are some questions you can ask: *Can everyone hear me?*   *Is my volume OK?*

C With your group, give your presentation to the class. Remember to speak at the right volume.   PRESENTING

Whitewater rafters,
Grand Canyon,
Arizona, USA

Dam-Release Rafting

BEFORE VIEWING

A Read the information about the video you are going to watch. Use your dictionary to help you with any words you don't know.

> **MEET JONNY PHILLIPS AND RICHARD AMBROSE.** They're industrial scientists from the United Kingdom. They are also the hosts of a BBC documentary television show called *I Didn't Know That*, and they're known for doing dangerous and exciting activities.
>
> In this video, Jonny and Richard introduce us to an unusual kind of water sport: dam-release[1] rafting. In a country that's not known for its mountainous landscapes, this may be the only way to experience the excitement of whitewater rafting[2].

[1]**release** (v): to let go or set free
[2]**whitewater rafting** (n): rafting that takes place on fast-moving rivers with rough water

PREDICTING **B** Check (✓) the things you think you will see or learn about in the video. Then compare your predictions with a partner's.

☐ a dam ☐ a mountain ☐ how water is released from a dam
☐ a raft ☐ a river or stream ☐ how to stay safe when rafting

WHILE VIEWING

C ▶ **1.7** Watch the video and check your predictions from exercise B.

CHECKING PREDICTIONS

D ▶ **1.7** Watch the video again and complete each quote from the video with the number that you hear.

UNDERSTANDING DETAILS

1. "This valve alone can release over _____ liters of water a minute."

2. "For water to be released for a whole day, it can cost _____ pounds."

3. "With the dam open, the amount of water flowing down this river increases to a massive _____ million liters."

4. "That's _____ times the normal amount, which means the boys will be traveling down it _____ times faster than normal!"

AFTER VIEWING

E Use the passive form of the verbs in parentheses to complete the steps for dam-release rafting.

1. First, a release of water __is requested__ (request).

2. Second, money _____ (pay) for the release of water.

3. Next, a valve inside the dam _____ (open) to release the water.

4. After that, people in the raft _____ (carry) on a wild ride down the river.

5. Finally, the valve _____, (close) and much of the water stays behind the dam again.

F Work with a partner. Close your books and take turns retelling the steps for dam-release rafting from exercise E. Use the passive voice.

G Work in a group. Discuss these questions.

CRITICAL THINKING: ANALYZING

1. The kind of rafting you saw in the video is somewhat risky, and people can be hurt if they do it. Why do you think some people enjoy risky or even dangerous activities?

2. Is rafting a sport you might want to do? Explain.

3. Do you think there are any disadvantages to releasing the water from a dam for a water sport? Explain.

B Vocabulary

PERSONALIZING   **A**   Work with a partner. Discuss these questions.

1. Have you ever experienced a water shortage? Explain.
2. Are there any rules in your country about using water? Explain.

MEANING FROM   **B**   🎧 1.31   Look at the map and read and listen to the information about "water-stressed
CONTEXT   areas" in the world. These are areas where the demand for clean water is greater than
the supply. Notice each word in **blue** and think about its meaning.

1. An **urgent** problem in the western United States is low levels of groundwater.

2. Water from rivers can be **distributed** to cities and farms where the water is needed.

3. Without adequate water for **agriculture**, a world food **crisis** is possible. If farmers do not have enough water for their crops, it could affect millions of people.

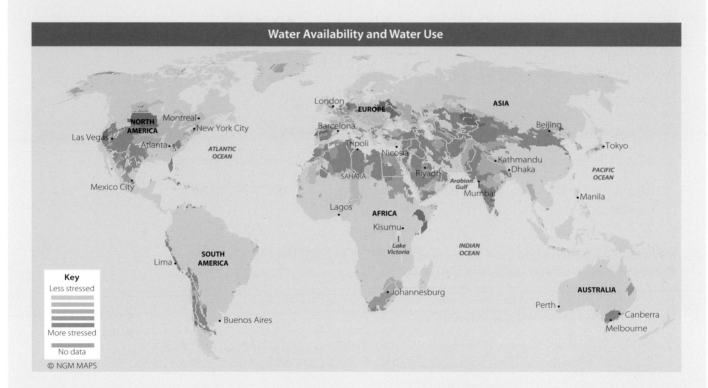

Water Availability and Water Use

Key
Less stressed

More stressed

No data

© NGM MAPS

4. Farmers can **reduce** the amount of water they use. Learning about and practicing water **conservation** will allow them to do the same work with less water.

5. Parts of northern Africa are **extremely** dry. For example, the **average** yearly rainfall in the Sahara Desert is less than 1 inch (25 mm).

6. Water is **scarce** in many regions of the world, and people in these areas often do not have access to clean water.

7. Australia has **experienced** both drought and floods in recent years. This has been very difficult for the farmers there.

C Complete each definition with the correct word in **blue** from exercise B.

1. If you _____ (v) something, you moved it from one place to many other places.

2. _____ (n) means not using too much of a natural resource.

3. If something is _____ (adj), it is usual and normal.

4. _____ (n) is the science of growing plants and raising animals on farms.

5. If something is _____ (adj), you need to take care of it very soon.

6. A _____ (n) is a large and serious problem.

7. To _____ (v) something means to make it smaller or less.

8. If you _____ (v) something, it happened to you.

9. "_____" (adv) means to a very great degree.

10. If something is _____ (adj), there isn't a lot of it available.

EVERYDAY LANGUAGE Showing Interest

In conversation, it is polite to show interest. Here are some phrases you can use:

Really?   *That's interesting.*   *Uh-huh.*   *I didn't know that.*   *Wow!*

D Work in a group. Say whether you agree or disagree with each of the statements below. Be sure to explain and give reasons for your opinions.

1. I need to reduce the amount of water I use.
2. When there's a water crisis, it's usually caused by nature.
3. Not having enough clean water is an urgent problem in my country.
4. Water conservation is extremely important.

PERSONALIZING

E Work with a partner. Look at the map and the key on the previous page and complete the exercise.

CRITICAL THINKING: INTERPRETING A MAP

1. According to the map, what are three places where the water situation is urgent (very water stressed)? _____ _____ _____

2. According to the map, what are three places that are not experiencing a water crisis. (less water stressed)?

   _____ _____ _____

3. List two places where the water situation is bad, but not extremely bad.

   _____ _____

4. Describe the water situation in your country according to this map. Do you agree with the information on the map? Explain.

Listening A Discussion about the Ogallala Aquifer

BEFORE LISTENING

A Read the information in the box. Then answer the questions below with a partner.

> ### AQUIFERS
>
> Aquifers are areas of rock under the ground that contain large amounts of water. Sometimes this water is easy to reach, but often it has to be pumped up out of the aquifer with a special device. In dry parts of the western United States, farmers use water from aquifers to irrigate their fields. Without this water, the fields might be too dry to grow certain food crops.

1. In your own words, what is an *aquifer*?
2. How do farmers in the western United States use the water from aquifers?
3. Why is the water from aquifers so important to these farmers?
4. Do you know of any other places where there are aquifers? If so, where?

WHILE LISTENING

LISTENING FOR
MAIN IDEAS

B 🎧 1.32 Listen to the students' discussion and choose the correct answers.

1. What is the topic of the group presentation?

   a. Better Ways to Distribute Water   c. How to Solve the Aquifer Crisis
   b. What Caused the Aquifer Crisis

2. There is an "aquifer crisis" because _____.

   a. the water in the aquifer is difficult to reach   c. the water in the aquifer isn't clean
   b. people are using the aquifer water too quickly

3. Dryland farming is a possible solution to the aquifer crisis because _____.

   a. it requires little water   c. it's a good way to grow corn
   b. it's less expensive for farmers

Tractors put corn into huge piles at a feedlot near Imperial, Nebraska, USA.

A mother gives her daughter a bath in a bucket using water distributed by the town of Clovis, New Mexico, USA.

LISTENING SKILL Listening for Problems and Solutions

When listening to a talk or discussion about an issue, being able to recognize and link problems to their solutions will help you understand key ideas about the topic. When listening, pay attention to words and phrases that signal when a speaker is going to talk about a problem or a solution. Here are some examples:

The problem is ...   *That's **one possible solution**, but* ...

Here's the issue.   *Maybe **the best approach** is* ...

C 🎧 **1.32** Listen to the discussion again and complete the notes in the T-chart.

LISTENING FOR PROBLEMS AND SOLUTIONS

The Ogallala Aquifer	
Problems	Possible Solutions
– Water in aquifers being pumped out quickly (past 70 yrs.)	– Better ways to _____
– In parts of the western U.S., not enough water for 1. _____ 2. _____	– Water _____

AFTER LISTENING

D Work in a group. Compare your notes from exercise C. Then discuss these questions.

CRITICAL THINKING: EVALUATING

1. Which of the two solutions do you think would have more of an impact?
2. What other solutions might there be to the problems the students discussed?
3. What experiences have you had with group projects? Do you think the three students you heard were working together well? Explain.

B Speaking

SPEAKING SKILL Asking for and Giving Opinions

Here are some expressions you can use to ask people for their opinions:

Do you think . . . ?   *What's your opinion of . . . ?*

What do you think about . . . ?   *How do you feel about . . . ?*

Here are some expressions you can use when giving your opinion:

I think . . .   I feel that . . .   In my opinion, . . .   I don't think . . .   If you ask me, . . .

ASKING FOR AND GIVING OPINIONS

A Work with a partner. Take turns asking for and giving opinions about the topics below. Then talk about some of your own ideas.

A: *What do you think is the most interesting sport to watch in the Olympic Games?*

B: *In my opinion, it's skiing. I love watching the skiing events. How about you?*

sports in the Olympic Games	traveling to other countries	the weather today
owning a car	classical music	online classes

CRITICAL THINKING: APPLYING

B Work in a group. Read the situation in the box, and look at the information in the chart below. Then discuss the questions on the next page. Use the expressions in the Speaking Skill box to ask for and express opinions.

Situation: Your family lives in a small house. A large water pipe in your city broke yesterday, so there will be less water available to you until the pipe is fixed. It will take the city one whole week to fix the pipe. Each person in your family can use only 13 gallons (50 liters) of water a day, or a total of 91 gallons (350 liters) a week.

How much water do you need to . . .

 . . . drink every day?
.5 gallons/2 liters a day

 . . . wash the dishes?
8 gallons/30 liters

 . . . wash fruits and vegetables?
2 gallons/8 liters

 . . . flush the toilet?
3.5 gallons/13 liters

 . . . do a load of laundry?
22 gallons/85 liters

 . . . take a four-minute shower?
30 gallons/113 liters

 . . . brush your teeth?
.25 gallons/.5 liters

 . . . wash your face or hands?
.5 gallons/2 liters

1. What uses of water do you think are absolutely necessary every day?
2. What uses of water do you think are important, but perhaps not necessary every day?
3. What do you think are the best ways for your family to conserve water?

> **CRITICAL THINKING** Prioritizing
>
> When you have to make difficult decisions, it's important to be able to prioritize and evaluate which of your options is most important. This can help you to determine which things are most important in a certain situation and which things you need to do first.

C Make a list of your family's water priorities. Then make a plan for how you will use water for a week. Remember to take notes and do the necessary arithmetic.

CRITICAL THINKING: PRIORITIZING

D Present your plan to the class. Explain how you prioritized your water usage.

PRESENTING

FINAL TASK Role-Playing a Meeting

> You are going to role-play a government meeting about how to manage the local water supply. In the meeting, you will try to decide how much water each of the different organizations should be allowed to use.

A Work in a group of four. Read the situation below and the roles. Assign a role to each member of your group.

> **Situation:** The government built a new dam near a large city, and now the reservoir behind the dam is filling with water. Scientists determined how much water the city can take from the reservoir every year. Now the government will have a meeting to decide how to use that water.

> **Role #1: Manager of the City Water Company**
>
> - The population of the city has increased by 200,000 people in the last 10 years.
> - Now there are strict rules about using water for gardens and washing cars.
> - The price of water is very high.
>
> Requested share: 30 percent of the total amount

A THIRSTY WORLD **79**

Role #2: President of the National Farmers' Association

- Most farms are very small, and farmers don't earn much money.
- With more water, farmers could start growing cotton to sell to other countries.
- Farmers have had problems because there has been very little rain during the past few years.

Requested share: 60 percent of the total amount

Role #3: President of the International Aluminum Company

- The company wants to build a large aluminum[1] factory next to the reservoir.
- The factory would provide new jobs for more than 1,000 people.
- This would be the biggest factory in the region.

Requested share: 50 percent of the total amount

[1]**aluminum** (n): a lightweight metal with many uses

Role #4: Director of the National Parks Service

- Several kinds of rare fish and birds live in lakes that are connected to the reservoir.
- Foreign tourists often come to see and photograph these animals. The tourist industry is important to the local economy.
- If there isn't enough water, all the animals will die, and tourists will stop coming.

Requested share: 20 percent of the total amount

ORGANIZING IDEAS

B Prepare a one-minute talk to introduce your organization and present your viewpoint to the other members of your group. Take notes to help you remember your ideas. Your talk should answer these questions:

- Who are you? What organization or company do you work for?
- How much water does your organization need?
- Why does it need this amount of water?

C With your group, role-play the meeting. Take turns presenting your organizations and viewpoints. Decide how much water each organization will get. The amount must total 100 percent. Then report your group's decision to the class.

REFLECTION

1. What are two phrases you learned in this unit to help you express your opinion?

_____

_____

2. What is the most useful thing you learned in this unit?

_____

_____

3. Here are the vocabulary words from the unit. Check (✓) the ones you can use.

☐ adequate AWL	☐ distribute AWL	☐ resource AWL
☐ agriculture	☐ experience	☐ risk
☐ amount	☐ extremely	☐ scarce
☐ average	☐ flow	☐ significant AWL
☐ collect	☐ manage	☐ supply
☐ conservation	☐ reduce	☐ urgent
☐ crisis	☐ require AWL	

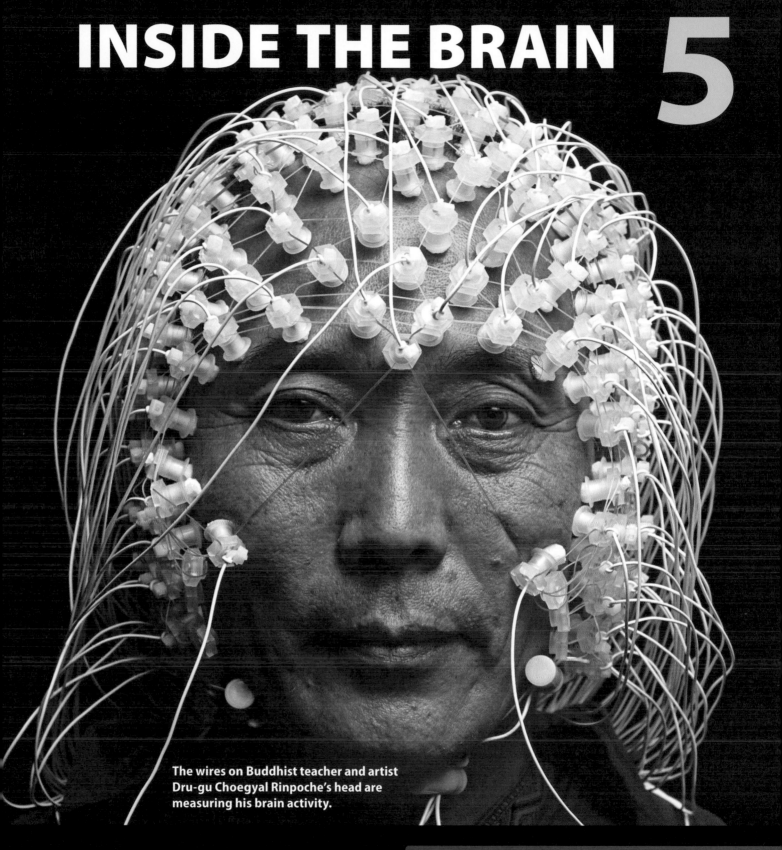

INSIDE THE BRAIN 5

The wires on Buddhist teacher and artist Dru-gu Choegyal Rinpoche's head are measuring his brain activity.

ACADEMIC SKILLS

LISTENING Listening for Reasons and Explanations
Recording the Steps in a Process
SPEAKING Making Suggestions
Linking
CRITICAL THINKING Identifying Solutions

THINK AND DISCUSS

1 What's happening in this photo? Why do you think scientists want to study this man?

2 What are some things you would you like to know about the human brain? Why?

Look at the photos and read the information. Then discuss these questions.

1. What activities are the people in the photos doing? Why do you think they're doing these activities?

2. Which of these activities can improve your memory? Make you feel happier? Reduce stress?

3. Do you exercise regularly? If so, how do you usually feel afterwards?

4. What other kinds of activities do you think "exercise" your brain?

EXERCISE YOUR BRAIN!

You probably already know that you can make your body stronger and healthier by exercising, but did you know that there are also ways to exercise your brain? Studies show that certain kinds of activities can increase memory, creativity, and even make us feel happier.

Studies show that playing chess can help improve memory, creativity, and even your IQ.

Physical exercise can improve your mood, making you feel happier and more positive. Studies show that it can also make it easier for you to learn.

Learning new skills, such as juggling or playing a musical instrument, can actually change the structure of your brain.

Creative activities, such as pottery and drawing, can help keep your brain "fit", reduce stress, and increase your sense of emotional well-being.

A Vocabulary

A **2.2** Read and listen to the information. Notice each word in **blue** and think about its meaning.

FACTS TO MAKE YOU THINK ABOUT YOUR BRAIN

1. Your brain is an extremely **complex** organ. It contains over 100 billion neurons[1] that are constantly sending messages. Different neurons send messages at different **speeds**—some faster and some slower.

5. Every time you think, laugh, or sneeze, chemical and electrical **signals** are moving between neurons. These messages make it possible for your brain to communicate with your body.

2. Every time you experience something new, your brain creates new **connections** and pathways between brain cells.

6. Learning changes the **structure** of the brain. When you learn a new skill, such as playing a musical instrument, your brain cells organize themselves in a new way.

3. The common belief that we use only a **tiny** amount (10 percent) of our brains is wrong. Each part of the brain has a **function**, so we use 100 percent of our brains.

7. Your brain is extremely powerful. When you're awake, it **generates** between 10 and 23 watts of electricity—enough to power a light bulb!

4. Even without words, you can figure out how someone is feeling. A part of your brain called the amygdala lets you "read" other people's faces and understand what kind of **mood** they are in.

8. The *hypothalamus* is the part of your brain that **controls** body temperature. It keeps you from getting too hot or too cold.

[1]**neuron** (n): a brain cell that is part of the nervous system

B Choose the correct word or phrase to complete each sentence.

1. Your brain controls your heartbeat and breathing, so you (need / don't need) your brain in order to live.
2. Brainstorming is a good way to generate ideas. You (can / can't) get many ideas from a good brainstorming session.
3. When you're riding a bicycle, use hand signals for left or right turns. This (will / won't) show other people on the road which way you plan to turn.
4. My country has a complex history. There were (a few / many) people and events that made my country what it is today.
5. If cars are moving at high speeds, they're moving quite (slowly / quickly).

6. The pineal gland is a tiny organ located inside your brain. It is one of the (smallest / largest) organs in the human body.
7. Babies usually have a strong connection with their parents, so they (feel / don't feel) close to their parents emotionally.
8. Your bones and muscles are important parts of your body's structure. Without bones and muscles, you (could / couldn't) stand or move around.
9. My brother just received some excellent news, so he is in a (bad / good) mood today.
10. The largest part of the human brain is the cerebrum, which allows us to think and move. Letting us think and move (are / aren't) among the cerebrum's functions.

C Work with a partner. Write each word in **blue** from exercise A in the correct column of the chart. Use grammar clues in the sentences in exercises A and B to help you.

CRITICAL THINKING: ANALYZING

Nouns	Verbs	Adjectives

D Work with a partner. Discuss these questions.

CRITICAL THINKING: ANALYZING

1. Which of the facts in exercise A do you think are most interesting? Explain.
2. Your amygdala helps you "read" other people's faces and understand what kind of mood they're in. How can doing this be useful?
3. What are some signals you can give to show someone you're happy? To show you understand? To show you agree?
4. Who is someone you have a strong connection with? How is that person important in your life?
5. What are some of the things you can control in your life? What are some things you cannot control?

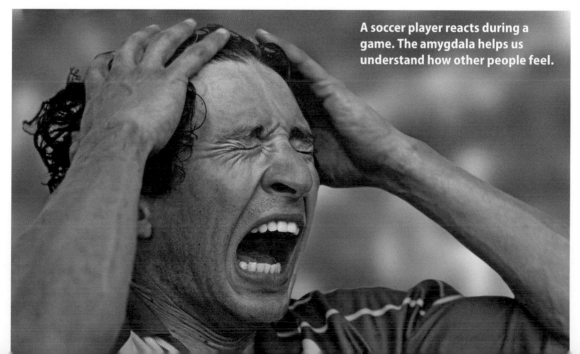

A soccer player reacts during a game. The amygdala helps us understand how other people feel.

A Listening A Podcast about Exercise and the Brain

BEFORE LISTENING

PREDICTING **A** Work with a partner. You are going to listen to a podcast about the effects of exercise on the human brain. Which of these topics do you expect to hear about? Check (✓) your ideas.

☐ brain surgery   ☐ intelligence   ☐ memory   ☐ neurons

☐ food/taste   ☐ learning   ☐ mood

WHILE LISTENING

LISTENING FOR
MAIN IDEAS **B** 🎧 2.3 ▶ 1.8 Listen to the podcast. Choose the correct answers.

1. According to the podcast, which <u>two</u> positive effects does exercise have on the brain?

   a. It helps reduce stress.   c. It improves your mood.   e. It repairs brain cells.
   b. It makes your brain larger.   d. It makes you smarter.

2. BDNF is a chemical produced by the brain _____.

   a. when we learn something new
   b. when our brain creates new neurons and pathways
   c. after we exercise

3. BDNF controls _____.

   a. processes in the brain   b. blood flow in the brain   c. heart rate and breathing

---

LISTENING SKILL Listening for Reasons and Explanations

Speakers often give reasons and explanations to support their ideas. Listening for reasons and explanations will help you decide whether the speaker's ideas are valid and well thought out. Speakers sometimes use signal phrases before giving an explanation. Here are some common signal phrases:

> *The reason for this . . .*   *To explain, . . .*   *Let me explain.*   *That's because . . .*

> *Scientists learned recently that exercise makes you smarter . . .* ***That's because*** *for some time after you've exercised, your body produces a chemical that actually makes it easier for your brain to learn.*

A man and woman ride mountain bikes on Adam's Gulch Trail in Ketchum, Idaho, USA.

C ⌂ 2.3 Listen again and match each idea with the correct reason or explanation.

LISTENING FOR DETAILS

Ideas

1. Exercise makes it easier to learn because _____.
2. Doing things repeatedly is a way to learn because _____.
3. BDNF supports learning because _____.
4. Aaron Fleming will probably continue to exercise regularly because _____.

Reasons and Explanations

a. it controls processes like the growth of new neurons
b. it creates new connections in the brain
c. he wants to keep his brain fit
d. your body produces a certain chemical afterwards

AFTER LISTENING

D Work in a group. Discuss these questions.

CRITICAL THINKING: REFLECTING

1. What new information did you learn from the podcast? Do you have any questions about it?
2. Based on your own experience, do you agree that exercise improves your mood? Explain.
3. Where and when do you prefer to study? What helps you learn and remember things?
4. Do you plan to change your exercise or study habits based on the podcast? Explain.

Speaking

GRAMMAR FOR SPEAKING Infinitives after Verbs

An *infinitive* is *to* plus the base form of a verb. We use infinitives after certain transitive verbs. *Transitive verbs* are verbs that take direct objects.

> My son is <u>learning</u> **to ride** a bicycle. He doesn't <u>want</u> **to fall** again.
>
> I <u>forgot</u> **to bring** my notebook to class. Did you <u>remember</u> **to bring** yours?

Note: Verbs cannot have other verbs as objects.

> **Incorrect:** ✗ *Volkan and Begum <u>plan</u> **take** a vacation in August.*
>
> **Correct:** ✓ *Volkan and Begum <u>plan</u> **to take** a vacation in August.*

Here are some verbs that can be followed by infinitives:

| agree | ask | choose | decide | forget | intend | need | pretend | promise | | try |
| appear | begin | continue | expect | hope | learn | plan | seem | | remember | want |

A Complete each sentence with an appropriate infinitive. Then work with a partner and compare your sentences.

1. I promise not _____*to spend*_____ too much money on my vacation.

2. Pablo tried _____ his friend John with his homework.

3. My daughter sometimes forgets _____ her teeth in the morning.

4. When Mehmet wants _____ a new vocabulary word, he writes it down.

5. Did the Nortons decide not _____ a new car?

6. Lee needs _____ after class today.

7. Do you plan _____ another English class next semester?

8. I really hope _____ London someday.

PERSONALIZING **B** Work with a partner. Take turns finishing these sentences about yourself. Use infinitives and your own ideas.

1. When I was a child, I wanted . . .

2. Next year, I plan . . .

3. In this class, I'm learning . . .

4. I really hope . . .

5. Yesterday, I forgot . . .

6. I've decided . . .

7. In the future, I don't want . . .

8. Next week, I need . . .

C Work in a group. Follow the instructions for the *Brain Game*.

Brain Game: Think Fast!

• The first person in the group chooses any verb from the Grammar for Speaking box and says a sentence using that verb plus an infinitive. Then he or she says the name of another person in the group and a verb from the chart.

- The next person must then say a sentence as quickly as possible using the verb plus an infinitive. Then he or she says the name of another person in the group and a verb, and so on. Repeat the process as many times as possible in two minutes.

    A: *intend.* *I intend to do my homework after dinner tonight.* *Marta—decide.*
    B: *I've decided to get a new phone.* *Toshi—appear.*

PRONUNCIATION Linking

⌢ 2.4 In English, speakers do not usually pronounce each word separately. They join, or *link*, words together. When two words are linked, they often sound like one word. Learning to recognize linking will help you understand what you hear, and linking words correctly will help you sound more fluent. Three common types of linking are:

1. Consonant sound to vowel sound: *It's a fascinating job.*

2. Vowel sound to vowel sound: *The book will certainly be interesting.*

3. Consonant sound to same consonant sound: *What was your reason for leaving?*

D **⌢ 2.5** Listen and complete the sentences with the linked words that you hear. Then listen again and check your answers.

1. Your brain _____ _____ you do.

2. Your brain _____ _____ energy to power a light bulb.

3. The activity in your _____ _____ stops.

4. I'm with _____ _____ that!

5. _____ _____ that makes your heart beat faster can help your mood.

6. Neurons carry the _____ _____ the brain.

E Work with a partner. Practice saying the sentences in exercise D. Use linking.

SPEAKING SKILL Making Suggestions

When you make suggestions, you want them to sound polite and not too forceful. One way you can do this is by using the modals *could*, *should*, and *might*.

    You **could** *talk to the professor and explain the problem.*
    Maybe we **should** *practice our presentation again before class.*
    You **might** *want to take the exam again.*

Here are some other words and phrases you can use to make suggestions:

    Let's *make a list of possible ideas first.*
    Why don't we *write our ideas on the board?*
    I suggest *we talk about our ideas first.*

F Work with a partner. Complete the conversation between two college students in any correct way. Then practice the conversation. Switch roles and practice it again.

> **Mike:** I have to pick my cousin up at the airport on Friday, so I can't go to class. Do you think Professor Harris will let me hand my psychology paper in on Monday instead?
>
> **Eric:** I'm not sure. Maybe you _____ hand it in on Thursday.
> 1
>
> **Mike:** I don't think I can finish it by then.
>
> **Eric:** Well, you _____ email it to her on Friday.
> 2
>
> **Mike:** Good idea. I'm going to try to talk to her after class.
>
> **Eric:** You _____ want to tell her before class starts because I think she has
> 3
> a class right after ours.
>
> **Mike:** OK, thanks. _____ stop at the Student Center before class and get
> 4
> something to eat.
>
> **Eric:** Sounds good. I haven't had lunch yet.

G In your notebook, write three problems or situations you need help with. Then take turns reading your situations and giving suggestions to your partner. Use the modals and phrases from the Speaking Skill box when appropriate.

> A: *I really want to get a pet, but my roommate is allergic to cats and birds.*
> B: *Why don't you get some tropical fish?*

LESSON TASK Discussing Problems and Solutions

A Work with a partner. Read the information about the different problems people have. Then think of some possible solutions for each problem. Write notes in your notebook to help you remember your ideas.

> **JOSH** "My wife and I are from different countries. We can't decide where to live after our children are born."

> **MAYA** "I already speak English. Now I want to learn Japanese, but I don't have time to take classes because of my busy work schedule."

KEN "I have a new job, and it's hard for me to remember the names of my new co-workers. I keep forgetting everyone's name!"

RENATA "I don't want to live alone in this house anymore. My husband died five years ago, and my son and daughter are married now and have their own houses and families. This house feels too big for me now."

TAMARA "I spend too much money on electronics. Every time a new version of my phone comes out, I want to buy it. I really can't afford to keep doing this!"

A woman takes photos with her mobile phone in a restaurant in downtown Amman, Jordan.

B Work with a new partner. Role-play conversations between each person in exercise A and one of his or her friends or family members. Take turns talking about "your" problems and making helpful suggestions. Use your own words and the expressions from the Speaking Skill box on page 89.

CRITICAL THINKING: APPLYING

C With your partner, choose one of the problems from exercise B and role-play the conversation for the class.

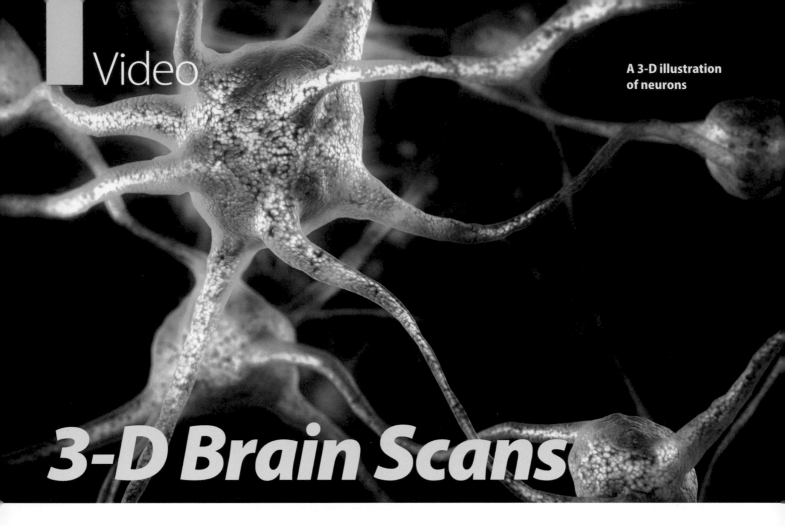

A 3-D illustration
of neurons

3-D Brain Scans

BEFORE VIEWING

A Work with a partner. Match the underlined part of each phrase from the video with its meaning. You may use a dictionary.

1. _____ <u>unconventional</u> science
2. _____ <u>gap</u> in our knowledge
3. _____ <u>map out</u> in detail
4. _____ <u>keep track of</u> something

a. to draw a visual representation
b. not what is usually done
c. to always know where something is
d. an empty space

CRITICAL THINKING:
ANALYZING

B Read the information about Dr. Jeff Lichtman. With a partner, discuss why you think Lichtman refers to neurons in the brain as "wires."

Dr. Jeff Lichtman and his team at the Lichtman Lab at Harvard University are working to reveal the structure of nerve cells in the brain. They're using a device that cuts very thin slices[1] of preserved[2] mouse brain. An electron microscope takes a picture of each slice, and a computer puts the slices in order. When they add bright colors, the result is an amazingly detailed three-dimensional view of what Lichtman calls the "wires[3]" inside the brain—and how they fit together.

[1]**slices** (n): thin pieces from a larger object, e.g., a slice of bread
[2]**preserved** (adj): treated with chemicals to keep fresh
[3]**wires** (n): long thin flexible pieces of metal that carry electricity

WHILE VIEWING

C ▶ **1.9** Read a partial summary of the video. Then watch and choose the correct phrases to complete the summary.

UNDERSTANDING MAIN IDEAS

When it comes to diseases of the nervous system, the only real sign that there is something wrong is the way (1) (the brain looks / the person is acting). If you look at the brain with the techniques we have, there's (2) (nothing to see / a visible difference). Dr. Lichtman says you have to (3) (see the wires / use maps) to understand where they come from and where they go.

The main goal is to understand how cells in the brain (4) (look on camera / communicate with each other). To see this level of detail, Dr. Lichtman's team is using (5) (slices / diagrams) of brain tissue. They're using 33,000 sections of brain tissue for every (6) (meter / millimeter) of depth. Looking at these sections (7) (in sequence / over a period of time) allows the team to generate a diagram of a tiny part of the brain. This diagram gives them the information they need to understand the wires in that section. They can then generate the connections of every (8) (cell / image) in that area of the brain.

D ▶ **1.9** Watch the video again and write the word(s) to complete each sentence.

UNDERSTANDING DETAILS

1. Dr. Lichtman says we _____ what the brain is made up of at the finest level of detail.

2. Playing the image frames in sequence is like seeing the brain over _____.

3. The colors that the team adds to the images have _____.

AFTER VIEWING

E Work in a group. Discuss these questions.

CRITICAL THINKING: ANALYZING

1. What makes it so difficult to study the human brain?

2. Even though Dr. Lichtman is studying mouse brains, do you think it will be helpful in understanding the human brain? Why or why not?

3. If you visited Dr. Lichtman's lab, what questions would you have for him? Think of two or three. Do you think he would be able to answer your questions? Explain.

B Vocabulary

MEANING FROM
CONTEXT **A** 🎧 2.6 Read and listen to the article. Notice each word in **blue** and think about its meaning.

ROMANTIC LOVE VS. LONG-TERM ATTACHMENTS

There are many different kinds of love. There is the strong **emotion** we feel when we fall in love. There is the **attachment** between parents and children, and the quiet feeling of **security** that develops slowly in **long-term** relationships, when couples are together for many years.

Your brain knows the difference between **romantic** love and other attachments. When we're in love, the amount of a brain chemical called *dopamine* increases. This increase gives us the extra energy we feel when we're in love.

On the other hand, an increase in dopamine can make the brains of people in love **similar** to the brains of people with OCD—Obsessive Compulsive Disorder.[1] People with OCD cannot stop thinking about something, and these thoughts can cause compulsive behaviors—actions the person cannot control, such as washing the hands again and again. Similarly, people who are in love often cannot stop thinking about the person they are in love with. Both kinds of people may find it difficult to **function** normally because of their thoughts.

Fortunately, this "lovesickness" is a **short-term** condition. With time, strong romantic feelings decrease, and we can **concentrate** on "real life" again. As time passes, couples have higher levels of *oxytocin*—a brain chemical connected with calm feelings of happiness and trust.

So is love only a matter of brain chemistry? In fact, while chemicals do affect the way we feel, **psychological** factors are also important. We might be attracted to someone who likes the same things we like, for example, or someone who makes us feel safe and secure.

[1]According to research by Donatella Marazziti at the University of Pisa in Italy

A newly married couple dances on Mendenhall Glacier in Alaska, USA.

VOCABULARY SKILL Using Context Clues

Context clues can help you understand the meanings of new words you read or hear. Here are some examples of context clues from the article on page 94:

Type of Context Clue	Example
A definition	… and these thoughts can cause **compulsive** behaviors—<u>actions the person cannot control</u>, …
Other words nearby	…, and the quiet feeling of security that develops slowly in **long-term** relationships, when couples are <u>together for many years.</u>
Your prior knowledge	The article mentions the **attachment** between parents and children.
	I feel love for my parents, so I understand that attachment may be a kind of love.

B Work with a partner. Find other words in **blue** from exercise A that have helpful context clues. Underline the context clues you find.

C Fill in each blank with one of the words in **blue** from exercise A.

1. They have a(n) _____ relationship. They've been married for 29 years.

2. They have _____ taste in music: both like classical music.

3. My teenage daughter has a strong _____ to her best friend. They have been friends since they were three years old.

4. I can't _____ on my homework when you're talking so loudly.

5. Love is a complex _____. There are many different aspects to it, and it can change over time.

6. Your brain and body cannot _____ well if you do not eat and sleep enough.

7. If something is _____, it involves thoughts and feelings.

8. Marc wanted to be _____, so he wrote a song and gave roses to his wife on their anniversary.

9. He got a(n) _____ job in an office. It's only for six weeks.

10. Charlene likes living near the police department. She says it gives her a feeling of _____ .

B Listening A Discussion about Memory, Learning, and Emotions

BEFORE LISTENING

A Work in a group. Discuss these questions.

1. What do you think "short-term memory" means? How about "long-term memory"?
2. What kinds of things do you think are easy to learn? Hard to learn? Explain.
3. In your opinion, what makes a marriage successful? Do you think couples need to have romantic feelings about each other in order to be happy?

WHILE LISTENING

LISTENING FOR MAIN IDEAS

B 🎧 2.7 Listen and complete the main ideas with words you hear.

1. Short-term memory allows us to _____ in the world.

2. When information moves to our long-term memory, it _____ a lifetime.

3. To learn new information, you have to concentrate on it and _____ it.

4. Emotions are also _____ —not just psychological.

LISTENING FOR DETAILS

C 🎧 2.7 Read the statements. Then listen again and choose T for *True* or F for *False* for each statement. Correct the false statements.

1. The memory process has four steps.	T	F
2. Memories become weaker when they travel down the same pathways in the brain again and again.	T	F
3. To learn how to do something, you need to repeat it.	T	F
4. Emotions are a result of our past experiences.	T	F
5. The level of dopamine in our brains decreases when we fall in love.	T	F

> **NOTE-TAKING SKILL** Recording the Steps in a Process
>
> Taking notes on the steps in a process can help you understand important information about a topic, such as how or why something happens. To identify the steps in a process, listen for words and phrases that signal order, such as *First, Second, Step one, The next step,* etc. Then record the steps in a way that will be clear when you review your notes later. Here are two ways you can indicate steps:
>
> 1st, ...   Step 1: ...
> 2nd, ...   Step 2: ...
> 3rd, ...   Step 3: ...

D 🎧 **2.8** Listen to the excerpt from the discussion and complete the notes.

The Process of Remembering

Step 1: _____ enters the brain through our _____ (taste, smell, touch, sight, hearing).

Step 2: Information we need _____ immediately moves to our _____ memory.

    <u>Example</u>: Remembering a question long enough _____ it.

Step 3: Information we try _____ or that our _____ decides is

    _____ moves to our _____ memory.

AFTER LISTENING

E Work with a partner. Discuss these questions.

1. What kinds of information can you remember easily (e.g., people's names, the lyrics to songs, information you read)?
2. In your opinion, what's the best way to remember new information?
3. The students in the listening mention emotions. Do you think emotions affect your ability to think, learn, or remember?

F Read the statements in the questionnaire. Decide how strongly you agree or disagree with each statement. Discuss your answers with a partner.

1 = strongly disagree; 3 = agree somewhat; 5 = strongly agree

---

QUESTIONNAIRE: WHAT HELPS YOU LEARN AND REMEMBER?

1. It was easier to learn something new when I was younger.   1 2 3 4 5
2. Even with practice, there are some things I just can't learn how to do.   1 2 3 4 5
3. I learn from mistakes more quickly than I learn in other ways.   1 2 3 4 5
4. It's easier for me to remember information if I write it down.   1 2 3 4 5
5. It's easier for me to learn something new if someone shows me rather than tells me how to do it.   1 2 3 4 5

◀ A surfing lesson on Woolacombe Beach in Devon, England

B Speaking

A Work with a partner. Read the assignment below. Then discuss these questions.

1. How would you feel if you needed to complete the *Group Presentation Assignment* below? Would you be excited about it? Feel stressed about it? Explain.
2. In the Listening section of this lesson, you heard a discussion among students in a study group. What experiences have you had with study groups and group projects?
3. Do you prefer to study and learn alone or in a group? Explain.

Psychology 201

Assignment: Group Presentation (Due October 23)

In small groups, generate a research question about one of the topics we have discussed this semester. Use the library and the Internet to find answers to your question. Then prepare a ten-minute presentation to give to the class. You will need to summarize the information you found and organize it into an interesting presentation.

Tasks

- Meet with group members to come up with an interesting question.
- Decide on a fair way to divide the research work.
- Share the research you find and decide which information to include in the presentation.

B With your partner, look at the list of tasks necessary to complete the assignment in exercise A. Then think of two more tasks and write them below.

_____

_____

C With your partner, brainstorm a list of the benefits and possible problems with study groups and group projects. Write your ideas in your notebook.

(+) Benefits	(−) Possible Problems
more people = more ideas	some people don't do any work

CRITICAL THINKING   Identifying Solutions

Identifying solutions to problems often requires you to use more than one critical-thinking skill. For example, you may need to reflect on your own experience to identify the causes of a problem and brainstorm possible solutions. Then you need to evaluate your ideas in order to identify which solution is the best.

D With your partner, look at your list of possible problems from exercise C. Follow these steps.

CRITICAL THINKING: IDENTIFYING SOLUTIONS

1. For each problem, ask yourselves these questions: What is my experience with this problem? What are the possible causes of this problem?
2. Brainstorm solutions for each problem. Write your ideas in your notebook.
3. Discuss your list of solutions and choose the best solution for each problem.

> **EVERYDAY LANGUAGE**   Expressing Understanding
>
> *That makes sense.*   *I see your point.*   *That's a good point.*   *I see what you mean.*

FINAL TASK   Planning a Presentation about the Human Brain

> You are going to plan a group presentation on an aspect of the human brain. You will then give your presentation during another class period.

A Work in a group. Choose one question from the chart to answer in your presentation. Then assign one of the roles below to each member of your group.

Brain Function	Brain Chemistry	Learning Styles and Strategies
What happens when parts of the brain are injured?	What happens when children don't receive enough love?	What is the best way to measure intelligence?
How can people improve their brain function?	How does exercise affect brain chemistry?	What are some important study skills for language learners?

> **Roles**
>
> Leader: Makes sure the assignment is done correctly and on time, and that all group members do their work.
>
> Secretary: Takes notes on the group's ideas and plans.
>
> Expert: Understands the topic well and checks the group's ideas before the presentation.
>
> Manager: Takes care of details such as the visual aid for the presentation and suggests place and time to meet outside of class.

B Discuss these questions with your group. Your group's secretary should take notes.

1. What do you already know about your topic, and what do you need to learn? What information will you present to the class?
2. Where and how can you find information about your topic? Will you research the topic individually or together as a group?
3. How will you organize the information you find?
4. What kind of visuals could you use to support your presentation?

ORGANIZING IDEAS **C** Prepare to present your ideas from exercise B to the class. Decide which member of your group will present which information.

PRESENTING **D** Present your group's ideas from exercise B to the class.

PRESENTATION SKILL Pausing to Check Understanding

When you present ideas, it's important to check to make sure your audience understands you. You can do this by pausing occasionally and looking at your audience. If they look confused, ask them if they need you to repeat any information or give clarification. Stop occasionally and ask your audience if they have any questions. Here are some questions you can ask:

Are there any questions at this point?   *Is there anything that needs clarification?*

E Your teacher will tell you when you will give your group presentation.

REFLECTION

1. Which skills did you find most helpful in this unit? Why?

   _____

   _____

2. What topics in this unit would you like to learn more about? Why?

   _____

   _____

3. Here are the vocabulary words from the unit. Check (✓) the ones you can use.

   ☐ attachment AWL   ☐ function (v) AWL   ☐ short-term
   ☐ complex AWL   ☐ generate AWL   ☐ signal
   ☐ concentrate AWL   ☐ long-term   ☐ similar AWL
   ☐ connection   ☐ mood   ☐ speed
   ☐ control   ☐ psychological AWL   ☐ structure AWL
   ☐ emotion   ☐ romantic   ☐ tiny
   ☐ function (n) AWL   ☐ security AWL

People gather around a huge pot to eat noodles at Bailongtan Temple Fair in Anyang, Henan Province, China.

LET'S EAT! 6

ACADEMIC SKILLS

LISTENING Listening for Numerical Data
Using a Split Page to Take Notes
SPEAKING Interrupting and Returning to a Topic
Intonation: Finished and Unfinished Sentences
CRITICAL THINKING Evaluating

THINK AND DISCUSS

1 What's happening in the photo? Would you like to eat like this? Why or why not?
2 What are some typical foods from your country?
3 What's your favorite kind of food?

Look at the photos and the pie chart, and read the information. Then discuss these questions.

1. What kinds of food do you see in the photos? How often do you eat these kinds of food?
2. According to the pie chart, do people get more of their daily calories from meat or from fruits and vegetables?
3. Does any information from the pie chart surprise you? Explain.
4. How well do you think the pie chart represents your daily diet? Explain.

WHAT THE WORLD EATS

A boy holds fish that he caught in Lake Langano, Ethiopia.

▶ Bread for sale at Kemeralti Market, Izmir, Turkey

THE WORLD'S DAILY DIET

How much of our diet consists of meat? Of fruits and vegetables? Of grains? This pie chart shows the world's daily diet in calories. A calorie is the unit used to measure the amount of energy in food.

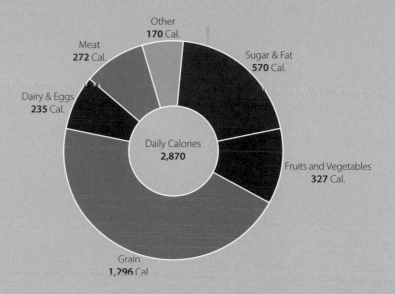

Other
170 Cal.

Meat
272 Cal.

Sugar & Fat
570 Cal.

Dairy & Eggs
235 Cal.

Daily Calories
2,870

Fruits and Vegetables
327 Cal.

Grain
1,296 Cal.

Source: http://www.nationalgeographic.com/what-the-world-eats/, Daily Diet 2011.

A Vocabulary

A 🎧 2.9 Listen and check (✓) the words you already know. Use your dictionary to help you with any new words.

☐ grains (n) ☐ protein (n) ☐ servings (n) ☐ specific (adj)
☐ guidelines (n) ☐ recommend (v) ☐ source (n) ☐ varied (adj)
☐ modernize (v) ☐ regional (adj)

MEANING FROM CONTEXT

B 🎧 2.10 Complete each sentence with a word from exercise A. Then listen and check your answers.

1. Today, many countries have produced _____ to teach their citizens about healthy diets.

2. Most doctors _____ eating a lot of fruits and vegetables.

3. _____ such as rice, wheat, and corn are basic parts of most people's diets.

4. It's OK to include a few _____ of sweets in your diet each week, but not too many.

5. Cheese is an excellent _____ of calcium; so are milk and yogurt.

6. Scientists believe the _____ food in Sardinia, Italy, helps the people who live there to have long, healthy lives.

7. A _____ diet includes many different kinds of food, not just the same foods again and again.

8. Foods that are high in _____ include fish, chicken, nuts, and beans.

9. This recipe calls for a _____ kind of red pepper. You can't use just any kind of pepper.

10. To _____ means to begin using the newest technology and methods.

▶ A man sells fresh fruits and vegetables in Oman.

C Complete the quiz. Give an explanation or example for each of your answers. Then work with a partner and compare and discuss your answers.

QUIZ: HOW WELL DO YOU EAT?	USUALLY	SOMETIMES	NEVER
1. I try to eat a varied diet.			
I eat several kinds of food every week.	☑	☐	☐
2. I eat a healthy amount of grains.			
_____	☐	☐	☐
3. I eat 3–5 servings of fruits and vegetables every day.			
_____	☐	☐	☐
4. I follow my country's diet guidelines.			
_____	☐	☐	☐
5. My diet includes protein.			
_____	☐	☐	☐
6. I drink the recommended amount of water (6–8 glasses per day).			
_____	☐	☐	☐
7. I eat foods that are good sources of calcium such as yogurt and cheese.			
_____	☐	☐	☐
8. I check food labels for specific ingredients such as sugar and sodium (salt).			
_____	☐	☐	☐

D Discuss these questions with a partner.

1. What do you know about your country's nutrition guidelines? What do they recommend?
2. What foods from your country are available everywhere in the world? What foods are regional and difficult to find in other places?
3. When a country modernizes, what aspects of food and eating can change?
4. Why do you think nutritionists encourage people to eat a varied diet? What can happen if you usually eat just a few kinds of food?
5. Why do you think it is hard for some people to eat a healthy diet?

A Listening A Presentation about the Korean Diet

BEFORE LISTENING

PRIOR KNOWLEDGE **A** Discuss these questions with a partner.

1. How has the diet in your country changed in the last 50 years? Is your diet similar to or different from your grandparents' diet?
2. What do you know about the foods eaten in South Korea?

WHILE LISTENING

LISTENING FOR
MAIN IDEAS

B 🎧 2.11 ▶ 1.10 Read the information in the box and the questions below. Then listen to a student's seminar presentation about changes in the Korean diet. Listen for the answers to the questions.

> A seminar is a small-group class where students and a professor share information about a subject. Often, the students give presentations about a research topic.

1. What was unhealthy about the Korean diet in 1969?
2. What foods had been added to the Korean diet by 1995?
3. How were Koreans in 1995 different physically from Koreans in 1969?
4. Which way of eating—traditional or modern—does the student think is healthier?

▼ **Meals in South Korea often include many different side dishes.**

C Discuss the questions in exercise B with a partner.

Listening for and understanding numerical data will help you better understand a speaker's ideas. In the presentation, the speaker wants to show exactly how the Korean diet changed between 1969 and 1995. She does this by providing numerical data.

You can see that in **1969**, *people were eating about* **37 ounces** *of food every day.*

Here are some ways we talk about numerical data:

two and a half = 2.5 OR 2 ½

two-point-three = 2.3

a quarter of... = 1/4 OR .25

D 🎧 2.11 Listen to the presentation again and complete the chart with the numbers you hear.

LISTENING FOR
NUMERICAL DATA

Change in Korean Eating Habits		
Kind of Food	Ounces per Day in 1969	Ounces per Day in 1995
Total Food	37	
Rice and Other Grains		
Vegetables		
Fruits		
Meat		
Milk and Other Dairy Products		

AFTER LISTENING

E Discuss these questions in a group.

CRITICAL THINKING:
ANALYZING

1. What information from Mi-Ran's presentation did you find most interesting? Explain.
2. According to the chart above, what kind of food showed the greatest decrease during the time period? The greatest increase?
3. How did the data in the presentation help you to understand Mi-Ran's main ideas?
4. Do you know other countries where the diet has changed a lot? How and why did it change? Are the people healthier now? Explain.
5. Do you think that you eat a healthier diet than your grandparents did when they were young?

Speaking

| GRAMMAR FOR SPEAKING | The Real Conditional: Present and Future |

Present Real Conditional

We use the present real conditional to talk about situations that are always or generally true.

        if clause (condition)   main clause (result)
*If I **have** chocolate in the house, I **eat** it.*

We often use *when* instead of *if* in the conditional clause.

    ***When** people have more fruit in their diet, they get more vitamins.*

Future Real Conditional

We use the future real conditional to talk about situations that are possible in the future.

      if clause (condition)   main clause (result)
*If you don't **eat** a varied diet, you **are not going to be** very healthy.*

    main clause (result)   *if* clause (condition)
*We **will call** you if we **see** Thomas at the festival.*

Notice that the *if* clause can come before or after the main clause.

    main clause (result)   *if* clause (condition)
*I won't be hungry for dinner **if I have a snack now**.*

A   Work with a partner. Use the words and phrases below to make sentences using the present real conditional.

>   *If I don't eat breakfast, I feel very hungry by late morning.*

Condition	Result
1. I / not eat / breakfast	I / feel very hungry / by late morning
2. I / arrive late / to class	I / enter the room / quietly
3. my sister / see / fresh oranges	she / always want / buy some
4. you / not like / fish	you / should not order / that dish
5. I / feel hungry / at night	I / sometimes order / a pizza
6. people / not like to eat / meat	they / can become / vegetarians

B   Work with a partner. Read the situations. Then talk about results for each situation. Use the future real conditional.

>   *You won't have healthy teeth if you eat a lot of sugar.*

1. you eat a lot of sugar
2. you drink coffee late at night
3. children eat a lot of fast food
4. you don't eat enough fruits and vegetables
5. people learn how to cook
6. I eat a very big lunch

C Work with a partner. Complete each sentence using the present or future real conditional and information about yourself. PERSONALIZING

> *When I have an important exam, I try to go to bed early the night before.*

1. When I have an important exam, . . .
2. When I can't sleep, . . .
3. If I don't feel well tomorrow, . . .
4. If someone asks for my help, . . .
5. I get upset . . .
6. I feel happy . . .

SPEAKING SKILL Interrupting and Returning to a Topic

Sometimes during a discussion, you need to interrupt a speaker to ask a question or express an idea. Here are some expressions you can use to interrupt politely:

Can/Could/May I . . . interrupt?   . . . stop you for a second?   . . . ask a question?
. . . say something here?

If you are speaking and someone interrupts you, here are some expressions you can use to return to your topic:

Anyway, . . .   Moving on, . . .   As I was saying, . . .   To continue, . . .

D 🎧 **2.12** Listen to excerpts from the presentation you heard. Mark the expressions used for interrupting and returning to a topic when you hear them.

1. Mi-Ran, may I say something here?
2. Moving on, . . . when we compare the kinds of food people ate, we see a significant difference.
3. Could I ask a question, Mi-Ran? Is that just milk, or does that include other dairy products, too?
4. To continue,—as the country developed, instead of just eating a lot of rice and vegetables, Koreans started including many other kinds of food in their diets, . . .

▼ **Drum majorettes eat during a break in Yeongwol, South Korea.**

PRONUNCIATION Intonation: Finished and Unfinished Sentences

2.13 Intonation refers to the way your voice rises and falls when you're speaking. In English, we use intonation to signal when we have finished a sentence or plan to continue speaking.

A falling intonation at the end of a sentence usually signals that the speaker has finished.

I have to go to the supermarket.

She lives in Tokyo.

If the intonation doesn't fall, it usually signals that the speaker probably hasn't finished and may have more to say.

I saw Pam yesterday. . . .

Mike's brother called. . . .

E **2.14** Listen to the intonation in each sentence. Choose U for *Unfinished* or F for *Finished* for each sentence.

1.	I really don't like milk	U	F
2.	Rick has two favorite restaurants	U	F
3.	I'll buy chicken if it looks fresh	U	F
4.	On my next vacation, I want to go to Seoul	U	F
5.	My mother is an excellent cook	U	F
6.	If the weather is nice, we usually go to the park	U	F

F Work with a partner. Choose one sentence from each pair and say it using the correct intonation. Your partner will say whether you said sentence a or b.

1. a. It's one of the most modern countries . . .
   b. It's one of the most modern countries.

2. a. We eat rice three times a day . . .
   b. We eat rice three times a day.

3. a. People were eating more . . .
   b. People were eating more.

4. a. A lot of Koreans love yogurt . . .
   b. A lot of Koreans love yogurt.

CRITICAL THINKING: ANALYZING

G Discuss these questions with a partner.

1. In your culture, is it OK to interrupt someone when they are speaking? If so, in what situations? When is it not OK to interrupt someone?
2. Do Americans interrupt more or less often than people in your culture? Explain.

LESSON TASK Participating in a Group Discussion

You are going to participate in a group discussion about vegetarian versus omnivorous diets. During the discussion, you will practice interrupting and returning to the topic.

A Work with a partner. Your teacher will assign you one of the opinions below. You will both have the same opinion. (This might not be your real opinion!) Brainstorm a list of ideas that support the opinion you were assigned. Think of reasons, explanations, and examples. Write your ideas in your notebook.

BRAINSTORMING

> **Opinion A:** A vegetarian diet with no meat, fish, or chicken is better than an omnivorous diet.

> **Opinion B:** An omnivorous diet that includes meat, chicken, and fish as well as fruits and vegetables is better than a vegetarian diet.

B With your partner, decide which of your ideas from exercise A are the best.

CRITICAL THINKING: EVALUATING

C Form a group with a pair of students that discussed the opposite opinion. Choose one person to be the timekeeper. Your teacher will tell you how much time you have. Follow these steps.

1. Pair A will explain and support their assigned opinion and give reasons, explanations, and examples.
2. While Pair A is speaking, Pair B will listen and try to politely interrupt once or twice using an expression from the Speaking Skill box on page 109.
3. Then switch roles and repeat.

D Have a discussion with the whole class. What is your real opinion about vegetarian and omnivorous diets?

▼ **A family has dinner together in Guangxi Province, China.**

Video

Maria Juana prepares corn
tortillas at a restaurant in
Oaxaca, Mexico.

The Food and
Culture of Oaxaca

BEFORE VIEWING

PRIOR KNOWLEDGE **A** In this video, you will learn about food from Oaxaca, Mexico. What are some foods from Mexico you know about? Tell a partner.

PREDICTING **B** Write five food words that you think you will hear in the video.

_____

WHILE VIEWING

CHECKING PREDICTIONS **C** ▶ 1.11 Watch the video. Check (✓) the words in exercise B that you heard.

UNDERSTANDING DETAILS **D** ▶ 1.11 Read the statements. Then watch the video again and choose T for *True* or F for *False*. Correct the false statements.

1. Oaxaca is famous for its traditional culture.	T	F
2. Oaxaca is one of the richest states in Mexico.	T	F
3. Susana Trilling went to Oaxaca to start her own restaurant.	T	F
4. *Mole* is a sauce made with chile peppers and spices.	T	F
5. People eat *mole* on chicken and meat.	T	F
6. The *Guelagetza* is a new dance from Oaxaca.	T	F

E ▶ **1.11** Watch the video again and complete the sentences with the words you hear.

UNDERSTANDING DETAILS

1. When you come to Oaxaca, beautiful _____ and wonderful _____ are all around you.

2. Oaxacan food is _____ around the world.

3. Susana Trilling _____ the chiles in Oaxacan food.

4. Many foreigners have come to _____ how to make real Oaxacan *mole* and other _____.

5. Susana's students _____ about Oaxacan food in their own _____.

6. Susana thinks Oaxacan food is as _____ and _____ to make as Thai food, or French food.

7. The buildings in the city are _____ and _____.

8. Oaxacan people say that a healthy person is _____ and loves to work and _____.

AFTER VIEWING

F Work in a group. Discuss these questions.

PERSONALIZING

1. Which ideas in exercise E above do you agree with? Why?
2. Do you think you would enjoy Oaxacan food? Why or why not?
3. Which region in your country has the best food? Give examples.
4. Have you ever taken a cooking class? If so, what kind of food did you learn to make? If not, are you interested in taking a cooking class? Explain.

G Match the beginning of each conditional sentence with the correct ending. Then practice saying the sentences with a partner.

1. Oaxacans think if a person is healthy, _____

2. If you go to Oaxaca, _____

3. If you feel cold in winter, _____

4. If you want to make *mole*, _____

a. beautiful colors and wonderful smells surround you.

b. you have to use chile peppers and spices.

c. you can warm up in Oaxaca.

d. he or she loves to work and eat.

▼ **Macedonio Alcala Street in Oaxaca, Mexico**

B Vocabulary

A 🎧 **2.15** Read and listen to the information about an experiment. Notice each word in **blue** and think about its meaning.

DR. ALIA CRUM'S MILKSHAKE EXPERIMENT

Introduction:

We know that seeing a picture of food can make us hungry, but Dr. Crum, a psychologist and researcher, wanted to find out whether reading food labels can affect the body. Her conclusion was that our attitude is **relevant** to the way our bodies respond to food.

To understand this experiment, it is important to understand the hormone[1] *ghrelin*. When you have not eaten, the level of ghrelin in your body rises. It **stimulates** feelings of **hunger** and "tells" us we need to eat. After we have eaten enough, the level drops, we feel full, and our bodies use the food for energy and **strength**.

Results:

Dr. Crum's research **strategy** was to give two groups of people the same milkshake but with two different labels. First, the team asked participants to read the label on the milkshake. Then participants drank the milkshake and rated the taste. The final step was a blood test.

The first group of participants read a label for "Sensi-Shake" and drank a milkshake they believed had 140 calories and 0 grams of fat. Blood tests afterwards showed very little change in their ghrelin levels.

The second group read a label for "Indulgence," a shake they thought had 620 calories and 30 grams of fat. The label **convinced** participants that they should feel full, and in fact, their ghrelin levels dropped significantly, so they did feel full and satisfied. The only **element** of the experiment that was different between the two groups was the label on the milkshake.

▲ **Strawberry milkshakes**

Discussion:

When food manufacturers **market** their products, they create labels to **appeal** to the tastes and interests of consumers. When they **target** people who want to be healthy, for example, their food labels might include a picture of someone exercising outdoors. Crum's experiment suggests that our ideas about a food product—even before we eat or drink it—may affect us in unexpected ways.

[1]**hormone** (n): a chemical from organs in the body that stimulates activity

B Write each word in **blue** from exercise A next to its definition.

Verbs

1. _____ : made someone believe something is true
2. _____ : to seem interesting or attractive
3. _____ : causes something to begin or develop
4. _____ : to organize the sale of something
5. _____ : to advertise a product to a certain group of people

Nouns

6. _____ : one part of something
7. _____ : physical energy, ability to do physical things
8. _____ : a plan to achieve something
9. _____ : a feeling of needing to eat

Adjective

10. _____ : important or significant

C Work with a partner. Take turns completing each sentence so that it is true for you. Explain your answers. Ask your partner follow-up questions to get more information.

PERSONALIZING

> *The smell of pizza always stimulates my appetite. It's my favorite food . . .*

1. The smell of … always stimulates my appetite.
2. Some kinds of foods that don't appeal to me are…
3. Companies use advertising to convince people to buy things. For example,…
4. I think the most important element in good cooking is . . .
5. A good kind of food to eat to increase your strength after an illness is . . .

VOCABULARY SKILL Recognizing Parts of Speech

In English, many words can function as either a noun or a verb. Use context clues to help you figure out the part of speech.

> The **market** for vegetarian burgers is growing. Therefore, the company **is marketing** its new soybean burger in several European countries.

Notice that the noun form of the word *market* follows the definite article *the*, while the verb form comes after the subject *company*.

D Read the sentences. Decide whether the underlined word in each sentence is a noun or a verb. Choose n for *noun* or v for *verb*. Then compare your answers with a partner's.

CRITICAL THINKING: ANALYZING

1. Researchers reported an increase (n / v) in the hunger level of some participants.
2. Young men are the main target (n / v) for some kinds of energy drinks.
3. Pictures of hot coffee or tea can appeal (n / v) to tired college students.
4. Let's experiment (n / v) with the way our minds affect our bodies.
5. High ghrelin levels may be a concern (n / v) for people who want to lose weight.
6. Mexican food has a strong appeal (n / v). It's my favorite kind of food.
7. The company is trying to find new ways to market (n / v) its health-food products.
8. Some fast-food restaurants target (n / v) children and teenagers.

Listening A Discussion about Food Psychology

BEFORE LISTENING

A Look at the photo and read the information in the box below. Then discuss the questions with a partner.

▶ **A variety of cakes in a pastry shop window**

> **FOOD PSYCHOLOGY**
>
> People who market and sell food—whether they're farmers selling vegetables at an outdoor market or large manufacturers selling packaged foods such as potato chips and breakfast cereals—understand food psychology. Before the food ever gets near our mouths, someone has developed a strategy to make the food appeal to us.

1. Does the food in the photo appeal to you? What does it make you want to do?
2. How do you decide what to order from a restaurant menu?
3. When you go grocery shopping, do you usually buy only the items on your list, or do you sometimes buy other items? Explain.

WHILE LISTENING

NOTE-TAKING SKILL Using a Split Page to Take Notes

Taking notes using a split page can be a helpful note-taking and study strategy. Begin by drawing a vertical line down the middle of a page in your notebook. On the right side, take notes on main ideas and details. On the left side write questions. These can be questions that are answered by your notes or questions for your professor. You can write your questions while you listen or later on as you review your notes.

Questions	Main Notes
— Are there other examples of this happening?	— Experiment with milkshakes: People got same milkshakes but different message.
— What happens when people learn they all had the same milkshake?	— Groups had different blood chemistry.

B 🎧 2.16 Listen to the discussion and complete the partial notes on the right-hand side of the split page below. NOTE TAKING

Questions	Main Notes
	Food psychology:
How do restaurants appeal to hungry people?	— descriptions and photos of food on menus
_____	— survey cards give customers a chance to _____
What other kinds of communication are important?	— social connections, (i.e., getting together for a meal with _____)
_____	— a variety of foods/having many options (e.g., at grocery store) makes us _____

C 🎧 2.16 Listen again for any information you missed the first time or any other ideas that seem important to you. Add your notes to the right-hand side of the split page. NOTE TAKING

AFTER LISTENING

D Read over your notes from exercises B and C. Then on the left-hand side of the split page, write any questions that are answered by your notes.

E Work with a partner. Compare and discuss your notes.

F Work in a group. Read the information. Use a dictionary to help you with any new words. Then discuss the questions below. CRITICAL THINKING: ANALYZING

> **Food and Flavor Trends: What's Popular Now?**
>
> - **Tropical Fruits**: Forget about pomegranates and açai berries, people around the world are discovering dragon fruit, jackfruit, and other tropical delights.
> - **Seaweed**: Expect to see this nutritious green food in everything from soup to dishes like Japanese seaweed salad and seaweed snacks.
> - **World Cuisine**: Look for Vietnamese *pho* (a main-dish soup), Peruvian *ceviche* (a seafood dish), or spicy North African dishes flavored with *harissa* (chile paste).

1. Which food trend appeals to you the most? Explain.
2. How might food psychology be a part of each food trend? For example, why would tropical fruits appeal to someone who lives in North America?
3. Based on your knowledge and experience, which food trend(s) do you think will last the longest? Which trend(s) might disappear quickly? Explain.

B Speaking

CRITICAL THINKING:
ANALYZING

A Look at the photo and read the caption. Then discuss these questions with a partner.

1. In your culture, is it common to buy food from street vendors (people who sell food outdoors)? Do you like getting food in this way? Explain.
2. What do you think are some of the advantages and disadvantages of owning a food truck versus a traditional restaurant?

Food trucks in
Los Angeles,
California, USA

B 🎧 2.17 Read and listen to the information.

TIPS FOR MARKETING YOUR FOOD TRUCK

Food trucks have become very popular, but attracting customers isn't always easy. According to Ross Resnick, who created a smartphone app to help customers find food trucks in their cities, "You can't just show up and expect to make a lot of money running a food truck. You have to have a brand and a strategy." Other tips include:

1. If you want to have a successful food truck, work on your photography skills as well as your cooking skills. Taking beautiful photos of your food for advertising or social media is essential in today's market.
2. Use social media to attract "followers." Then if you send regular updates such as an e-newsletter, customers will remember to stop by for a bite to eat.
3. Learn to cook creatively. International foods in new combinations—from Korean-style tacos to fried-chicken sandwiched between breakfast waffles—add to the fun of food-truck dining.
4. Use a creative brand strategy. For example, choose a memorable name and a colorful truck design. This will make you unforgettable to customers.
5. Set up the truck in places where customers can socialize and have fun while they eat. This will encourage them to return and will help you be successful in the food-truck business.

C Work in a group and discuss the marketing tips in exercise B. Follow these steps.

CRITICAL THINKING: EVALUATING

1. What do you think is helpful about each marketing tip?

2. Rank the tips from 1 (most important) to 5 (least important) according to your group's discussion.

EVERYDAY LANGUAGE   Managing a Group Discussion

Here are some questions and expressions you can use during a group discussion to make sure everyone has an opportunity to participate and you keep to the time limit:

Shall we get started?   *Who has a suggestion?*   *Omar, what do you think?*
We don't have much time left.   *Does everyone agree?*

D Compare your rankings of the marketing tips with another group's.

FINAL TASK Presenting a Marketing Plan

You are going to work with a partner to create a marketing plan for opening a new food truck. You will then present your plan to the class.

A With a partner, look at the ideas for different kinds of food trucks. Add two or three of your own ideas.

healthy sandwiches	fruit drinks	Middle Eastern kebabs
_____	_____	_____

B Evaluate the options from exercise A, and choose the food-truck idea you think is best.

CRITICAL THINKING: EVALUATING

C With your partner, brainstorm a list of the foods or drinks your food truck will serve. In your notebook, write brief descriptions to make the foods and drinks appeal to people. Then discuss ways to market your food truck. Think about the following topics.

- a creative name for the truck
- artistic ideas for painting the truck
- good locations for the truck (places where you will attract a lot of customers)
- other ways to attract and appeal to customers

PRESENTATION SKILL Starting Strong

Your introduction is the time to get the attention of your audience and get them interested in your ideas. You can begin with a question, an interesting photo or fact, or a brief story. In addition, you might include a sentence or two that explains what you will do in the presentation. These techniques encourage your audience to start thinking about your topic, and make them want to listen and learn more. Here is the introduction from the presentation in Lesson A; it begins with a question and an explanation of what the presenter will talk about in her presentation:

Hello, everyone… As you know, I'm from South Korea, and people from my country love food! So today I'll be talking about what else? Food! Specifically, I'll be talking about changes in the Korean diet in the twentieth century.

ORGANIZING IDEAS **D** Use the outline below to organize your ideas from exercise C and plan your presentation. Decide who will present which information. Then practice your presentation. Make sure you have a strong introduction.

Food Truck Presentation

I. Introduction

II. Foods and/or Drinks You'll Sell _____

III. Marketing Plan

    a.   name and appearance of food truck: _____

    b.   where you will go to sell food/drinks: _____

    c.   how you will attract customers: _____

IV. Conclusion and Thanks

PRESENTING **E** Present the marketing plan for your food truck to the class. Remember to start with a strong introduction.

REFLECTION

1. What technique did you learn in this unit for taking notes? When do you think you will use it?

_____

_____

2. Which listening topic was more interesting to you: changes in the Korean diet or the psychology of food? Why?

_____

_____

3. Here are the vocabulary words from the unit. Check (✓) the ones you can use.

☐ appeal	☐ modernize	☐ specific AWL
☐ convince AWL	☐ protein	☐ stimulate
☐ element AWL	☐ recommend	☐ strategy AWL
☐ grain	☐ regional AWL	☐ strength
☐ guideline AWL	☐ relevant AWL	☐ target AWL
☐ hunger	☐ serving	☐ varied AWL
☐ market	☐ source AWL	

OUR ACTIVE EARTH

On June 15, 1991, Mount Pinatubo in the Philippines erupted, destroying everything in its path and killing 847 people.

ACADEMIC SKILLS

LISTENING	Listening for Transitions
	Using a Chart to Take Notes
SPEAKING	Using Transitions
	Syllable Number and Syllable Stress Review
CRITICAL THINKING	Predicting Exam Questions

THINK AND DISCUSS

1 What's happening in the photo?

2 Can you name any other volcanoes? Where are they?

3 Look at the unit title. What are some topics you think you will learn about in this unit?

Look at the photo and the map. Then discuss these questions.

1. Have you ever heard of the San Andreas Fault? If so, what do you know about it?

2. What does the color red mean on this map?

3. In which places are earthquakes most likely to occur? Least likely?

4. What does the map show about your country?

THE WORLD'S EARTHQUAKE ZONES

The San Andreas Fault cuts across the Carrizo Plain in San Luis Obispo County, California, USA.

This map shows the world's earthquake zones, or areas of the world where earthquakes are most likely to occur.

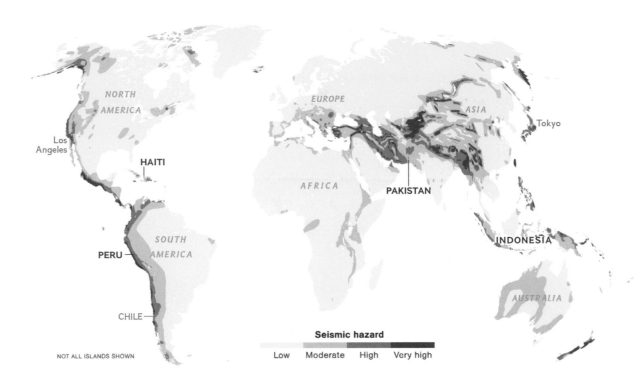

NORTH AMERICA

Los Angeles

HAITI

PERU

SOUTH AMERICA

CHILE

NOT ALL ISLANDS SHOWN

EUROPE

AFRICA

ASIA

Tokyo

PAKISTAN

INDONESIA

AUSTRALIA

Seismic hazard

Low   Moderate   High   Very high

A Vocabulary

INEXPENSIVE BUILDINGS FOR EARTHQUAKE ZONES

The earth's outer layer consists of several pieces called tectonic plates. The places where these plates meet are called **boundaries**. Tectonic plates are always moving. Sometimes the plates "jump" as they move. When this happens, **earthquakes** can occur.

Regions where earthquakes are more likely to occur are called earthquake **zones**. Some of the countries inside these zones are Pakistan, Haiti, Peru, and Indonesia. All of these countries have experienced **major** earthquakes, and many people have died because of unsafe buildings. Fortunately, we can **construct** inexpensive houses that will allow more people to **survive** earthquakes in developing parts of the world.

Pakistan

Light walls: Lightweight walls are less affected by earthquakes and are less likely to fall when the ground **shakes**. In Pakistan, a **material** called plaster is used to help **reinforce** the inside and outside of straw walls.

Haiti

Light roofs: Metal roofs are lighter than concrete and won't **collapse** when an earthquake occurs.

Small windows: Small windows mean that walls are stronger.

Peru

Reinforced walls: Walls do not have to be reinforced with steel[1] or other kinds of metal. In Peru, plastic is sometimes used to reinforce walls.

Indonesia

Enclosed[2] materials: In Indonesia, concrete[3] and metal rods hold brick walls together so that in an earthquake, the whole wall moves as one piece.

[1]**steel** (n): strong, hard material [2]**enclosed** (v): to be inside or within something [3]**concrete** (n): a hard material made of sand, water, and cement

B Choose T for *True* or F for *False* for each statement. Correct the false statements. Use the context in exercise A to help you.

1. If a house or building collapses, it falls down.   T   F

2. When something shakes, it doesn't move.   T   F

3. If someone survives an earthquake, it means they are killed in it.   T   F

4. A boundary marks an area's limits.   T   F

5. When you construct something, you take it down.   T   F

6. Construction materials include concrete, metal, and bricks.   T   F

7. A zone is similar to an area.   T   F

8. We reinforce walls to make them weaker.   T   F

9. Major earthquakes are powerful and dangerous.   T   F

10. Earthquakes are caused by the movement of tectonic plates.   T   F

C Fill in each blank with the correct form of a word in **blue** from exercise A.

1. Buildings that _____ during an earthquake are dangerous. People can be killed or seriously injured when walls and roofs fall down.

2. It does not have to be expensive to _____ earthquake-safe houses. In Peru, for example, people use plastic to _____ walls and make them stronger.

3. You can protect your head by covering it with your arms during an earthquake. What are some other things you can do in order to _____ an earthquake?

4. When the earth _____, you can feel it. It's very scary!

5. In some places, people use natural _____ such as bamboo to make their walls stronger.

6. My country is in an earthquake _____, so I have experienced several earthquakes during my lifetime.

7. Occasionally earthquakes happen outside the _____ of earthquake zones. A rare earthquake in Washington, D.C., for instance, damaged the Washington Monument.

8. If you live in a(n) _____ zone, keep a bag of emergency supplies ready to go.

9. I've experienced a small earthquake but never a(n) _____ one, fortunately.

D Work in a group. Discuss these questions.

CRITICAL THINKING: ANALYZING

1. How does each house on page 124 keep people safe during an earthquake? Explain.
2. Which house on page 124 do you think would be the cheapest to construct? Explain.
3. Have you ever experienced an earthquake? If so, what happened?

A Listening An Earth Science Lecture

BEFORE LISTENING

CRITICAL THINKING:
INTERPRETING
A MAP

A Work with a partner. Look at the map and discuss the questions below.

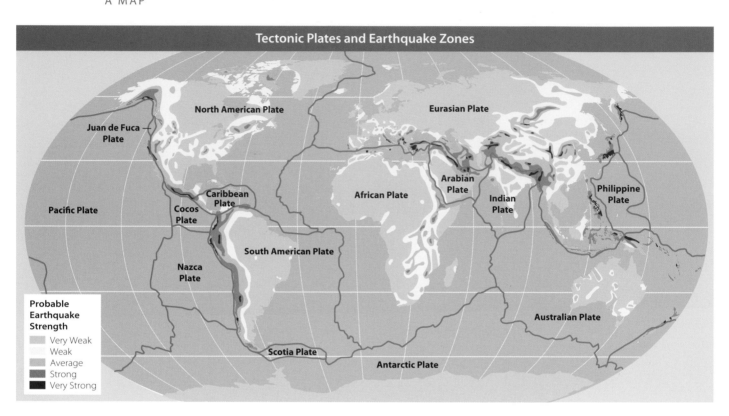

Tectonic Plates and Earthquake Zones

North American Plate

Juan de Fuca
Plate

Eurasian Plate

Pacific Plate

Caribbean
Plate

Cocos
Plate

African Plate

Arabian
Plate

Indian
Plate

Philippine
Plate

Nazca
Plate

South American Plate

Australian Plate

Scotia Plate

Antarctic Plate

Probable
Earthquake
Strength

- Very Weak
- Weak
- Average
- Strong
- Very Strong

1. What do the colors on this map represent?
2. What do you think the green lines on the map represent?
3. What are some areas of the world that have very strong earthquakes?

WHILE LISTENING

LISTENING FOR
MAIN IDEAS

B 🎧 2.19 ▶ 1.12 Read the questions. Then listen to the lecture and write the answers.

1. What is the main topic of the lecture? _____

2. According to the speaker, what are *boundaries*? _____

3. How many types of boundaries are there? _____

4. How did buildings in Chile keep people safe during a 2010 earthquake?

_____

NOTE-TAKING SKILL Using a Chart to Take Notes

When you're listening to a lecture, it is sometimes helpful to use a chart to take notes. You can also use a chart after you listen to organize the information from your notes. As you review your notes, look for pieces of information that you can organize into categories. Using a chart to take and organize your notes will help you better understand and remember the most important information from the lecture.

C 🎧 2.19 Look at the chart. What information do you need in order to complete the chart? Listen again and take notes on the missing information.

Types of Tectonic Boundaries

Boundary Type	Convergent		Transform
Movement	Plates come together; one plate can move under or over another.	Plates move apart.	
Results		A body of water can form between the two plates.	

AFTER LISTENING

CRITICAL THINKING Predicting Exam Questions

Predicting exam questions is a helpful technique for learning and remembering key ideas about a topic. As you review your notes and textbook, think about which information is the most important. That's the information that is most likely to be on an exam. Even if you are not studying for an exam, thinking about possible exam questions can help you succeed on other types of assignments.

D Look at the information from exercises A , B, and C. With a partner, think of at least five questions that might be on an exam and write them below. Some questions could be general, and others might be more specific.

1. _____

2. _____

3. _____

4. _____

5. _____

E Form a group with another pair of students and take turns asking and answering each other's exam questions.

A Speaking

> **SPEAKING SKILL** Using Transitions
>
> *Transitions* are words and phrases that show the relationship between ideas. Using transitions will help your listeners follow and understand your ideas more easily. Here are some examples of common transitions and how they are used:
>
> **To give additional information:**   *Furthermore, . . .*   *In addition, . . .*
>
> *These areas are places where earthquakes occur most often.* **Furthermore,** *the biggest, most dangerous earthquakes happen in these zones.*
>
> **To show contrast:**   *However, . . .*   *On the other hand, . . .*   *In contrast, . . .*
>
> *These houses—with lightweight walls and roofs—are still standing, and the people who live there are safe.* **In contrast,** *living in a part of the world where the buildings don't have these features can be quite dangerous.*
>
> **To give examples:**   *For example, . . .   For instance, . . .*
>
> *Buildings can be constructed with lighter materials.* **For instance,** *straw weighs much less than concrete.*
>
> **To talk about a result:**   *Therefore, . . .   As a result, . . .*
>
> *One plate can move under another plate.* **As a result,** *the mountains are pushed up even higher.*

A Fill in each blank with an appropriate transition. Then work with a partner and compare your answers.

1. I didn't sleep much last night. _____, I'm very tired today.

2. The food at that restaurant isn't very good. _____, it's near my house, so I go there pretty often.

3. There are ways to help people after natural disasters. _____, you can donate money to humanitarian relief organizations.

4. That grocery store has a large selection of foods. _____, the prices are low, so we usually shop there.

5. This house is well constructed and big enough for our whole family. _____, it would be a safe place for all of us during an earthquake.

A woman in Aceh, Sumatra, Indonesia, walks on pieces of coral she brought into her house when it was flooded after an earthquake and a tsunami.

B Work with a partner. Take turns completing each statement with your own ideas.

1. We (do / don't) live in an earthquake zone. Therefore, . . .
2. We sometimes experience extreme weather here. For instance, . . .
3. I keep important papers in a backpack in case I need to leave the house suddenly during an emergency. Furthermore, . . .
4. I don't worry very much about earthquakes. On the other hand, . . .
5. After an earthquake, you may not be able to use your cell phone. In addition, . . .
6. California had dangerously high temperatures in 2015. As a result, . . .

GRAMMAR FOR SPEAKING Gerunds as Subjects and Objects

A *gerund* is the base form of a verb plus *-ing*. Gerunds act as nouns. We often use them as the subjects of sentences. Notice that a gerund subject is always singular.

> ***Walking*** *is my favorite form of exercise.*
> ***Using*** *lightweight materials for houses helps keep people safe.*

We also use gerunds as the objects of verbs or prepositions.

> *Today we're going to* <u>continue</u> ***talking*** *about plate tectonics.*
> *Lisa is interested* <u>in</u> ***studying*** *geology.*

Verbs that are often followed by a gerund object include:

admit	*consider*	*dislike*	*finish*	*(don't) mind*	*postpone*	*suggest*
avoid	*discuss*	*enjoy*	*keep*	*miss*	*recommend*	

C Fill in each blank with the gerund form of the verb in parentheses.

1. _____ (predict) an earthquake is not possible, unfortunately.

2. I never worry about _____ (be) killed in an earthquake. I don't live in an earthquake zone.

3. They suggest _____ (go) outside as soon as you feel an earthquake.

4. _____ (have) an earthquake safety plan is important for people in earthquake zones.

5. Sorry, would you mind _____ (repeat) that? I wasn't paying attention.

6. Are you interested in _____ (get) a degree in geology?

D Work with your partner. Take turns interviewing each other using the questions below. Practice using gerunds. Take notes on your partner's answers.

1. What are some things you enjoy doing in your free time? Why?
2. What are some things you are considering doing in the future? Why?
3. What are some things you dislike doing on the weekends? Why?

CRITICAL THINKING: **E** Form a group with another pair of students. Take turns telling the group about your
APPLYING   partner. Use your notes from exercise D to help you. Practice using gerunds.

LESSON TASK Interviewing a Partner about an Experience

A 🎧 2.20 Look at the photo, and read the caption and information in the box on page 131. Then listen to information about a photographer and complete the sentences on page 131 with the gerunds you hear.

▶ **Surfers at Kirikiri Beach in Otsuchi-cho, Japan stand near a protective wall that was destroyed in the 2011 tsunami. In 2016, photographer Alejandro Chaskielberg took photos of places damaged by Japan's 2011 tsunami.**

On March 11, 2011, a strong earthquake under the Pacific Ocean caused a *tsunami*—a powerful ocean wave that moved onshore over a large area of Japan's eastern coast. The tsunami destroyed buildings and vehicles and caused major damage to a nuclear power plant. It also killed more than 16,000 people and injured many others.

Sadly, the death and destruction following a major natural disaster are not quickly forgotten. This story focuses on a photographer from Argentina and what he did to help the people of Japan.

1. _____ in Japan means _____ a lot about earthquakes.

2. Today, some Japanese people avoid _____ about the horror and sadness of the tsunami of 2011.

3. A photographer from Argentina went to Japan in 2016 with the goal of _____ survivors think about the tsunami in new ways.

4. _____ around the world is nothing new to Alejandro Chaskielberg.

5. He asked people to consider _____ to the places they lived or the places they went before the tsunami.

6. According to Chaskielberg, _____ these photos was "... a way to help them create new memories."

B Work with a partner. Discuss these questions. Use gerunds and transitions when appropriate.

CRITICAL THINKING: ANALYZING

1. Living anywhere in the world involves some kind of danger, from tsunamis and earthquakes to crime or dangerous roads. What are some of the dangers of living in your country?
2. Look at the photo on page 130. Why do you think Chaskielberg decided to take a photo of these people?
3. Why do you think Chaskielberg decided to go to a place damaged by the tsunami to take this picture? What questions do you think he asked the people in the photo?

C Work with a different partner. Interview your partner about a difficult experience in his or her life. In your notebook, take brief notes on the answers. Then switch roles and repeat.

1. What difficult event have you experienced? What happened? What did you do?
2. How did this experience affect you afterwards?
3. (your own question) _____

D Form a group with another pair of students. Tell the group about your partner's experience. Use your notes from exercise C to help you.

CRITICAL THINKING: APPLYING

Video

Volcano Trek

A climber stands above the lava lake inside the Erta Ale volcano in Ethiopia.

BEFORE VIEWING

CRITICAL THINKING:
INTERPRETING
A DIAGRAM

A Look at the diagram below. Use the words from the diagram to complete the paragraph.

A VOLCANIC ERUPTION

A volcano is a mountain with a large hole at the top. This hole is called a(n) _____. A volcano produces very hot, melted rock. When it is underground, this hot, melted rock is called _____. When it leaves or comes out of the volcano, it is called _____. When the lava stays in the crater, it forms a(n) _____. When lava leaves a volcano, we say the volcano erupts. We call it a(n) _____.

1 2 3 4 5

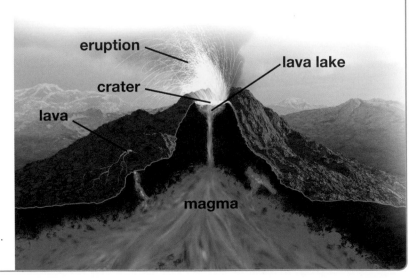

eruption

lava lake

crater

lava

magma

B Read the information about Dr. Franck Tessier and Dr. Irene Margaritis. With a partner, discuss what you know about volcanoes. Are there volcanoes in your country? Are they popular places to visit?

> **MEET DR. FRANCK TESSIER AND DR. IRENE MARGARITIS.** They're National Geographic Explorers, geologists, and professors. They've traveled from France to Ethiopia to study a very unusual volcano: Erta Ale. It has the world's oldest lava lake, which is also one of the lowest points on Earth. Collecting and analyzing samples of the material in the lava lake could help the scientists learn more about the earth's beginnings.

WHILE VIEWING

C ▶ 1.13 Read the statements. Then watch the video and choose T for *True* and F for *False*. Correct the false statements.

1. The temperature of the lava is more than 2,000° F.   T   F
2. The team uses horses to help them reach the lava lake.   T   F
3. The geologists are from the University of Paris.   T   F
4. Erta Ale is in the Afar area of Ethiopia.   T   F
5. As lava cools, it becomes red in color.   T   F
6. The team returns from the crater at 1:00 a.m.   T   F

D ▶ 1.13 Watch the video again and take notes on the information you see or hear that helps you answer this question: Do Dr. Franck Tessier and Dr. Irene Margaritis enjoy their work as geologists?

_____

_____

AFTER VIEWING

E Write two questions you'd like to ask the geologists in the video.

_____

_____

F Work in a group. Share your questions from exercise E.

B Vocabulary

A **2.21** Read and listen to the information. Notice each word or phrase in **blue** and think about its meaning.

THE PACIFIC RING OF FIRE: FAST FACTS

1. The Ring of Fire consists of many volcanoes in a near-circle around the Pacific Ocean.
2. **Active** volcanoes are dangerous. People choose to live near them, however, because volcanic **soil** is rich and good for farming.
3. In Indonesia, more people live near active volcanoes than in any other country. On the island of Java alone, there are more than 30 volcanoes and about 140 million people.
4. One of the world's worst natural **disasters** occurred in Indonesia in 1883. The **eruption** of Mount Krakatau, a volcanic island near Java, caused a tsunami that killed more than 36,000 people. In addition, it produced enough volcanic ash[1] to **affect** the earth's weather for several months.

An aerial view of Mount Tavurvur, an active volcano in Rabaul, Papua New Guinea

5. In Kinarejo, Java, many farmers live near a volcano called Mount Merapi. A man there named Mbah Marijan was known as the "Gatekeeper of Merapi." **According to** tradition, the Gatekeeper knew the volcano very well, and his job was to tell people when it became dangerous so that they could **evacuate**. Sadly, Marijan and many others were killed when Mount Merapi erupted violently in 2010.
6. For people who live near volcanoes, evacuating means **leaving behind** their homes, animals, and daily lives. Therefore, they often wait for **definite** news about the volcano that will **justify** their leaving. However, sometimes the news doesn't come in time to save lives.

---

[1]**ash** (n): burnt material

B Match each word or phrase from exercise A with its definition.

1. _____ active (adj)
2. _____ soil (n)
3. _____ disasters (n)
4. _____ eruption (n)
5. _____ affect (v)
6. _____ according to (prep)
7. _____ evacuate (v)
8. _____ leaving behind (v)
9. _____ definite (adj)
10. _____ justify (v)

a. unlikely to be changed
b. things that have very bad effects or results
c. to make right or necessary
d. phrase that tells us where information comes from
e. to leave an area because of some danger
f. not taking something with you when you leave
g. a sudden explosion of rocks, ash, and lava
h. the material on the earth's surface in which plants grow
i. with volcanoes, having recently erupted or likely to erupt
j. to influence or change something

C Complete each sentence with two or more words. Use your own ideas. Then work with a partner and take turns saying your sentences.

1. Volcanic eruptions are dangerous because _____.
2. According to my parents, _____.
3. If we ever need to evacuate this building, I'll _____.
4. The worst natural disaster that I remember was _____.
5. Active volcanoes are _____.
6. _____ affects my life every day.

VOCABULARY SKILL Using *Affect* and *Effect*

It's easy to confuse the words *affect* and *effect* since they look and sound so similar. However, *affect* almost always acts as a verb, and *effect* almost always acts as a noun.

verb: Sunshine **affects** the way I feel.
noun: Sunshine has a positive **effect** on my mood.

D Choose the correct word to complete each sentence.

1. Natural disasters in the Ring of Fire (affect / effect) a large number of people.
2. What are the (affects / effects) of a major earthquake?
3. A major hurricane actually (affects / effects) ocean life in the area.
4. Volcanic eruptions have a positive (affect / effect) on the soil.
5. How did seeing those photos of the earthquake (affect / effect) you?
6. Fortunately, the storm didn't (affect / effect) our area.
7. The documentary showed the (affects / effects) of the 2015 earthquake in Nepal.
8. Volcanic ash can have an (affect / effect) on the weather.

Listening A Discussion about Volcanoes

BEFORE LISTENING

PREDICTING **A** You are going to listen to a group of students discussing volcanoes during a study session for an Earth Science class. Discuss this question with a partner: What topics related to volcanoes do you think the students will discuss, (e.g., the dangers of volcanoes, magma and lava)?

WHILE LISTENING

LISTENING FOR MAIN IDEAS **B** 🎧 2.22 Listen to the discussion. Choose the three topics the speakers discuss. Did they mention any of the topics you discussed in exercise A?

    a. the material inside volcanos

    b. why volcanos are dangerous to people

    c. how to tell when a volcano will erupt soon

    d. the Gatekeeper in Indonesia

    e. the number of people killed when Mount Merapi erupted

C 🎧 2.22 Listen again and complete each sentence with the information you hear.

LISTENING FOR DETAILS
1. When melted rock is _____ the earth, it's called magma.

2. When it comes *out* of the earth, it's called _____ .

3. According to Professor Lopez, lava can kill people and _____ .

4. U.S. government geologists told everyone to _____ before Mount Saint Helens erupted.

5. _____ people were killed when Mount Saint Helens erupted.

6. The Gatekeeper is an important part of village _____ .

Mount Nyiragongo, Democratic Republic of the Congo

It's important to listen for transitions in speech so that you have an idea of what the speaker is going to say next.

Remember, if you hear *in addition* and *furthemore,* the speaker is going to provide more information.

> There will be two exams this semester. **In addition,** we'll have three quizzes.

When you hear *in contrast, however,* or *on the other hand*, the speaker is going to talk about a contrast or an exception.

> Living near volcanoes isn't always safe. **However,** the land near volcanoes is excellent for farming.

When you hear *for example* or *for instance*, the speaker is going to provide an example.

> There are other ways to communicate. **For example,** you can mail a letter if you don't have an Internet connection.

When you hear *therefore* or *as a result*, the speaker is going to talk about a result.

> The prime minister has a serious illness. **Therefore,** she has canceled the trip.

D 🎧 **2.23** Work with a partner. Discuss these excerpts from the conversation. Which kind of transition do you think each speaker used? Complete each excerpt with a transition. Then listen and check your answers.

LISTENING FOR TRANSITIONS

1. **Khaled:** Professor Lopez said that when there's an eruption, hot lava can kill people

   and start fires. _____ , he talked about huge rocks and hardened lava. I

   ₁

   wouldn't want to be nearby when those fly out!

   Tony: Me neither! _____ , all of that stuff from inside volcanoes

   ₂

   makes good soil eventually.

2. **Ann:** … Personally, I'd rather get my volcano news from scientists. After all,

   it was geologists working for the U.S. government who told everyone in the area

   to evacuate before Mount Saint Helens erupted. … Some people stayed, and

   _____ , 57 people were killed when the volcano erupted.

   ₃

AFTER LISTENING

E Work with a partner. Discuss these questions.

CRITICAL THINKING: REFLECTING

1. Do you think the study group was helpful for the students? Why or why not?
2. Have you ever seen a volcano? If so, describe it. If not, would you like to? Why or why not?

Speaking

> **PRONUNCIATION** Syllable Number and Syllable Stress Review
>
> 🎧 2.24
>
> **Syllable Number**
>
> Part of learning to pronounce a word is learning how many syllables the word has. Pay attention to the number of syllables in these examples:
>
> | | | | |
> |---|---|---|---|
> | *col lapse* | *sur vive* | *dan ger ous* | *ma te ri als* |
> | 2 syllables | 2 syllables | 3 syllables | 4 syllables |
>
> **Syllable Stress**
>
> In words with more than one syllable, one syllable receives the primary stress, which means it is louder and clearer than the others. Pay attention to the syllable stress in these examples:
>
> e**nough**   **prac**tical   **in**terested   ac**cor**ding   af**fect**

A 🎧 2.25 Work with a partner. Say each word aloud. Underline the stressed syllable in each word. Then count the number of syllables in each word and write it on the line. Listen and check your answers.

1. common _____
2. practical _____
3. circumstances _____
4. flow _____
5. summarize _____

6. clothes _____
7. psychological _____
8. recommend _____
9. reinforce _____
10. definitely _____

B Work with a partner. Say either option *a* or *b* for each item below. Your partner will listen and tell you which one you said. Then switch roles and repeat.

A: *You can turn it.*
B: *You said b.*
A: *That's right!*

1. a. You can return it.
2. a. We demand it.
3. a. common
4. a. It's likely.
5. a. definite
6. a. We need a research team.

b. You can turn it.
b. We demanded it.
b. Come in.
b. It's unlikely.
b. Define it.
b. We need a search team.

FINAL TASK Giving a Presentation about a Natural Disaster

> You are going to give an individual presentation about a natural disaster. You will choose a natural disaster and present it to the class.

A Work with a partner. Discuss whether you think each statement in the quiz is true or false. Choose T for *True* or F for *False* for each statement. Use expressions from the Everyday Language box when necessary. Then check your answers below.

CRITICAL THINKING: EVALUATING

QUIZ: WHAT DO YOU KNOW ABOUT NATURAL DISASTERS?

1. A tornado can produce the fastest winds of any storm on Earth. T F
2. An avalanche can be caused by the movement of tectonic plates. T F
3. The strongest earthquake in history occurred in Indonesia. T F
4. Your chances of being hit by lightning in a given year are 1 in 7,000. T F
5. An island near Long Island was completely destroyed by a hurricane. T F
6. Landslides can hit any country with steep mountains and heavy rain. T F
7. One forest fire in the United States killed more than 1,700 people. T F
8. Tiny particles of frozen water fall from the sky during ice storms. T F

EVERYDAY LANGUAGE Making Guesses

It could be …   It's probably …   It might be …   I guess …   I think …

Answers: **1.** T (up to 300 mph/500 kph) **2.** T **3.** F (in Chile in 1960) **4.** F (1 in 700,000) **5.** T (Hog Island in 1893) **6.** T **7.** T (the Peshtigo Fire in 1871) **8.** F (cold liquid raindrops freeze as soon as they touch a surface)

Trees and a car covered in ice in Versoix, on the shore of Lake Geneva, Switzerland

B Work in a group. Discuss the natural disasters below. What do you know about them? Which topic is the most interesting to you? Explain.

avalanche	flood	heat wave	ice storm	tornado
drought	forest fire	hurricane	landslide	tsunami

C Work on your own. Choose one of the natural disasters from exercise B as the topic for your presentation. Do some research to learn about your topic. You can use the Internet, an encyclopedia, information from this book, or interview someone you know to get information.

D Use the questions below to help you organize the information about your topic. In your notebook, write brief notes to answer each question. Then think about which transitions might be helpful to connect your ideas.

1. Where and when does this kind of natural disaster usually occur (e.g., in cold places, warm places, during certain times of the year)?
2. What are the causes of this kind of natural disaster?
3. What happens when this kind of disaster occurs?
4. What are some things people should or shouldn't do when this natural disaster occurs?

PRESENTATION SKILL Speaking at the Right Pace

Many people get nervous and speak too quickly when they give a presentation. When you do this, your audience might not understand everything you are saying. When you give a presentation, it's important to remember to slow down and pause occasionally so that your audience has time to think about what you are saying.

It's also important not to speak too slowly. This can make your speech sound unnatural. It's OK to slow down occasionally to emphasize an important idea, but in general, try to find the right pace for speaking to an audience—not too fast and not too slow.

E Present your topic to the class. Remember to speak at the right pace. Use transition words and phrases when necessary.

REFLECTION

1. What are two ways that predicting exam questions might be useful to you?

_____

_____

2. What events from your life did the topic of natural disasters make you remember or think about?

_____

_____

3. Here are the vocabulary words and phrases from the unit. Check (✓) the ones you can use.

☐ according to	☐ disaster	☐ material
☐ active	☐ earthquake	☐ reinforce AWL
☐ affect AWL	☐ eruption	☐ shake
☐ boundary	☐ evacuate	☐ soil
☐ collapse AWL	☐ justify AWL	☐ survive AWL
☐ construct AWL	☐ leave behind	☐ zone
☐ definite AWL	☐ major AWL	

WONDERS FROM THE PAST

8

An ancient Moai statue
on Easter Island

THINK AND DISCUSS

1 Look at the photo. Why do you think this statue was made? What would you like to know about it?

2 Look at the title of this unit. What do you think you will learn about in this unit?

Look at the photos and read the information. Then discuss these questions.

1. Which of the ancient civilizations mentioned on these pages have you heard of? What do you know about them?

2. Which of the artifacts on these pages do you find most interesting? Why?

3. What kinds of "clues" or information do you think the artifacts on these pages can give us about the ancient civilizations they come from?

4. What other ancient civilizations do you know about? What do you know about them?

CLUES TO THE PAST

What was daily life like for the ancient Egyptians, the ancient Greeks, or the Maya? What did they eat and drink? How did they dress and spend their free time? These are some of the questions that archaeologists try to answer through their work. And although we may never have all of the answers, the artifacts left behind by these ancient civilizations provide some clues to what life may have been like for people hundreds and thousands of years ago.

A gold female rhyton, or drinking cup , from the Panagyurishte era, Greece

A decorated container from the Maya civilization, Mexico

A gold bracelet that was discovered in the burial chamber of Egyptian Queen Hetepheres, mother of Cheops, of the IV Dynasty, Egypt

A Vocabulary

MEANING FROM CONTEXT **A** 🎧 **3.2** Look at the images, and read and listen to the information. Notice each word in **blue** and think about its meaning.

AN AMAZING DISCOVERY

Every career has a high point, and according to National Geographic Explorer William Saturno, being the first human being in 2,000 years to view a beautiful Maya mural[1] in Guatemala was probably that point for him. Saturno, an **archaeologist** and an expert on the Maya **civilization**, discovered the mural inside a room that was once next to a pyramid[2]. The mural room and pyramid were later covered by a larger pyramid— part of the **ruins** of an **ancient** Maya city, now called San Bartolo.

At first, Saturno could see only a small part of the mural. He had to **dig** through earth and stone in order to **reveal** the rest. Then, instead of using a camera, Saturno used his scanner[3] to take digital **images** of the mural. He took about 350 scans!

The mural wasn't the only important find at San Bartolo. The archaeologists also uncovered a **tomb**. It was a **royal** tomb, where the bones of a Maya king were **buried**, along with objects such as a bowl in the shape of a frog and an image of the Maya rain god Chac.

[1]**mural** (n): a picture painted on a wall
[2]**pyramid** (n): a huge building used as a tomb or ceremonial site
[3]**scanner** (n): a device that "reads" an image and changes it to digital information

B Write each word in **blue** from exercise A next to its definition.

1. _____ (n) a place that contains the body of a dead person

2. _____ (n) pictures

3. _____ (v) to use the hands or a tool to make a hole in the ground

4. _____ (v) put into the ground and covered with earth or stone

5. _____ (n) a person who studies the past by uncovering ancient sites and
    objects

6. _____ (adj) having to do with kings, queens, princes, or their families

7. _____ (adj) extremely old

8. _____ (n) broken parts of buildings that still exist after a long time

9. _____ (v) to show or uncover something so that people can see it

10. _____ (n) a human society with a complex social organization

C Work with a partner. Take turns asking and answering these questions.

CRITICAL THINKING:
REFLECTING

1. Where in the world can you see pyramids?
2. What ancient cultures have you studied? What do you remember about them?
3. What famous archaeological site would you like to visit? Why?
4. What kinds of things do archaeologists dig for? What do they hope to find?
5. What ancient civilizations are there in your part of the world?

VOCABULARY SKILL Using Antonyms

An *antonym* is a word that means the opposite of another word. Learning antonyms
can help you build your vocabulary and better express your ideas.

| ancient / modern | reveal / hide | buried / uncovered |

D Work with a partner. Discuss the meaning of the underlined word in each statement.
Then match the correct antonym with each underlined word.

Antonyms

1. _____ In years with enough rain, food was <u>abundant</u>.   a. similar

2. _____ The Great Pyramid at Giza is <u>enormous</u>, rising more than   b. scarce
    450 feet into the air.

3. _____ We have some <u>general</u> ideas about the ruins, but few details.   c. tiny

4. _____ The Egyptian pyramids all have the same shape, but the   d. specific
    Pyramid of the Magician in Mexico is <u>distinct</u>.

5. _____ Before people lived in cities, human societies had a <u>simple</u>   e. complex
    structure: Adults either hunted animals or gathered plants for food.

BEFORE LISTENING

PRIOR KNOWLEDGE

A Work with a partner. Discuss these questions.

1. Where did the ancient Maya people live?
2. What do you know about the Maya? For example, did they live in cities?

WHILE LISTENING

LISTENING FOR
MAIN IDEAS

B 🎧 **3.3** Listen to the guided tour. Choose the correct answer to each question.

1. Which Maya site are the tourists visiting?

    a. Tulum
    b. Palenque
    c. Uxmal

2. Why is this one of the most popular Maya historical sites?

    a. It has several pyramids and other structures.
    b. It has a ball court.
    c. It's easy to get to.

3. Why is the Pyramid of the Magician unusual?

    a. It has rounded sides.
    b. It has triangular sides.
    c. It has flat sides.

The Pyramid of the Magician and the ball court at Uxmal, Yucatán, Mexico

The stone goal ring from the ball court at Uxmal, Yucatán, Mexico

C 🎧 **3.3** Listen again and write notes to answer the questions.

LISTENING FOR DETAILS

1. From which period of Maya history is this site? _____

2. According to an old story, how long did it take to build the Pyramid of the Magician?
   _____

3. Around how many years did it actually take to build the pyramid? _____

4. How many different structures make up the pyramid? _____

5. Where does the group go after seeing the pyramid? _____

6. What is in front of the Governor's Palace? _____

7. What is a *jaguar*? _____

AFTER LISTENING

D Work with a partner. Imagine that you are going to speak to the tour guide at Uxmal. Write three questions about the Maya civilization to ask him. These questions can be about any part of Maya life (e.g., food, clothing, housing).

1. _____?

2. _____?

3. _____?

E Form a group with another pair of students. Share your questions from exercise D. Explain why you want to know the answers to your questions.

A | Speaking

PRONUNCIATION Question Intonation

🎧 **3.4** Intonation can help people understand the kind of question you are asking.

1. In *yes/no* questions, the speaker's voice usually rises at the end of the question.

   Is the Maya ball game still played here?

2. In questions that offer choices, the speaker's voice rises for each option except the last one, where the speaker's voice falls.

   Would you rather leave now or later?

3. In *wh-* questions, the speaker's voice rises on the stressed syllable of the last content word and then falls at the end.

   *When was Uxmal **discovered**?*

A 🎧 **3.5** Listen and draw rising or falling arrows according to the intonation you hear.

1. What time are we leaving?

2. Have you ever been to Kazakhstan?

3. How was the walking tour?

4. Did you go there on Friday or Saturday?

5. Is the mural from the early, middle, or late period?

6. Does this story make sense to you?

7. Is the mural in Mexico, Guatemala, or Honduras?

8. Where's the pyramid?

B Work with a partner. Compare your answers from exercise A. Then practice asking and answering the questions using the correct question intonation.

C With your partner, think of new questions to ask each other using the question words in the box.

Are…?	Is…?	Do…?	Does…?	Which…?
Why…?	Where…?	When…?	How many…?	Who…?

A: *Are you going to have lunch after class?*
B: *No, I have another class at 1:30.*

GRAMMAR FOR SPEAKING The Passive Voice with the Past

We form the passive voice in the past with *was/were* and the past participle of a verb.
The walking tour **was given** *by an archaeologist yesterday.*

Notice how questions are formed in the passive voice with the past.
Were *a lot of people* **buried** *in the tombs?*

As you learned in Unit 4, we use *by* with the passive when we want to specify who or what did the action. We generally use the passive voice without the *by* phrase when:

1. the agent (the "do-er") of an action is not known or not very important.
   The Pyramid of the Magician definitely **wasn't built** *in one night.*

2. the agent is clear from the context.
   Corn **was grown** *near the city of Uxmal.*

D Read the information about the Seven Wonders of the Ancient World. Then complete each sentence below using the passive with the past form of the verb in parentheses.

> The Seven Wonders of the Ancient World were remarkable structures in the Mediterranean region. They were listed in tourist guidebooks around 2,000 years ago. Today, the Great Pyramid at Giza in Egypt is the only "wonder" that is still standing.

1. The Temple of Artemis at Ephesus _____ (build) to honor a Greek goddess.

2. The Hanging Gardens of Babylon _____ (plant) by King Nebuchadnezzar II.

3. The Lighthouse of Alexandria _____ (construct) in the third century BC.

4. The Colossus of Rhodes _____ (destroy) by an earthquake.

5. The Statue of Zeus at Olympia _____ (keep) inside its own temple.

6. About eight hundred tons of stone _____ (need) every day to build the Great Pyramid at Giza.

7. The Mausoleum at Halicarnassus _____ (design) by Greek architects.

A man leads camels in the desert near the pyramids at Giza in Egypt.

CRITICAL THINKING: APPLYING KNOWLEDGE

E **Work in a group. Compare your answers from exercise D. Then discuss these questions.**

1. The Colossus of Rhodes and the Statue of Zeus at Olympia were large statues. What are other large statues you know about? Why do you think those statues were built?
2. The Hanging Gardens of Babylon are the only "living wonder." Why do you think the gardens were planted? What are some similar places that exist today? What do you know about them?
3. The Lighthouse of Alexandria may be the only wonder with an everyday purpose. Why do you think it was built?
4. The Great Pyramid at Giza and the Mausoleum at Halicarnassus were built to serve as tombs for important leaders. How are important leaders in your culture honored when they die?

LESSON TASK Presenting Ancient Artifacts

CRITICAL THINKING: ANALYZING

A **Work in a group of three. Look at the photos and read the captions on this page and the next about three ancient artifacts. Discuss these questions about each artifact.**

1. Where was the artifact found?   3. What material was it made from?

2. When was it made?   4. What do you think it was used for?

1.

▲ This artifact is from the Anasazi civilization. It is either a spoon or a shovel made from the horn of an animal. The Anasazi lived in the southwestern United States, where this artifact was found.

2.

▲ This Maya mask was found in Mexico. It was the death mask of a Maya king named Pakal. It's made of jade, which is a smooth green stone.

3.

▲ This necklace was found on the Island of Crete, Greece. It was buried with a woman from ancient Greece. It's made of glass and gold.

EVERYDAY LANGUAGE Expressing Certainty and Uncertainty

More certain:
I'm fairly sure…
I'm almost positive…
I'm certain…

Less certain:
I'm not really sure…
I'm not positive…
I don't know…

> *I'm certain this artifact was made from the horn of an animal, but I don't know what kind of animal the horn came from.*

B With your group, prepare a short presentation about the artifacts from exercise A. Write notes on your ideas in your notebook. Your presentation should include the following: ORGANIZING IDEAS

1. information that answers the questions from exercise A
2. some additional details from your own ideas. Use your imagination. (What words describe the artifact? Who do you think found it? What other artifacts do you think were found with it?)

C Practice your presentation with your group. Each student in your group should present one artifact.

D Get together with another group. Take turns presenting your artifacts.   PRESENTING

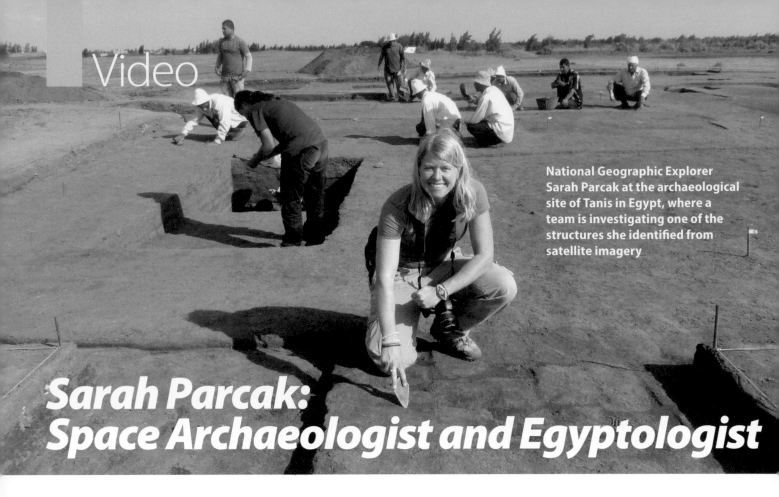

Video

National Geographic Explorer Sarah Parcak at the archaeological site of Tanis in Egypt, where a team is investigating one of the structures she identified from satellite imagery

Sarah Parcak:
Space Archaeologist and Egyptologist

BEFORE VIEWING

A Match each word or phrase from the video with its meaning. You may use a dictionary.

1. _____ archaeology
2. _____ satellite images
3. _____ excavate

4. _____ Egyptologist
5. _____ curiosity
6. _____ settlement

a. photos taken from a satellite in space
b. interest in knowing about things
c. the study of human history and pre-history and the materials and remains of ancient civilizations
d. to remove soil carefully in order to uncover things
e. a person who studies ancient Egypt
f. a place where a group of people live

B Work with a partner. Which of these facts about archaeology and space archaeology did you already know? Which fact is the most surprising to you? Explain.

1. Archaeologists spend a lot of their time working outdoors.
2. Space satellites can take pictures of what is under the earth's soil.
3. Archaeology helps us learn about people and civilizations of the past.

CRITICAL THINKING:
MAKING INFERENCES

C Read the information about Sarah Parcak on the next page. With a partner, discuss how you think she feels about her job and why you think so.

MEET SARAH PARCAK. She's a National Geographic Explorer, a Space Archaeologist, and an Egyptologist. She's been interested in ancient history since childhood. She describes the moment she first saw the Great Pyramids of Egypt as "magical." These days, Parcak directs the Laboratory for Global Observation at the University of Alabama in the United States. There, she analyzes satellite images in order to locate ancient archaeological sites.

WHILE VIEWING

D ▶ 1.14 Watch the video and choose the correct answers.

UNDERSTANDING MAIN IDEAS

1. What does Sarah Parcak say is the most important thing about being an explorer?

   a. getting the necessary education in archaeology
   b. doing research on computers and smartphones
   c. being outside and looking at the world around us

2. What does Parcak say about her philosophy of archaeology?

   a. It's about finding gold jewelry and other treasures.
   b. It's about asking questions in order to understand the past.
   c. It's about understanding how the environment affected ancient people.

3. According to Parcak, what does archaeology help us understand?

   a. who we are and why we're here
   b. how to keep our past knowledge
   c. why life today is better than in the past

E ▶ 1.14 Read the statements. Then watch the video again and choose T for *True* or F for *False*. Correct the false statements.

UNDERSTANDING DETAILS

1. Parcak grew up doing activities outside, including camping and hiking.   T   F
2. She says curiosity motivates us to explore the world.   T   F
3. Parcak uses satellites to look into outer space.   T   F
4. She uses information that works like a space-based X-ray to see beneath the soil.   T   F
5. She has found more than 4,000 ancient settlements in Egypt.   T   F
6. Parcak can point to a single moment when she decided to be an archaeologist.   T   F

AFTER VIEWING

F Discuss these questions with a partner.

CRITICAL THINKING: REFLECTING

1. Do you enjoy being outdoors and exploring the world? Explain.
2. What are two questions you would like to ask Sarah Parcak?

B Vocabulary

A 🎧 **3.6** Read and listen to the information. Notice each word in **blue** and think about its meaning.

NEW CLUES ABOUT TUTANKHAMEN: HIS LIFE AND DEATH

In 1922, British Egyptologist Howard Carter found the **remains** of a young man in a tomb filled with royal **treasures** in the Valley of the Kings, Egypt. Newspapers around the world **reported** the **discovery** and described the gold jewelry, **precious** stones, and beautiful art found in the tomb. Everyone wanted to know who this important man was.

We now know Tutankhamen was the son of Akhenaten, and he **ruled** Egypt from 1332–1322 BC. He became pharaoh[1] as a child, and he died young. Yet many questions are still unanswered. Was "Tut" ill? Was he murdered[2]? What did he look like when he was **alive**?

In 2005, scientists began to **analyze** Tut's remains with computer tomography (CT) and modern forensic medicine—a science usually used to **investigate** and solve murder cases. Tut's remains were scanned in a CT machine, which created 3-D images. Using this technology, scientists **determined** that Tut was probably not murdered and was about 19 when he died.

Scientists also worked with an artist to construct a life-like model of Tut. Not everyone likes the result, but according to the CT scans, he probably looked a lot like modern Egyptians.

[1]**pharoah** (n): a ruler or king of ancient Egypt
[2]be **murdered** (v): to be killed by someone

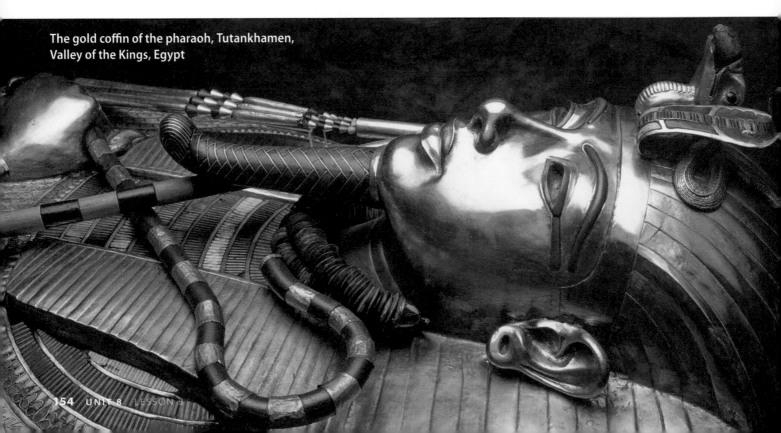

The gold coffin of the pharaoh, Tutankhamen, Valley of the Kings, Egypt

B Write each word in **blue** from exercise A next to its definition.

1. _____ (n) valuable objects

2. _____ (v) to look at something carefully in order to understand it

3. _____ (adj) very valuable

4. _____ (n) the finding of something new

5. _____ (v) told about something (e.g., an event)

6. _____ (adj) living, not dead

7. _____ (v) controlled (e.g., a country)

8. _____ (v) to search for facts and information

9. _____ (n) parts or things that are left after death or destruction

10. _____ (v) concluded or decided

C Complete each sentence with the correct form of a word from exercise B.

1. She's a statistician. She _____ numerical data.

2. Our country's most important _____ are in our National Museum.

3. Tutankhamen _____ Egypt as pharoah for a very short time before he died.

4. Your bike was stolen? You should _____ it to the police.

5. The _____ of Machu Picchu in Peru in 1911 caused a lot of excitement.

D Work with a partner. Discuss these questions.

CRITICAL THINKING:
REFLECTING

1. What do you think King Tut probably looked like when he was alive?
2. King Tut's tomb was a major discovery. What are some other important discoveries that you know about?
3. What are some famous treasures from your country, and where can people go to see them?
4. What are some things you own that are precious to you? Explain.
5. What factors help you determine where to live? For example, is it more important to live in a place with good weather, or to live close to family members?
6. What are some things and places that you would like to investigate in order to learn more about them? Explain.

B Listening A Conversation about an Assignment

BEFORE LISTENING

A Work with a partner. Read the notes that a college student wrote while watching a documentary film. Then talk about the documentary film.

> *The documentary was about the discovery of a historical site in Hanoi.*

Documentary Title: Uncovering the Past in Hanoi

- 2002, government plan - a new building in Hanoi, Vietnam
- They started construction, then found: ancient palaces & meeting halls & 1,000's of artifacts
- Name: Thang Long Imperial Citadel / (citadel = a safe place for royals)
- Gov't chose new site for its building; Thang Long Imperial Citadel now a UNESCO World Heritage site (popular for tourists)

WHILE LISTENING

LISTENING FOR
MAIN IDEAS

B 🎧 **3.7** **Listen to the conversation. Choose the correct answers.**

1. The class assignment is to give an oral summary of a _____.

   a. movie or documentary film

   b. class lecture on the Thang Long Imperial Citadel

   c. historical site in Southeast Asia

2. Professor Norton told Silvio that _____.

   a. he should have taken a lot more notes

   b. his notes were not very helpful

   c. he had already begun to summarize the information

3. Professor Norton suggests that Silvio _____.

   a. write out his notes as complete sentences

   b. ask himself questions about the documentary he watched

   c. talk to some of the archaeologists on campus

4. Professor Norton says including a few examples can _____.

   a. make a summary very confusing

   b. help support the main ideas

   c. take too much time in a presentation

LISTENING SKILL Listening for Examples

Listening for examples can help you better understand a speaker's main ideas. Here are some common expressions used to introduce examples:

> *For example,…   For instance,…   To give an example,…   such as…*
>
> *Artifacts **such as** large jars for storing grains helped archaeologists locate the kitchen areas in the ancient city.*

NOTE-TAKING SKILL Recording Examples

When you record an example, write it near the main idea it supports, and use a clear abbreviation or symbol before the example. One easy way to do this is to indent the example under the main idea and use *e.g.,* or *ex:* to indicate the example.

> *Old objects show how people lived in past.*
>
>> *e.g., a plate (how made; preference for plain or colorful)*

C 🎧 **3.7** Look at the notes below for three key ideas from the conversation. Then listen again and take notes on the examples you hear for each key idea. Use indentation and *e.g,.* or *ex:* to indicate each example.

NOTE TAKING

1. Ruins found at hist. site in Hanoi, Vietnam

3. Archaeologists found many artifacts at site

2. Wh- question technique for summarizing

AFTER LISTENING

D Work with a partner. Compare and discuss your notes from exercise C. How do the examples that you recorded in your notes help you to understand the key ideas of the conversation?

The Imperial Citadel of Hanoi, Vietnam

Speaking

> **SPEAKING SKILL** Summarizing
>
> Summarizing means to briefly give the key points about something such as a movie, a book, an article, or a talk using your own words. When you give a summary, you should include only the most important information in order to answer the questions *Who*, *What*, *When*, *Where*, *How*, and *Why*? You should not include your own opinion in a summary—just the key facts about the topic.

NOTE TAKING **A** 🎧 3.8 Listen to Silvio's oral summary of the documentary film he watched. As you listen, take brief notes in your notebook to answer each question.

1. Where was the site discovered?
2. When was it discovered?
3. How was it discovered?
4. Who was involved?
5. What did the Vietnamese government do, and why?
6. What happened in 2010?

CRITICAL THINKING: EVALUATING **B** Work with a partner. Compare your notes from exercise A. Then discuss Silvio's presentation. Do you think he did well on the oral-summary assignment? Explain.

CRITICAL THINKING: APPLYING **C** You are going to summarize the information about the San Bartolo discovery from Lesson A in this unit. Follow these steps.

1. Look back at the information about the San Bartolo discovery on page 144.
2. Decide which information you should include in a summary about the discovery. Use *wh-* questions to help you.
3. Use the chart below to take notes about the discovery. Use your own words.

Who?	What?	When?
Where?	**How?**	**Why?**

D Work with a partner. Take turns summarizing the information about the San Bartolo discovery. You can use your notes from exercise C to help you.

SUMMARIZING

E Think about your partner's summary from exercise D. Choose Y for *Yes* or N for *No* for each question. Then share and discuss your answers with your partner.

CRITICAL THINKING: EVALUATING

1. Did your partner answer the questions *Who, What, When, Where, How,* and *Why*?   Y   N
2. Was any important information missing?   Y   N
3. Did your partner include any unnecessary information?   Y   N
4. Did your partner include his or her opinion?   Y   N

FINAL TASK   Giving a Presentation about a Historical Site

> You are going to give a short presentation about a historical site that interests you. It could be a place in your country that you have visited, or another place in the world.

A Brainstorm some interesting ancient or historical places in your country or in other parts of the world. Make a list in your notebook. Then choose one place you are interested in as the topic for your presentation.

BRAINSTORMING

The Great Wall of China

B If you need more information about your topic, do some research and take brief notes. Include the most important facts about the site and a few interesting details.

> ### PRESENTATION SKILL Using Index Cards
>
> Index cards can be useful for organizing your notes for a presentation. Here are some ways to use index cards when preparing for and giving a presentation:
>
> - First, number your index cards. This will help you keep them in order later.
> - Write only a few important ideas on each index card.
> - Write only key words and phrases, not complete sentences.
> - Practice your presentation using the index cards. Decide if you need to reorder any of the ideas in your presentation.
> - As you present, look down at the cards only briefly to help you remember your ideas. Don't read directly from your cards.

C Prepare index cards to use during your presentation. Refer to the information in the Presentation Skill box to help you.

D Practice giving your presentation in front of a mirror or for friends or family members. After you finish, ask them these questions: *Were my ideas clear? Did I speak too quickly or too slowly?*

E Give your presentation to the class. When you give your presentation, remember to:

- Look at your notes or slides only occasionally.
- Look up and make eye contact with your audience.
- Ask your audience if they have any questions.

REFLECTION

1. How do you think you might use summarizing in the future?

   _____

   _____

2. Which ancient civilization from the unit was the most interesting to you? Why?

   _____

   _____

3. Here are the vocabulary words from the unit. Check (✓) the ones you can use.

☐ alive	☐ dig	☐ reveal ᴀᴡʟ
☐ analyze ᴀᴡʟ	☐ discovery	☐ royal
☐ ancient	☐ image ᴀᴡʟ	☐ ruins
☐ archaeologist	☐ investigate ᴀᴡʟ	☐ rule
☐ bury	☐ precious	☐ tomb
☐ civilization	☐ remains	☐ treasure
☐ determine	☐ report	

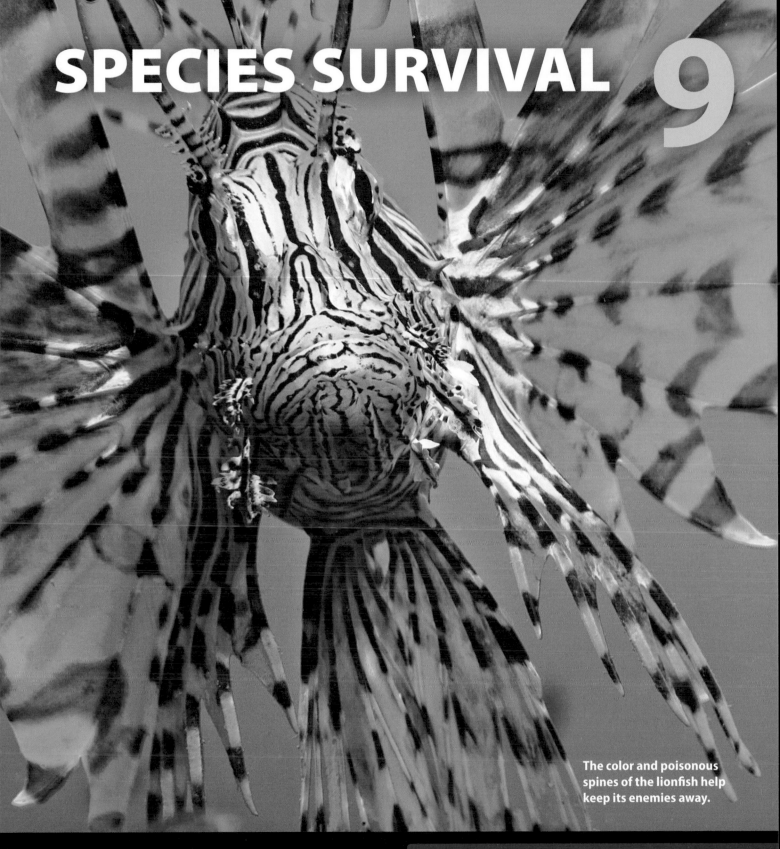

SPECIES SURVIVAL

9

The color and poisonous spines of the lionfish help keep its enemies away.

THINK AND DISCUSS

1 Look at the photo. What helps this fish survive, or live?
2 Look at the title of this unit. What do you think it means?
3 Do you enjoy learning about animals? Why or why not?

Look at the photos and read the information. Then discuss these questions.

1. What are some ways that animals use color in order to survive?
2. What are two ways that the giraffe's long neck helps it survive?
3. Which of the animals on these pages do you find most interesting? Why?
4. Can you think of any other animals that have adapted in some way in order to survive?

AMAZING ANIMAL ADAPTATIONS

The lichen katydid from Central and South America uses its perfect camouflage to hide from predators. It looks exactly like the lichen it eats.

A male Wilson's bird-of-paradise displays his colors to attract a female. Finding a mate will allow him to pass on his genes and help the species continue.

The strawberry poison dart frog's bright colors tell its predators (animals that eat other animals) that it's poisonous and not safe to eat.

The giraffe's long neck is one of the adaptations that helps it survive. Having a very long neck enables it to reach leaves at the tops of trees and see predators from far away.

A Vocabulary

MEANING FROM CONTEXT **A** 🎧 **3.9** Look at the map, and read and listen to the information. Notice each word in **blue** and think about its meaning.

THE *BEAGLE* IN SOUTH AMERICA

The *Beagle* expedition's priority was to map the harbors and coastlines of South America. Charles Darwin also spent a lot of his time on land, exploring parts of the Argentine Pampas, the Atacama Desert, and the Andes mountains.

1 **Argentina, 1832:** At both Punta Alta and Monte Hermoso, Darwin found fossils of large prehistoric animals. He could not **identify** the fossils, but they were similar to modern animal **species** from the area. This might have been the beginning of his now famous idea that species could change over time.

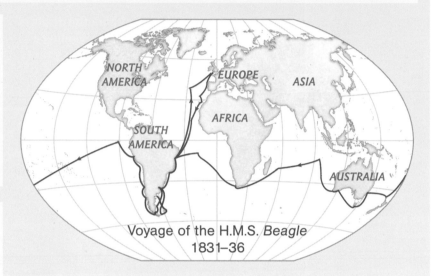

Voyage of the H.M.S. *Beagle*
1831–36

2 **Chile, 1833:** In South America, the men on Darwin's ship the *Beagle* sometimes ate a bird called a *rhea*. Darwin heard about a smaller type of rhea. It lived mostly in southern Patagonia, while the larger rhea lived in the north. Darwin wondered why the southern rhea **differed** from the northern one. At this time, Darwin became interested in the **diversity** of animal life. Could an animal's environment affect **traits** such as size?

3 **Galápagos Islands, Ecuador, 1835:** Here, Darwin began to develop his ideas about why and how the diversity of species occurred. In a **process** he called natural selection, an animal with a useful trait was more likely to survive, and therefore, more likely to **reproduce**. The animal's **offspring** would then **inherit** the useful trait. In contrast, animals of that same species with a different trait might die and not reproduce. In this way, a species would **adapt** to its environment and change over time.

B Write each word in **blue** from exercise A next to its definition.

1. _____ (v) was unlike something else
2. _____ (v) to recognize someone or something
3. _____ (n) a person's children or an animal's young
4. _____ (n) a variety of things that are different from each other
5. _____ (n) things one gets from one's parents, such as eye color
6. _____ (v) to produce young animals or plants
7. _____ (v) to change in order to be successful in a new situation
8. _____ (n) a certain kind of animal or plant
9. _____ (n) a series of actions or events that leads to a certain result
10. _____ (v) to be born with something because one's parents also had it

C 🎧 3.10 Read the article and fill in each blank with the correct form of a word from the box. Then listen and check your answers.

| diversity | inherit | process | reproduce | trait |

OUT OF AFRICA

Anthropologists, scientists who study human beings, have long said that modern humans first lived in Africa and then moved east toward Asia, north across the Mediterranean, and later throughout the world.

Now, a large genetic[1] study supports that theory. The study looked at nearly 1,000 people in 51 places around the world. It found the most genetic _____ in Africa and
1
less farther away from Africa. How did this happen? When small groups of people moved away, they took only a small amount of all the possible genetic information with them. People in the small groups _____. Their offspring _____
2 3
their parents' more limited set of genes. Therefore,

Human Migration

☒ Fossil or artifact site   40,000 Migration years ago date   ➜ Generalized route

Anthropological evidence shows that human beings first lived in Africa and then moved to different places around the world.

their _____ were very similar to those of
4
their parents. This _____ continued as
5
small groups of people moved farther and farther from Africa.

[1]**genetic** (adj): related to genes (small pieces of DNA) and heredity

D Work with a partner. Discuss these questions.

1. How do you differ from other people in your family? In what ways are you similar?
2. What are some of the traits you inherited from your parents and grandparents?
3. What are some species of animals that live in your country?
4. Can you identify many species of birds? Of plants? Explain.
5. What parts of the world have a large diversity of plant and animal species?

CRITICAL THINKING: ANALYZING

A Listening A Talk about Birds

BEFORE LISTENING

PRIOR KNOWLEDGE **A** You are going to listen to a biologist in the UK give a presentation before a bird-watching trip. Discuss these questions with a partner.

1. Bird-watching is a hobby that involves viewing birds outdoors in their natural environment. Do you know anyone who enjoys this hobby?
2. What are some good places in your country to see birds and other animals? Do you enjoy going to those places? Explain.

WHILE LISTENING

> **LISTENING SKILL** Listening for Repeated Words
>
> Speakers often use repetition to emphasize key points. When you are listening to a talk, pay attention to words (including words from the same family, e.g., *differ, different, difference*) and phrases that the speaker repeats. These are usually ideas that the speaker wants listeners to remember.
>
> The **males** and **females** of this bird species don't **differ** much in their appearance. But the one we saw in the last slide is definitely a **male**. One **difference** is that the **female's** beak is a little shorter, so she can't reach as many kinds of flower seeds as the **male** can.
>
> Key point: The males and females of this species have different beaks.

LISTENING FOR MAIN IDEAS **B** 🎧 3.11 ▶ 1.15 Listen to the talk. Check (✓) the words when you hear them and notice how the speaker repeats them. Then listen again and check (✓) the speaker's main idea.

☐ goldfinch   ☐ trait(s)   ☐ seeds   ☐ beak   ☐ greenfinch

_____ Goldfinches fly to warmer parts of Europe during September and October.

_____ Greenfinches have larger, stronger beaks than goldfinches, so they can eat larger seeds.

_____ Different finches have different traits that help them survive and reproduce.

A European goldfinch with a seed in its beak sits on a thistle plant.

C 🎧 3.11 Listen to the talk again and complete the notes in the chart below.

Type of Finch	goldfinch	
Where It Lives		Most of Europe + NW Africa and Turkey
Special Traits		
What It Eats	Male: seeds from inside flower Female: other seeds	
Other Habits		Lives diff. places in diff. seasons Summer: parks & forests Winter: gardens and farm fields

AFTER LISTENING

D Work with a partner. Compare your notes from exercise C.

> **NOTE-TAKING SKILL** Re-Writing Your Notes
>
> Since note-taking is usually done quickly—using only key words and phrases, abbreviations, and symbols—it can be helpful to rewrite your notes in sentence form after class. Rewriting your notes will help you remember key ideas. By doing this, you create a set of notes that are easy to read and study from later.
>
> **Original Notes:** *Lives diff. places in diff. seasons*
>
> **Re-Written Notes:** *The greenfinch doesn't leave the UK in the winter, but it does live in different places during different seasons.*

E Re-write your notes from exercise C. Use complete sentences. Then work with a partner and compare your notes.

F Discuss these questions in a group.

1. Do you enjoy watching TV shows or documentary films about nature? Explain.
2. Have you ever gone on a nature hike? If so, where did you go, and what kind of wildlife did you see? If not, would you like to do this in the future?

A Speaking

A 🎧 **3.12** Listen to the following words. Then answer the questions below.

banana	demand	identify	reproduce

1. How many syllables are in each word?
2. Which is the stressed syllable in each word?
3. How many different vowel sounds are in each word?

PRONUNCIATION Stress in Multi-Syllable Words

🎧 **3.13**

Primary Stress
In words with two or more syllables, one syllable is stressed, or stronger than the others. It has a full vowel sound.

lo cal	**fac** tor	**sea** son
/oʊ/	/æ/	/i/

Secondary Stress
Sometimes in a word with more than two syllables, another syllable is also stressed, but not as fully as the syllable with primary stress. In *analyze*, for example, the primary stress is on the first syllable, and the third syllable has the secondary stress. It has the full vowel sound /aɪ/.

a na lyze
/aɪ/

Unstressed Syllables
Syllables without stress are said more quickly, and often have the schwa /ə/ sound.

lo cal	**fac** tor	**sea** son
/ə/	/ə/	/ə/

B 🎧 **3.14** Listen to the words below. Underline the stressed syllable(s) in each word. Then take turns saying the words with a partner.

1. practical
2. compare
3. attachment
4. available
5. proportion
6. support

C 🎧 **3.15** Listen to the words below. Underline the syllable with the most stress in each word. Circle the syllable with secondary stress. Then practice saying the words with a partner.

1. recommend
2. classify
3. atmosphere
4. quantity
5. romantic
6. disappear

CRITICAL THINKING:
ANALYZING

D With your partner, analyze your name or the name of a famous person.

1. How many syllables are there?
2. Which syllables have primary or secondary stress?
3. Which syllables are unstressed?
4. Which vowel sounds are full, and which are reduced (schwa) sounds?

We use *because, since,* and *due to (the fact that)* to talk about causes.

> **Since** polar bears live in snowy places, they have developed white fur to help hide them from their prey, or the animals that they kill for food.

We use *so, as a result (of this), therefore,* and *consequently* to talk about effects or results.

> Over time, finches' beaks have become very strong. **As a result,** they can eat hard seeds.

> Polar bears have white fur, **so** their prey doesn't always notice them in the snow and ice.

Polar bears' white fur is a helpful trait because it makes it difficult for their prey (the animals they eat) to see them in the snow.

E 🎧 3.16 Read and listen to the information about the process of natural selection. Write down the words and phrases you hear that signal causes and effects.

The Process of Natural Selection

1. First, the environment affects animals in some way.

2. _____, the animals that have certain helpful traits do well in their environments.

3. And _____, they survive and reproduce.

4. The offspring of these animals inherit the helpful trait from their parents.

5. This process continues and _____, over time, most of the animals in the species have the helpful trait.

F With a partner, explain the process of natural selection using the sentences and the signal words and phrases you wrote in exercise E.

> *Because the environment affects animals in some way, species develop certain helpful traits.*

G Work with a partner. Look at the photos and read the information. Then discuss these questions.

1. What are the threats, or dangers, to each animal's survival?
2. What does each animal do in response to these dangers?
3. Which animal behavior is the most surprising or interesting to you? Explain.

ANIMAL SURVIVAL BEHAVIORS

Speed: The blue wildebeest of southern, central, and eastern Africa is a favorite food for lions, leopards, and other large predators. It's also one of the fastest land animals with a top speed of about 50 mph (80 kph)—just a little faster than its predators, most of the time.

Surprise: The Texas horned lizard can actually shoot a stream of blood from its eyes when it is disturbed by predators such as snakes, hawks, and coyotes[1]. The surprise can be enough to give the lizard a chance to escape.

Camouflage: The dead leaf butterfly lives in tropical parts of Asia. When its wings are open, it's colorful and beautiful. But when its wings are closed, it looks exactly like a dead leaf, which birds and other hungry insects are not interested in eating.

Playing Dead: The opossum of North America is nocturnal (active at night) and lives in trees. In addition, if it is disturbed by people, cats, or other predators, it can "play dead" —and even smell bad! It's enough to make anyone walk away!

[1] **coyotes** (n): a kind of North American wild dog

H With your partner, take turns finishing these sentences about the animals in exercise G. Then say some sentences using your own ideas.

> *Since lions like to eat blue wildebeests, …the wildebeests need to run very fast.*

1. Since lions and leopards eat blue wildebeests, . . .
2. The butterfly looks like a dead leaf, so . . .
3. The lizard can surprise its predators; as a result, . . .
4. The opossum has several survival behaviors. Consequently, . . .
5. Because the opossum seems to be dead, . . .

I With your partner, talk about some other animals you know about (including your own pets if you have any). What survival behaviors do they use? Use words and phrases to talk about causes and effects

TALKING ABOUT CAUSES AND EFFECTS

> *Because birds can fly, cats and other animals can't catch them.*

LESSON TASK Presenting a Life Lesson

A Work with a partner. Read the information below. Then discuss this question: What are some ways that our human intelligence has helped us survive (e.g., getting food, traveling over long distances)?

CRITICAL THINKING: ANALYZING

> One of the most important human traits is intelligence. Our large brains have allowed us to survive and adapt to our environment in different ways. Some other animals are also quite intelligent, but human beings' ability to create and have an impact on the world sets us apart from other species.

B You are going to give a short, informal presentation about a helpful life lesson you have learned. Follow these steps:

ORGANIZING IDEAS

1. Brainstorm some important life lessons you have learned from your family that have helped make your life better in some way. Then choose one of the life lessons from your list.
2. In your notebook, write brief notes about the life lesson you chose. Answer these questions in your notes:

   • What was the lesson?

   • Who did you learn this lesson from?

   • When did you learn this lesson? (How old were you? When did it happen?)

   • Has your life been different as a result of this lesson? How?

C Work in a group. Take turns presenting your life lessons. Practice using expressions for talking about causes and effects.

PRESENTING

> *My mother taught me not to form opinions about people too quickly. When I was six, I decided that I didn't like the girl next door even though I didn't know her. I told my mother this, and the next day she invited the girl and her mother over to our house for lunch. We've been best friends ever since…*

Video

Amazing Chameleons

Panther chameleon, Madagascar

BEFORE VIEWING

MEANING FROM CONTEXT

A Read the information. Notice each underlined word and think about its meaning.

> ### KEYS TO CHAMELEON SURVIVAL
>
> **Skin:** Chameleons' best-known ability is being able to change their skin color. We used to think they did this mostly for camouflage, to match their <u>background</u> and avoid being seen by predators.
>
> **Eyes:** Chameleons' eyes can <u>rotate</u> independently, with one eye looking in one direction and the other eye in another direction.
>
> **Feet:** The shape of chameleons' feet allows them to hold onto tree <u>branches</u>.
>
> **Tongue:** Chameleons have long tongues that they can <u>project</u> out of their mouths at high speeds to catch insects.
>
> **Movements:** Chameleons move in a slow, deliberate way in order to <u>mimic</u> the movement of leaves in the wind—a kind of behavioral camouflage.

B Write each underlined word from exercise A next to its definition. You may use a dictionary.

1. _____ (n) the smaller parts of trees that grow out from the trunk
2. _____ (v) to turn with a circular movement
3. _____ (v) to imitate or pretend to be something we are not
4. _____ (v) to throw or cause to move forward
5. _____ (n) the surroundings or scene behind something

WHILE VIEWING

C ▶ **1.16** Read the statements. Then watch the video and choose T for *True* or F for *False*. Correct the false statements.

1. For chameleons, changing colors is a communication strategy.   T   F

2. Female chameleons change colors when they are interested in a male.   T   F

3. Chameleons move in a way that mimics their predators.   T   F

4. Scientists are still learning about chameleons.   T   F

D ▶ **1.16** Watch the video again and fill in each blank with the number you hear.

1. Of the _____ chameleon species …, _____ percent occur on Madagascar.

2. Chameleons can project their tongues up to _____ body lengths.

3. This is done at speeds of about _____ miles per hour.

4. _____ percent of chameleon species are threatened with extinction (in danger of dying out or becoming extinct).

5. There are _____ species which are regarded as critically endangered, and _____ species that are regarded as endangered.

AFTER VIEWING

E Work in a group. Read the information. Then discuss the questions below.

> **THREATS TO CHAMELEON SURVIVAL**
>
> **Changes to Habitat:** Human activity results in changes to the places where chameleons live.
>
> **Deforestation:** Trees are cut down and removed by people.
>
> **Range Restriction:** Some chameleons are found only in one specific location. They don't live in many parts of Madagascar.
>
> **Other Pressures on Habitat:** Factors such as climate conditions, farming, and a growing human population can make it more difficult for chameleons to survive.

1. Which of the threats to chameleon survival are directly related to human activity?
2. What are some ways that people could help reduce some of these threats to chameleon survival?
3. Some people keep chameleons as pets. How do you feel about this? Would you want to have a chameleon as a pet? Explain.

B Vocabulary

A **3.17** Read and listen to the article. Notice each word in **blue** and think about its meaning.

BAR CODING LIFE ON EARTH

Paul Hebert is a biologist at the University of Guelph in Canada. As a young man in the 1970s, part of his job was to **classify** thousands of different species of moths[1]. Finding tiny **variations** in the moths in order to describe each species scientifically was not easy, however.

In 2003, Hebert suggested something a bit **controversial**. Instead of using descriptions to identify different species, why not use DNA? Hebert **argued** that a bar code—similar to the bar codes on products in a store—could be created for every living thing on Earth. This was a major break from scientific tradition.

Hebert suggested using part of a **gene** called *CO1*, which nearly every form of life has, to create bar codes. This gene is made up of four chemical **substances** known as *G, T, C,* and *A,* and the **sequence** of these substances differs for each species. Using bar codes and an electronic catalog, scientists or anyone else can identify a plant or animal by testing a **sample** of its DNA.

Hebert's bar code **technique** is not only a good way to identify species, the electronic catalog has also become a public resource that makes people more **aware** of biodiversity[2].

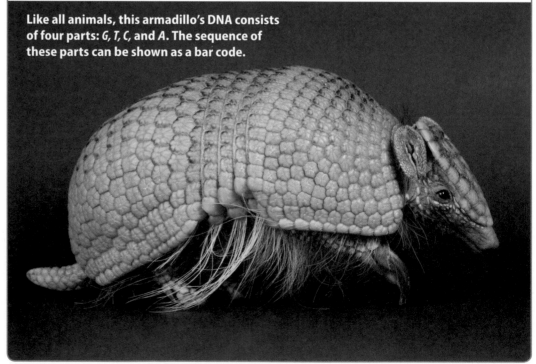

Like all animals, this armadillo's DNA consists of four parts: *G, T, C,* and *A.* The sequence of these parts can be shown as a bar code.

[1]**moth** (n): a winged insect that is similar to a butterfly

[2]**biodiversity** (n): many kinds of plants and animals existing in the environment

B Complete each sentence with the correct form of a word in **blue** from exercise A.

1. Most people aren't _____ (adj) of the number of species on Earth.

2. Paul Hebert thinks it's difficult to _____ (v) all the species using descriptions.

3. In some cases, there are only very small _____ (n) between one species and another.

4. A different _____ (n) for classifying species is to use their DNA.

5. Hebert's technique is somewhat _____ (adj). Some people don't agree with it.

6. DNA can be taken from a small blood _____ (n).

7. The _____ (n) that researchers are using is called *CO1*.

8. *G, T, C,* and *A* are the _____ (n) that make up DNA.

9. Different _____ (n) of *G, T, C,* and *A* carry different genetic information.

10. Hebert _____ (v) that all species on Earth should be bar coded.

C Work with a partner. Take turns asking and answering these questions.

CRITICAL THINKING: ANALYZING

1. What's one technique you use for learning new vocabulary words?
2. Which genes do you think you inherited from your mother or from your father?
3. What's a controversial topic in your country or in the news today?
4. What can be done to make people more aware of endangered species?

VOCABULARY SKILL Identifying the Correct Definition

Many words in English have more than one meaning. Dictionaries list the most frequently used definition first, but it's important to read all of the possible definitions so you can identify the correct one. Use information provided in the dictionary such as the part of speech and the example sentences to help you.

sub·stance /ˈsʌbstəns/ *n.* **1** [U] anything one can touch: *This face cream is a white, sticky substance.||Tires are made of rubber and other substances.* **2** *usu. sing.* [C;U] meaning, truth: *What she says has substance because of her knowledge and experience.* **3** [U] wealth, possessions: *The family owns a successful business; they are people of substance.*

THESAURUS substance **1** material, matter, stuff *infrml.* **2** significance **3** means, resources.

D Work with a partner. Discuss these questions.

1. Look at the dictionary definition. In the article on page 174, which definition of *sample* does the author use? _____

2. Look up each word in a dictionary. How many definitions do you find for each word?

argue (v) _____   nail (n) _____

fair (adj) _____   draft (n) _____

bear (v) _____

sam·ple /ˈsæmpəl/ *v.* [T] **-pled, -pling, -ples** to try s.t.: *I sampled each dessert on the menu. ||I sampled life in Hong Kong and loved it.* —*n.* **1** a single thing that shows what a larger group is like: *The tailor showed us samples of silk, wool, and cotton.* **2** a small amount of s.t. to try: *The clerk gave me a sample of cheese to taste; it was so delicious that I bought a pound.* **3** a small part of a larger group, used to study the larger group: *The teacher asked a sample of students if the school should build a new library.*

THESAURUS sample *v.* to taste, test. —*n.* **1** an example, a specimen, swatch | piece **2** a taste, trial amount **3** a cross section, subgroup.

B Listening A Conversation about a Photo Project

BEFORE LISTENING

PRIOR KNOWLEDGE **A** Read the information about photographer Joel Sartore. Then discuss the questions with a partner.

> **JOEL SARTORE** is a National Geographic photographer. He grew up in Nebraska in the United States His family loved nature and enjoyed spending time outdoors together. He remembers receiving a book about birds as a gift from his mother. In the part of the book about extinction[1], there was a picture of a passenger pigeon called Martha—the last living member of her species. Says Sartore about the disappearance of these birds, "I was amazed that you could go from billions to none."

[1]**extinction** (n): the death of all members of a species

1. What animal species can you name that have gone extinct? What do you know about the causes of their extinction?
2. What are some endangered animal species you know and care about? For example, are you concerned about the survival of polar bears, tigers, or other animals?

WHILE LISTENING

LISTENING FOR MAIN IDEAS **B** 🎧 3.18 Read each statement. Then listen to the conversation and choose T for *True* or F for *False*. Correct the false statements.

1.	Joel Sartore wants to photograph all of the world's animal species.	T	F
2.	Sartore wants to photograph the animals before some of them become extinct.	T	F
3.	His Photo Ark images show animals in their natural habitats.	T	F
4.	The photos Sartore takes are making people more aware of endangered species.	T	F

A critically endangered red ruffed lemur photographed by Joel Sartore at the Plzen Zoo in the Czech Republic

National Geographic photographer Joel Sartore photographs a gray wolf on the beach on Vargas Island, British Columbia, Canada.

C 🎧 3.18 Listen to the conversation again. Which of these points do the speakers make? Choose Y for *Yes* or N for *No* for each statement.

LISTENING FOR DETAILS

1. Sartore is publishing more photos now than he used to.   Y   N

2. Sartore's photographic techniques require natural light.   Y   N

3. Sartore can't possibly photograph every animal species.   Y   N

4. Sartore's photo of a bird helped wildlife groups get more money from the government.   Y   N

AFTER LISTENING

CRITICAL THINKING   Personalizing

When you personalize information, you think about it in relation to yourself, your life, and your knowledge and experiences. Personalizing information helps you to internalize it and process it more deeply. You are also more likely to remember information that is connected to you in some way.

D Work in a group. Discuss these questions.

PERSONALIZING

1. Based on your knowledge, do you think the extinction of animal species is a major problem for human beings, or are there other problems we should be more concerned about? Explain.

2. How do you feel when you hear about an endangered species? Are there any species you care more about than others? Explain.

3. Is there anything you are doing now or plan to do in the future to help protect endangered species? For example, are there any products or foods you avoid? Other actions you can take? Explain.

Speaking

GRAMMAR FOR SPEAKING Phrasal Verbs

Phrasal verbs are formed with a verb plus a particle, for example, *up, down, in, out,* and *at.*

> Stanley **gets up** at five thirty every morning.
>
> She **looked up** the meaning of the word.

Phrasal verbs have their own meanings. These meanings are different from the usual meaning of the verb plus a preposition.

Phrasal verbs can be transitive or intransitive.

Transitive	Intransitive
Victor **wrote down** the information.	The finches **come back** in the spring.

Some transitive verbs can be separated from their particles while others cannot.

Separable	Inseparable
Please **turn down** the volume.	√ Jemila really **takes after** her mother.
Please **turn** the volume **down**.	X Jemila really ~~takes her mother after~~.

A 🎧 3.19 Read and listen to the phone conversation. Notice the underlined phrasal verbs and think about their meanings.

Matt:	Jessica? It's me!
Jessica:	Matt! It's great to hear your voice! Are you back home now?
Matt:	Yes, and I really missed you, but I'm so happy you <u>talked</u> me <u>into</u> going on the expedition! I can't believe I almost <u>turned down</u> such a great opportunity.
Jessica:	Tell me all about it!
Matt:	Well, we were high up in the Foja Mountains. No human beings have ever lived there!
Jessica:	How exciting! Did you get a lot of work done?
Matt:	We did! We <u>set up</u> a tent as our laboratory. It was small but fine.
Jessica:	Did it rain a lot?
Matt:	Every day. Well—one afternoon the sky <u>cleared up</u> for a while, but the clouds were back by that evening. It was OK, though. The frogs didn't mind the rain.
Jessica:	Oh, tell me about the frogs!
Matt:	Can you believe there are 350 frog species in New Guinea? The best time to find them is at night. When I <u>turned on</u> my flashlight, I could see them easily and <u>pick</u> them <u>up</u> with my hands.
Jessica:	How interesting! It sounds like it was a great trip.
Matt:	It was, and the lead scientist was really happy with my work.
Jessica:	That's great! Congratulations, Matt!

A spurred big-eyed tree frog from New Guinea's Foja Mountains

B Work with a partner. Discuss the meanings of the phrasal verbs from exercise A.

C Practice the conversation from exercise A with your partner. Then switch roles and practice it again.

D Complete each statement with the correct form of a phrasal verb from exercise A.

1. I didn't want to do it, but my friend _____ me _____ it.

2. Your bag is on the floor. You should _____ it _____. The floor in here is very dirty!

3. Let's _____ the laboratory for our experiment so that it's ready tomorrow.

4. It was raining this morning, but now the sky has _____.

5. When I drive to work, I always _____ the radio and listen to the news.

6. I _____ Lara's invitation to go to the movies tonight because I have to study for the test tomorrow.

EVERYDAY LANGUAGE Congratulating Someone

Well done!   *Congratulations!*   *I'm happy for you!*   *Way to go!*

FINAL TASK Presenting a Research Proposal

> You are going to collaborate in a group to plan a research proposal. You will then present your proposal as a group to the class.

A Work in a group. Read the information and follow the steps on the next page.

> **Situation:** Your group is going on a scientific research field trip! And the best news is that you have received a government research grant, so you have plenty of travel money. However, before you actually receive the grant money, you must submit your research proposal.

1. Brainstorm a list of several interesting places you might go to do your research. What could you research in those places (e.g., what species of plants or animals)? Choose one of the ideas from your list, and write it in your Research Proposal.

> Research Proposal
>
> A. Destination: _____
>
> B. Research Topic: _____

2. Think about and discuss what you will need in order to travel to your destination and do your research.

> C. Travel Plans: _____
>
> D. Equipment Requests: _____

3. Because you're getting a government grant, you'll be expected to do something with your research after you return home. How will you use your research?

> E. Follow-Up Plans: _____

PRESENTATION SKILL Timing Your Presentation

Presentations often have a time requirement or a time limit. When you plan and practice your presentation, it's important to know how long your presentation needs to be. You want to be sure your presentation is long enough but doesn't go over the time limit. When you're planning a group presentation, first decide how much time each person needs for their part of the presentation. Practice and time yourself speaking individually, and then practice your presentation as a group.

ORGANIZING IDEAS **B** Find out how much time you will have to present your research proposal. Decide which information each member of your group will present. Each person should plan to include some details about the information that he or she will present. Then practice and time your presentation.

PRESENTING **C** Present your research plan to the class.

REFLECTION

1. When are you likely to use the expressions for talking about causes and effects?

   _____

   _____

2. How did the information about species survival in this unit change or add to your ideas about wildlife?

   _____

   _____

3. Here are the vocabulary words from the unit. Check (✓) the ones you can use.

   ☐ adapt AWL   ☐ gene   ☐ sequence AWL
   ☐ argue   ☐ identify AWL   ☐ species
   ☐ aware AWL   ☐ inherit   ☐ substance
   ☐ classify   ☐ offspring   ☐ technique AWL
   ☐ controversial AWL ☐ process AWL   ☐ trait
   ☐ differ   ☐ reproduce   ☐ variation AWL
   ☐ diversity AWL   ☐ sample

ENTREPRENEURS AND INNOVATORS 10

Mitsunobu Okada holds a model of the satellite ADRASI, which collects space garbage. Okada founded Astroscale, a start-up company committed to cleaning up trash in space.

THINK AND DISCUSS

1 Look at the photo and read the caption. What does Okada's company do?
2 Look at the title of this unit. What are entrepreneurs and innovators? What do they do?

181

EXPLORE THE THEME

Look at the photos and read the information. Then discuss these questions.

1. What are some words you would use to describe entrepreneurs?
2. Which of the inventions or ideas on these pages do you find most interesting? Why?
3. Which of the inventions or ideas do you think is most useful? Least useful? Explain.
4. Would you like to be an entrepreneur? Why or why not?

THE ENTREPRENEURIAL SPIRIT

Designer Arturo Vittori stands near a WarkaWater tower, a lightweight structure that collects water from the air. Each tower costs about 500 US dollars and produces 90 liters of clean water per day.

British inventor Charlie Harry has created a machine that allows you to inhale tastes such as chocolate, apple pie, or lobster. The Edible Mist Machine produces delicious edible mist in a range of over 200 flavors.

Archel Bernard teaches an employee how to use a sewing machine in her factory in Monrovia, Liberia. After she graduated from Georgia Tech, Bernard moved to Liberia where she opened her own boutique. She hopes to help Ebola survivors rebuild their lives.

An entrepreneur is someone who starts a business with a new idea, makes it grow, and takes the risk of failure. In general, entrepreneurs prefer to be their own bosses rather than working for someone else. The entrepreneurial spirit is a positive attitude toward risking time and money in order to find new and better ways of doing business.

A Vocabulary

MEANING FROM CONTEXT

A 🎧 3.20 Read and listen to the information. Notice each word or phrase in **blue** and think about its meaning.

SIX TRAITS OF SUCCESSFUL ENTREPRENEURS

Brothers Kieran and Sean Murphy serve what is widely considered the best ice cream in Ireland.

What does it take to be a successful entrepreneur? Here are six common traits.

1. **Caring about More than Money:** Making money is usually not the main **motivation** for successful entrepreneurs. Instead, they are driven by a strong belief in their product or service and its potential to improve people's lives in some way.

2. **Not Giving Up:** Good entrepreneurs are **persistent**. They don't give up easily and are willing to try out new ideas and take risks. Doing this **leads to** some **failures** along the way, but the entrepreneurs who **eventually** succeed are the ones who do not quit when things go badly.

3. **Having a Vision:** True entrepreneurs see opportunities where most people do not. Then they need to convince **investors** to lend money for new kinds of products and services.

4. **Dealing with Change:** Being open-minded and flexible is another important trait for entrepreneurs. The product they imagined in the beginning is likely to **evolve** over time, so they need to be flexible.

5. **Tolerating Uncertainty:** Entrepreneurs must be able to live with **uncertainty**. Nobody can predict the future, but good entrepreneurs keep moving ahead with their ideas rather than worrying about the unknown.

6. **Having Self-Confidence:** The sixth **essential** trait of successful entrepreneurs is psychological—having **confidence** in oneself. The best entrepreneurs believe in themselves and their ideas.

B Choose T for *True* or F for *False* for each statement. Correct the false statements.

1. Your motivation is your reason for doing something. T F

2. A persistent person will try and try again. T F

3. If one thing leads to a second thing, it causes the second thing to happen. T F

4. Failures in business are when things go well and you get what you want. T F

184 UNIT 10 LESSON A

5.	Events that happen eventually happen very soon.	T	F
6.	Investors are people who lend you money that you must pay back later.	T	F
7.	When something evolves over time, it stays the same.	T	F
8.	If we have uncertainty about something, we are not sure about it.	T	F
9.	If something is essential, you don't really need it.	T	F
10.	People with a lot of confidence feel sure about themselves and their abilities.	T	F

C Work with a partner. Take turns asking and answering these questions.

CRITICAL THINKING: REFLECTING

1. What are three things that are essential for your happiness? Why are they so important to you?
2. Talk about a time you chose to do something challenging. What was your motivation for doing it?
3. People's ideas and opinions often change during their lives. How have your ideas and opinions evolved over the years?

VOCABULARY SKILL Recognizing Adjectives and Adverbs

Recognizing different word forms such as adjectives and adverbs can help you expand your vocabulary and better understand information you hear and read.

Adjectives describe or modify nouns.

> A **persistent** businessperson will last longer than any **temporary** problem.

Common adjective suffixes include:

> -al (personal)   -ous (famous)   -ary (voluntary)   -ant/-ent (reluctant)
> -able (sociable)

Adverbs describe or modify verbs, adjectives, or other adverbs.

> We **eventually** found the office even though the door was not **well** marked.

Most adverbs have an -ly suffix, but irregular adverbs include very, almost, well, and too.

D Choose the correct words to complete the sentences. Then work with a partner and compare your answers.

1. I recently applied for a (permanent / permanently) position in the company's (regional / regionally) office.
2. The job interview went (good / well), even though I didn't feel (confident / confidently) at first.
3. The company is looking for a (persistent / persistently) salesperson who doesn't give up easily. The (ideal / ideally) candidate will have at least five years of sales experience.
4. The job requires a (capable / capably) person who can work (independent / independently). It's currently a part-time postion, but it may (eventual / eventually) become full time.
5. This is a (perfect / perfectly) job for a (high / highly) qualified person. The salary and benefits are very (good / well), too.

A Listening A Presentation about a Success Story

BEFORE LISTENING

PRIOR KNOWLEDGE **A** Discuss these questions with a partner.

1. What are some large, successful companies you know about? What do you think makes these companies so successful?
2. When you purchase a product, for example, a phone or a new pair of shoes, how do you decide which item to buy?

WHILE LISTENING

LISTENING FOR
MAIN IDEAS **B** 🎧 3.21 ▶ 1.17 Listen to the presentation. Which of these points does the speaker make? Choose Y for *Yes* or N for *No* for each statement.

1. Howard Schultz wanted to bring European coffee culture to the United States.   Y   N

2. It was difficult for Schultz to find investors for his company.   Y   N

3. Starbucks' profits are mostly due to the high quality of its coffee drinks.   Y   N

4. Starbucks employees earn more than workers in other service jobs.   Y   N

5. The company had problems after Schultz quit his job in 2000.   Y   N

6. Schultz plans to remain the CEO of the company until he retires.   Y   N

LISTENING SKILL Distinguishing Facts and Opinions

When listening to a talk or lecture, it is important to be able to distinguish facts from opinions.

Facts are statements that can be proved or verified. We can do this by checking several reliable sources of information.

Fact: *The people who work at Starbucks are called "partners" rather than "employees."*

Opinions show a speaker's viewpoint or bias. It is possible to disagree with someone's opinion.

Opinion: *I guess Starbucks wants to show its employees how important they are to the company.*

Here are some common expressions used for giving opinions:

For me, . . .	*If you ask me, . . .*	*Personally, . . .*	*I believe . . .*
I think . . .	*In my opinion, . . .*	*I guess . . .*	

▶ A barista prepares a coffee drink at a Starbucks Corp. store in Beijing, China.

C 🎧 3.21 Listen again and complete the statements from the talk. Fill in each blank with the two words that you hear.

LISTENING FOR DETAILS

1. And although _____ isn't actually "little" anymore, it did start out that way.

2. Now, of course, _____ like the world was just waiting for a good caffè latte to come along.

3. If you _____ , focusing only on making money is a great way to make a business fail.

4. Not only are Starbucks wages a little higher than in other service jobs, partners who work enough hours can _____ in the company.

5. I mean— _____ is that?

6. Schultz has given up his position as CEO on more than one occasion over the years. The first time was _____ .

D Work with a partner. Compare your answers from exercise C and decide whether each statement is a fact or an opinion. How do you know?

AFTER LISTENING

E Work in a group. Discuss the meaning of each idea from a business point of view. Do you agree or disagree with each statement? Explain.

CRITICAL THINKING: ANALYZING

1. The customer is always right.
2. Constant improvement is the way to success in business.
3. People who don't wait for someone to tell them what to do make more money.
4. In business, we spend too much time on what is urgent and not enough time on what is important.

A Speaking

GRAMMAR FOR SPEAKING The Present Perfect and Signal Words

We use the present perfect to talk about:

1. actions or situations that began in the past and continue until now.

   *Lydia's parents **have worked** there for 20 years.* (They still work there now.)

2. actions or situations that have happened one or more times in the past and relate to the present. The exact time that the action or situation happened is not stated or important.

   *Schultz **has quit** his position as CEO twice in the past 20 years.*

   *We **have** never **gone** to a business conference before, so we want to go to one.*

We often use signal words and phrases with the present perfect to give extra information about when something happened or about the speaker's attitude. Here are some examples of signal words and phrases that are commonly used with the present perfect:

> for   since   already   so far   (not) yet
>
> up to now   ever   never   always

   *We're a new company, but we **have already grown** a lot.* (We've grown faster than I expected.)

   *We **have earned** profits totaling $71,000 **so far** this year.* (We might still earn more.)

   ***Has** it really **been** five years **since** the company introduced a new product?* (Was the last time really five years ago?)

   ***Have** you **ever eaten** at that restaurant?* (Have you eaten there at any time in the past?)

A Complete the sentences using the present perfect form of the verbs and the signal words in parentheses.

1. Rosa _____ (be) the bank manager since 2013.

2. I _____ (call) customer service three times, and they still _____ (not, answer) the telephone.

3. _____ you _____ (ever, stay) at that hotel before? Is it a nice place?

4. Nabil _____ (always, want) to open his own furniture store.

5. We _____ (own) the restaurant for 17 years.

6. I _____ (buy) coffee at that shop several times, and so far the service _____ (be) fast and friendly. It _____ (never, be) slow.

7. Sandra _____ (work) at the same company for 25 years.

8. I _____ (not, send) the report yet, but I'll do it today.

B Work with a partner. Take turns asking and answering questions about the topics below. Use *ever* and the present perfect in your questions. Give details about your answers to keep the conversation going.

A: *Have you ever taken a class in business or economics?*
B: *No, I haven't, but I'd like to.*

1. take a class in business or economics
2. buy a coffee drink at Starbucks
3. visit your country's capital city
4. get paid for your work
5. be interviewed for a job
6. think about starting your own company

PRONUNCIATION Thought Groups

🎧 3.22 In English, speakers organize their ideas into chunks or *thought groups*. Thought groups can consist of a single word (*Exactly!*), a phrase (*for 20 years*), a clause (*The company experienced . . .*), or a short sentence (*It's a beautiful city.*). Each thought group usually has one focus word. There is a slight pause between thoughts groups. Using thought groups will make your speech sound more fluent and will help your listeners understand you.

> *In the early days, / Schultz was like / every entrepreneur.*
> *The company experienced / some major problems / as a result.*

C 🎧 3.23 Listen to each statement, and put a slash (/) at the end of each thought group you hear. Then practice saying the sentences with a partner. Use thought groups.

1. My best friend started her own company about five years ago right after college.
2. Her son wants to study business and then work at a bank.
3. Running a successful business is not easy because you work a lot and have to take risks.
4. I got a job at the new café on Main Street.
5. If you work hard and treat people well you'll be successful.
6. After work I usually take a walk so I can relax and get some exercise.

REPHRASING **D** **Work with a partner. Take turns saying each sentence and then rephrasing it in a new way.**

>   *I need to get something to eat. In other words, I'm hungry.*

1. I need to get something to eat.
2. What's your motivation for learning English?
3. Our English teacher knows a lot about grammar.
4. I'm interested in starting my own business.
5. Do you have a lot of self-confidence?
6. I have never shopped online.

E **Work with a partner. Partner A will read Part A of the article about the city of Detroit. Partner B will read Part B.**

PART A

The city of Detroit in the United States used to be called "the motor city." It was the home of the American automobile industry, and Ford, Chrysler, and General Motors all had enormous factories there. Jobs were not hard to find, and they came with high wages and good benefits such as health insurance and time off with pay.

PART B

However, since the 1970s, Detroit has lost thousands of jobs. Many people have left the city, and neighborhoods are full of empty houses. Poverty and crime are serious problems in Detroit as well. Recently, though, entrepreneurs are finding new opportunities here. They are buying inexpensive homes and businesses and turning them into success stories through their persistence and hard work.

George Higgins plays piano and sings in downtown Detroit.

F With your partner, take turns retelling your part of the article about Detriot. Practice rephrasing.

REPHRASING

G Discuss these questions with your partner.

PERSONALIZING

1. What interests you about the information in the article? What surprises you?
2. What city or cities in your country are doing well economically? What kind of work do people do there?

LESSON TASK Interpreting Quotations

A Work in a group. Read the quotations below from famous entrepreneurs and innovators, and discuss these questions.

CRITICAL THINKING: INTERPRETING QUOTATIONS

1. What do you think each quotation means? How might you rephrase it in your own words?
2. Discuss whether you agree or disagree with each quotation. Use examples from your own life to explain and support your ideas.
3. What do you know about each of these entrepreneurs and innovators? Which person do you find most interesting? Explain.

> a. Henry Ford (automobile manufacturer): *"The short successes that can be gained in a brief time and without difficulty are not worth much."*

> b. Nikola Tesla (engineer and inventor): *"Be alone, that is the secret of invention; be alone, that is when ideas are born."*

> c. Marissa Meyer (CEO of Yahoo): *"When you need to innovate, you need collaboration[1]."*

> d. Marie Curie (physicist and chemist): *"I was taught that the way of progress is neither swift[2] nor easy."*

> e. Albert Einstein (theoretical physicist): *"Play is the highest form of research."*

> f. Steve Jobs (co-founder of Apple): *"Being the richest man in the cemetery[3] doesn't matter to me. Going to bed at night saying we've done something wonderful—that's what matters to me."*

[1]**collaboration** (n): working together to accomplish a goal
[2]**swift** (adj): fast
[3]**cemetery** (n): a place where dead people are buried

B Discuss some other famous entrepreneurs and innovators that you know about.

CRITICAL THINKING: REFLECTING

Video

National Geographic Explorer Sanga Moses's goal is to provide inexpensive cooking fuel for Africans while improving socioeconomic outcomes and reversing deforestation.

Eco-Fuel Africa

Uganda

BEFORE VIEWING

A Read the information about Sanga Moses. Then with a partner, discuss how you think a "social entrepreneur" differs from other entepreneurs.

> **MEET SANGA MOSES.** He's a National Geographic Explorer and a social entrepreneur who quit a job at a bank in Kampala—Uganda's capital city—in order to work on solving a real problem in his country. He saw that girls, especially, had to find and carry wood for fuel intead of spending their time at school. Today, thousands of families in Uganda use Moses's clean-burning cooking fuel every day. And because the fuel is made from farm waste[1], for example, from corn crops, around 3,000 farmers and retailers[2] earn extra income each month by working with Moses's company, Eco-Fuel Africa.

[1]**farm waste** (n): parts of crop plants not used for food
[2]**retailers** (n): people who sell products to the public

PERSONALIZING **B** Work with a partner. Discuss these questions.

1. When you were a child, did you have household chores to do? For example, did you do some of the shopping, cleaning, or cooking for your family?
2. In your country, what kind of fuel do most people use for cooking? Do you think the fuel is convenient? Environmentally friendly? Is it expensive or inexpensive?

WHILE VIEWING

C ▶ **1.18** Read the statements. Then watch the video and choose the correct word to complete each statement.

UNDERSTANDING MAIN IDEAS

1. Moses got the idea for his company when he saw his (sister / brother) carrying wood.
2. When he quit his job at the bank, people were (upset / shocked).
3. He sold his (furniture / car).
4. Moses is now the (president / CEO) of Eco-Fuel Africa.
5. His advice is to (listen to / follow) your heart and believe in your dreams.

D ▶ **1.18** Watch the video again and fill in each blank with the number that you hear.

UNDERSTANDING DETAILS

1. After _____ months, Moses had spent all of his savings.

2. Eco-Fuel is _____ percent cheaper than other fuels.

3. Today, about _____ families use Moses's product.

4. Moses's goal in the next _____ years is to reach _____ million families.

AFTER VIEWING

> **CRITICAL THINKING**   Interpreting Data
>
> Interpreting data can increase your knowledge and understanding of a topic. To interpret data, look at the title and categories of the information included. Then look at the numbers and ask yourself questions such as: *What information does this data provide? How is this data important or relevant to the topic or situation?*

E Work in a group. Look at the data about Uganda and discuss the questions below.

CRITICAL THINKING: INTERPRETING DATA

> **Data about Uganda**
>
> **Population:** around 35 million
> **Percent of Population Under 30 Years Old:** 78%
> **Literacy Rate:** 78% (male 85%, female 72%)
> **Access to Electricity:** 20% of households
> **Cooking Fuel:** 94% use firewood or charcoal
> **Percent of Households Involved in Agriculture:** 80%

1. Based on your knowledge or an Internet search, how does this data compare with the numbers for your country? For example, does your country have a smaller or larger population than Uganda?
2. What do you notice about the literacy rate in Uganda? How does this information support Sanga Moses's concern about his sister not spending time at school?
3. How does the data help you understand information from the video?

Vocabulary

A 🎧 3.24 Read and listen to the information. Notice each word in **blue** and think about its meaning.

CHANDA SHROFF

When Chanda Shroff visited a part of India known as Kutch, she saw the **potential** for village women there to earn an **income** by selling their beautiful embroidery[1] work. Shroff thought there was a strong **probability** that other people would **appreciate** the beautiful embroidery as much as she did, so she commissioned[2] 30 embroidered *saris*[3] before she left Kutch. **Evidently**, she was right. The saris caused **considerable** excitement at an art exhibit in Mumbai. Shroff sold all 30 of them within a few hours.

▲ **Social entrepreneur Chanda Shroff, 1933–2016**

Kutch, India

Shroff eventually **founded** an innovative organization called Shrujan. Its **mission** is to market this traditional craft and help the Kutch people become more self-sufficient and to keep the craft alive and evolving. Since the Shrujan organization was founded, it has helped over 22,000 women earn sustainable, home-based income for their work and **achieve** more financial security. Shrujan has received a lot of **recognition** for its work, and Shroff herself received a Rolex Award for Enterprise in 2006. Shroff died in 2016, but the Kutch people still love and respect this woman who made a significant difference in so many people's lives.

[1]**embroidery** (n): decorative work done with a needle and colorful thread
[2]**commissioned** (v): formally asked for something to be done
[3]**saris** (n): traditional clothing worn by women in southern Asia

B Write each word in **blue** from exercise A next to its definition.

1. _____ (n) the chance that something will happen

2. _____ (v) to reach something positive such as success or happiness

3. _____ (n) credit or praise for doing something well

4. _____ (n) the possibility of being or doing something

5. _____ (n) money earned from working, investments, etc.

6. _____ (adv) as it appears, seemingly

7. _____ (v) to value or be thankful for something

8. _____ (v) started an organization

9. _____ (adj) much, a lot

10. _____ (n) the goals and purpose of a person, organization, or business

Young women sewing in Kutch, Gujarat, India

C Read each statement and choose T for *True* or F for *False*. Correct the false statements.

1. If there Is a strong probability of rain tomorrow, you should carry an umbrella.   T   F

2. If a company earns considerable profits, they are not making much money.   T   F

3. Someone who founded a company closed it down.   T   F

4. Investors will probably not lend you money if your company has the potential to succeed.   T   F

5. People who have achieved a lot in their lives usually feel good about themselves.   T   F

D Work with a partner. Discuss these questions.

CRITICAL THINKING: ANALYZING

1. In your own words, describe what Chanda Shroff achieved.
2. Do you think Chanda Shroff's mission is similar to Sanga Moses's? To Howard Schultz's? Explain.
3. One way that Shroff was innovative was in creating a completely new way for people to earn money. How do you think the new income has affected people's lives?

Listening A Conversation about Jack Andraka

BEFORE LISTENING

A Read the information. Then discuss the questions below with a partner.

> **JACK ANDRAKA** is a National Geographic Explorer who developed a test that can detect[1] certain types of cancer. He has won several awards for the test and has been a guest at the White House. He has been on TV shows and has been the subject of documentary films.
>
> Andraka invented the cancer test when he was only 15 years old. His motivation was the death of a close family friend from pancreatic cancer. Thanks to Andraka's work, doctors will soon be able to test for that type of cancer more cheaply and accurately, and they'll be able to detect the cancer much sooner.

[1]**detect** (v): to find or notice something

1. Have you heard about Jack Andraka before? If so, what do you know about him?
2. Why do you think he is getting so much recognition for his work?
3. Andraka had a strong motivation for trying to do something about cancer. What other innovative people can you think of who wanted to solve a problem?

National Geographic Explorer Jack Andraka works in his lab. Andraka created a new test for detecting pancreatic, lung, and ovarian cancer.

WHILE LISTENING

B 🎧 **3.25** Listen to the conversation and complete the notes about Jack Andraka.

LISTENING FOR
MAIN IDEAS

Jack Andraka's mission: find _____

If Dr.s detect cancer early → higher probability treated and _____

Andraka's test: 1. cheap (costs _____)   2. fast (takes _____)

          3. better than existing test; existing test = _____ + _____

Test not available yet (still needs _____)

C 🎧 **3.25** Listen to the conversation again. Add any important details about Jack Andraka to the main ideas you wrote in exercise B.

LISTENING FOR
DETAILS

AFTER LISTENING

> **NOTE-TAKING SKILL**   Reviewing and Editing Your Notes
>
> As soon as possible after you have taken notes, read through them and think about the information you heard in the talk or discussion. Doing this will confirm your understanding and help you remember the information later and for longer. As you review your notes, you can also do some editing to ensure the notes will be useful to you later. Here are some ways to do this:
>
> - Add any information that is missing.
> - Rewrite or replace any notes that are difficult to read.
> - Use highlighters to mark key ideas and important details.

D Review and edit the notes you took in exercises B and C. Follow the suggestions from the Note-Taking Skill box.

E Work with a partner. Compare your edited notes from exercise D. Did you miss any important information? If so, add it to your notes.

F With your partner, discuss the different aspects of Jack Andraka's achievement. Rank them in order (1–4) of how impressive or important they seem to you (1 = the highest; 4 = the lowest).

CRITICAL THINKING:
RANKING

_____ Andraka's age   _____ being able to detect cancers earlier

_____ the low cost of the test   _____ the short time the test takes

G Form a group with another pair of students. Compare and discuss how you ranked the factors in exercise F.

Speaking

> **GRAMMAR FOR SPEAKING** Infinitives to Show Purpose
>
> We use the infinitive of purpose to give a reason or purpose for doing something.
> The infinitive of purpose can come at the beginning or end of a sentence.
>
> > Elias borrowed a lot of money **in order to start** his new business.
> > Elias borrowed a lot of money **to start** his new business.
> >
> > **In order to get** a good grade, Freya studied for nine hours before the test.
> > **To get** a good grade, Freya studied for nine hours before the test.

A With your partner, think of one or more ways to complete each statement using infinitives to show purpose.

> *Howard Schultz chooses to pay employees a little more to make their lives better.*

1. Howard Schultz chooses to pay employees a little more . . .
2. Starbucks partners write the customer's name on the coffee cup . . .
3. Chanda Shroff commissioned 30 saris from Kutch women . . .
4. Shroff founded the Shrujan organization . . .
5. Jack Andraka invented a new cancer test . . .
6. The test uses a special kind of paper . . .
7. Many people become doctors…
8. People go to business school…
9. We are meeting with potential investors…
10. The company hired ten new sales people…

B Work with a partner. Take turns asking and answering the questions. Use infinitives to show purpose in your answers.

> *People take test preparation courses to improve their test scores.*

1. Why do people take test preparation courses?
2. Why do people spend time with their friends?
3. Why do businesses have to advertise?
4. Why do people drink coffee or tea in the morning?
5. Why do people go to the library?
6. Why do you take notes in class?
7. Why are you learning English?
8. Why do you use the Internet?
9. Think of one of the apps on your phone. Why do you use it?
10. Think of a popular tourist spot in your country. Why do people visit it?

FINAL TASK Presenting a New Product

You are going to participate in a role-play about an innovative product. First, with a partner, you are going to think of an innovative product or service. Then you will present your idea to another pair of students who will play the role of potential investors. You will ask the investors for money in order to start your new business. The investors will consider your idea carefully and decide whether or not to lend you the money you need.

A Work with a partner. Brainstorm a list of ideas for new products or services. Discuss these questions to help you get started. Write your ideas in your notebook.

BRAINSTORMING

1. What kinds of problems or difficulties do you experience in your everyday life at home or at school? What kind of product or service might solve some of those problems?
2. What are some problems that employees at schools, hospitals, offices, and other workplaces experience? What product or service could improve those people's lives?
3. What are some problems in cities or in the natural environment? What product or service could help to solve those problems?

EVERYDAY LANGUAGE   Complimenting Someone's Work

Good job!　　　　　*I like that idea!*　　　　　*Great idea!*
That was an interesting presentation!

▼ **Edwin Van Ruymbeke, inventor and developer of the Bionic Bird, a flying toy that can be operated by smartphone, holds one of his bird-shaped drones.**

ORGANIZING IDEAS **B** With your partner, look at your list of ideas from exercise A and decide which product or service you want to present. Then complete your business proposal.

> **Business Proposal**
>
> Name of product or service: _____
>
> Purpose of the product or service: _____
>
> How much will it cost? _____
>
> Who will want to buy it, and why? _____
>
> How will you market it? _____
>
> Will the product or service need to be tested? Manufactured? How much money do you need from investors to get started with your business?
>
> _____

> **PRESENTATION SKILL** Thinking about Your Audience
>
> When you give a presentation, thinking about your audience can help you decide which information to include and how best to present that information. Here are some questions you can ask yourself when you are preparing for a presentation.
>
> - *Who is my audience? What do I know about them?*
> - *What do they already know about my topic?*
> - *What do they want to learn or gain from my presentation?*

C Practice your presentation. Your audience will be potential investors for your new product or service. Think about your audience as you practice your presentation.

PRESENTING **D** Form a group with another pair of students. Follow these instructions.

1. Pair A: Present your proposal for an innovative product or service to the investors. Ask them for the money you need to start your new business.
2. Pair B: Listen to the entrepreneurs' presentation. Decide if you will lend them the money for their new product or service. Explain your decision.
3. Switch roles and repeat.

REFLECTION

1. What techniques did you learn to help you with note taking?

   _____

   _____

2. Which entrepreneur or innovator in the unit was the most interesting to you? Why?

   _____

   _____

3. Here are the vocabulary words and phrases from the unit. Check (✓) the ones you can use.

   ☐ achieve AWL ☐ evolve AWL ☐ motivation AWL

   ☐ appreciate AWL ☐ failure ☐ persistent AWL

   ☐ confidence ☐ found AWL ☐ potential AWL

   ☐ considerable AWL ☐ income AWL ☐ probability

   ☐ essential ☐ investor AWL ☐ recognition

   ☐ eventually AWL ☐ lead to ☐ uncertainty

   ☐ evidently AWL ☐ mission

Independent Student Handbook

Table of Contents

LISTENING SKILLS

Predicting

Speakers giving formal talks usually begin by introducing themselves and their topic. Listen carefully to the introduction of the topic so that you can predict what the talk will be about.

Strategies:

- Use visual information including titles on the board or on presentation slides.
- Think about what you already know about the topic.
- Ask yourself questions that you think the speaker might answer.
- Listen for specific phrases that indicate an introduction (e.g., *My topic is…*).

Listening for Main Ideas

It's important to be able to tell the difference between a speaker's main ideas and supporting details. It is more common for teachers to test students' understanding of main ideas than of specific details.

Strategies:

- Listen carefully to the introduction. Speakers often state the main idea in the introduction.
- Listen for rhetorical questions, or questions that the speaker asks, and then answers. Often the answer is the statement of the main idea.
- Notice words and phrases that the speaker repeats. Repetition often signals main ideas.

Listening for Details (Examples)

A speaker often provides examples that support a main idea. A good example can help you understand and remember the main idea better.

Strategies:

- Listen for specific phrases that introduce examples.
- Listen for general statements. Examples often follow general statements.

Listening for Details (Reasons)

Speakers often give reasons or list causes and/or effects to support their ideas.

Strategies:

- Notice nouns that might signal causes/reasons (e.g., *factors, influences, causes, reasons*) or effects/results (e.g., *effects, results, outcomes, consequences*).
- Notice verbs that might signal causes/reasons (e.g., *contribute to, affect, influence, determine, produce, result in*) or effects/results (often these are passive, e.g., *is affected by*).

Understanding the Structure of a Presentation

An organized speaker uses expressions to alert the audience to important information that will follow. Recognizing signal words and phrases will help you understand how a presentation is organized and the relationship between ideas.

Introduction

A good introduction identifies the topic and gives an idea of how the lecture or presentation will be organized. Here are some expressions to introduce a topic:

I'll be talking about . . .	*My topic is* . . .
There are basically two groups . . .	*There are three reasons* . . .

Body

In the body of a lecture, speakers usually expand upon the topic. They often use phrases that signal the order of events or subtopics and their relationship to each other. Here are some expressions to help listeners follow the body of a lecture:

The first/next/final (point/reason) is . . .	*First/Next/Finally, let's look at* . . .
Another reason is . . .	*However,* . . .

Conclusion

In the conclusion of a lecture, speakers often summarize what they have said. They may also make predictions or suggestions. Sometimes they ask a question in the conclusion to get the audience to think more about the topic. Here are some expressions to give a conclusion:

In conclusion, . . .	*In summary,* . . .
As you can see. . .	*To review,* + *(restatement of main points)*

Understanding Meaning from Context

When you are not familiar with a word that a speaker says, you can sometimes guess the meaning of the word or fill in the gaps using the context or situation itself.

Strategies:

- Don't panic. You don't always understand every word of what a speaker says in your first language, either.
- Use context clues to fill in the blanks. What did you understand just before or just after the missing part? What did the speaker probably say?
- Listen for words and phrases that signal a definition or explanation (e.g., *What that means is*…).

Recognizing a Speaker's Bias

Speakers often have an opinion about the topic they are discussing. It's important for you to know if they are objective or subjective about the topic. Objective speakers do not express an opinion. Subjective speakers have a bias or a strong feeling about the topic.

Strategies:

- Notice words like adjectives, adverbs, and modals that the speaker uses (e.g., *ideal, horribly, should, shouldn't*). These suggest that the speaker has a bias.
- Listen to the speaker's voice. Does he or she sound excited, angry, or bored?
- Notice if the speaker gives more weight or attention to one point of view over another.
- Listen for words that signal opinions (e.g., *I think…*).

NOTE-TAKING SKILLS

Taking notes is a personalized skill. It is important to develop a note-taking system that works for you. However, there are some common strategies to improve your note taking.

Before You Listen

Focus

Try to clear your mind before the speaker begins so you can pay attention. If possible, review previous notes or think about what you already know about the topic.

Predict

If you know the topic of the talk, think about what you might hear.

Listen

Take Notes by Hand

Research suggests that taking notes by hand rather than on a computer is more effective. Taking notes by hand requires you to summarize, rephrase, and synthesize information. This helps you *encode* the information, or put it into a form that you can understand and remember.

Listen for Signal Words and Phrases

Speakers often use signal words and phrases (e.g., *Today we're going to talk about…*) to organize their ideas and show relationships between them. Listening for signal words and phrases can help you decide what information to write in your notes.

Condense (Shorten) Information

- As you listen, focus on the most important ideas. The speaker will usually repeat, define, explain, and/or give examples of these ideas. Take notes on these ideas.

    Speaker: *The Itaipu Dam provides about 20% of the electricity used in Brazil, and about 75% of the electricity used in Paraguay. That electricity goes to millions of homes and businesses, so it's good for the economy of both countries.*

    Notes: Itaipu Dam → electricity: Brazil 20%, Paraguay 75%

- Don't write full sentences. Write only key words (nouns, verbs, adjectives, and adverbs), phrases, or short sentences.

    Full sentence: *Teachers are normally at the top of the list of happiest jobs.*

    Notes: teachers happiest

- Leave out information that is obvious.

> Full sentence: *Photographer Annie Griffiths is famous for her beautiful photographs. She travels all over the world to take photos.*
>
> Notes: *A. Griffiths travels world*

- Write numbers and statistics. (*9 bil; 35%*)
- Use abbreviations (e.g., *ft., min., yr*) and symbols (=, ≠, >, <, %, →)
- Use indenting. Write main ideas on the left side of the paper. Indent details.
> *Benefits of eating ugly foods*
>> *Save $*
>>> *10-20% on ugly fruits & vegs. at market*

- Write details under key terms to help you remember them.
- Write the definitions of important new words.

After You Listen

- Review your notes soon after the lecture or presentation. Add any details you missed.
- Clarify anything you don't understand in your notes with a classmate or teacher.
- Add or highlight main ideas. Cross out details that aren't important or necessary.
- Rewrite anything that is hard to read or understand. Rewrite your notes in an outline or other graphic organizer to organize the information more clearly.
- Use arrows, boxes, diagrams, or other visual cues to show relationships between ideas.

ORGANIZING INFORMATION

You can use a graphic organizer to take notes while you are listening, or to organize your notes after you listen. Here are some examples of graphic organizers:

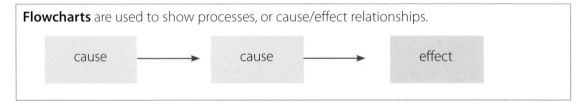

Flowcharts are used to show processes, or cause/effect relationships.

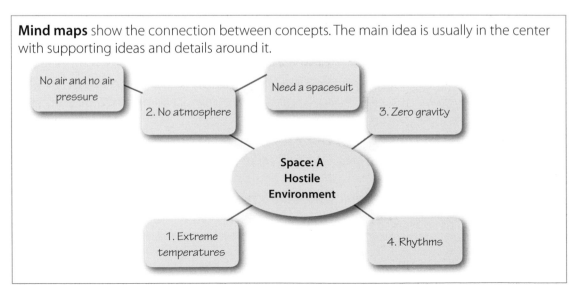

Mind maps show the connection between concepts. The main idea is usually in the center with supporting ideas and details around it.

Outlines show the relationship between main ideas and details.

To use an outline for taking notes, write the main ideas at the left margin of your paper. Below the main ideas, indent and write the supporting ideas and details. You may do this as you listen, or go back and rewrite your notes as an outline later.

> **I. Introduction:** How to feed the world
>
> **II. Steps**
>
> > Step One: Stop deforestation
> >
> > > a. stop burning rainforests
> > >
> > > b. grow crops on land size of South America

T-charts compare two topics.

Climate Change in Greenland	
Benefits	**Drawbacks**
shorter winters	rising sea levels

Timelines show a sequence of events.

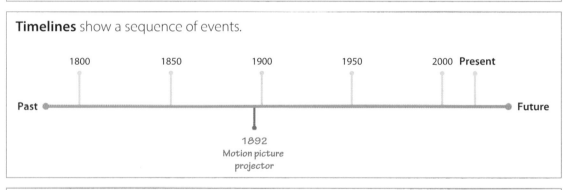

Venn diagrams compare and contrast two or more topics. The overlapping areas show similarities.

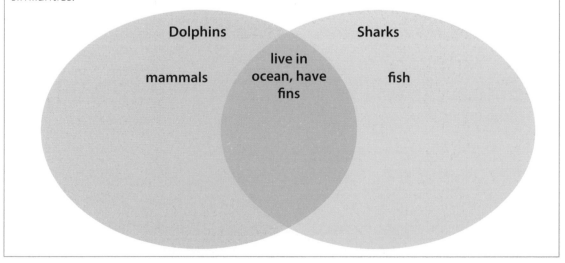

SPEAKING: PHRASES FOR CLASSROOM COMMUNICATION

Phrases for Expressing Yourself

Expressing Opinions	**Expressing Likes and Dislikes**
I think…	*I like…*
I believe…	*I prefer…*
I'm sure…	*I love…*
In my opinion/view…	*I can't stand…*
If you ask me,…	*I hate…*
Personally,…	*I really don't like…*
To me,…	*I don't care for…*
Giving Facts	**Giving Tips or Suggestions**
There is evidence/proof…	*Imperatives (e.g., Try to get more sleep.)*
Experts claim/argue…	*You/We should/shouldn't…*
Studies show…	*You/We ought to…*
Researchers found…	*It's (not) a good idea to…*
The record shows…	*I suggest (that)…*
	Let's…
	How about… + (noun/gerund)
	What about… + (noun/gerund)
	Why don't we/you…
	You/We could…
Agreeing	**Disagreeing**
I agree.	*I disagree.*
True.	*I'm not so sure about that.*
Good point.	*I don't know.*
Exactly.	*That's a good point, but I don't agree.*
Absolutely.	*I see what you mean, but I think that…*
I was just about to say that.	
Definitely.	
Right!	

Phrases for Interacting with Others

Clarifying/Checking Your Understanding

So are you saying that…?
So what you mean is…?
What do you mean?
How's that?
How so?
I'm not sure I understand/follow.
Do you mean…?
I'm not sure what you mean.

Asking for Clarification/Confirming Understanding

Sorry, I didn't catch that. Could you repeat it?
I'm not sure I understand the question.
I'm not sure I understand what you mean.
Sorry, I'm not following you.
Are you saying that…?
If I understand correctly, you're saying that…
Oh, now I get it. You're talking about…, right?

Checking Others' Understanding

Does that make sense?
Do you understand?
Do you see what I mean?
Is that clear?
Are you following/with me?
Do you have any questions?

Asking for Opinions

What do you think?
We haven't heard from you in a while.
Do you have anything to add?
What are your thoughts?
How do you feel?
What's your opinion?

Taking Turns

Can/May I say something?
Could I add something?
Can I just say…?
May I continue?
Can I finish what I was saying?
Did you finish your thought?
Let me finish.
Let's get back to…

Interrupting Politely

Excuse me.
Pardon me.
Forgive me for interrupting…
I hate to interrupt but…
Can I stop you for a second?

Asking for Repetition

Could you say that again?
I'm sorry?
I didn't catch what you said.
I'm sorry. I missed that. What did you say?
Could you repeat that please?

Showing Interest

I see.	*Good for you.*
Really?	*Seriously?*
Um-hmm.	*No kidding!*
Wow.	*And? (Then what?)*
That's funny / amazing / incredible / awful!	

SPEAKING: PHRASES FOR PRESENTING

Introduction

Introducing a Topic

I'm going to talk about…
My topic is…
I'm going to present…
I plan to discuss…
Let's start with…

Today we're going to talk about…
So we're going to show you…
Now/Right/So/Well, (pause), let's look at…
There are three groups/reasons/effects/ factors…
There are four steps in this process.

Body

Listing or Sequencing

First/First of all/The first (noun)/To start/To begin,…
Second/Secondly/The second/Next/Another/ Also/Then/In addition,…
Last/The last/Finally,…
There are many/several/three types/kinds of/ ways,…

Signaling Problems/Solutions

One problem/issue/challenge is…
One solution/answer/response is…

Giving Reasons or Causes

Because + (clause): Because the climate is changing…
Because of + (noun phrase): Because of climate change…
Due to + (noun phrase)…
Since + (clause)
The reason that I like hip-hop is…
One reason that people listen to music is…
One factor is + (noun phrase)
The main reason that…

Giving Results or Effects

so + (clause): so I went to the symphony
Therefore, + (sentence): Therefore, I went to the symphony.
As a result, + (sentence).
Consequently, + (sentence).
…causes + (noun phrase)
…leads to + (noun phrase)
…had an impact/effect on + (noun phrase)
If…then…

Giving Examples

The first example is…
Here's an example of what I mean…
For instance,…
For example,…
Let me give you an example…
…such as…
…like…

Repeating and Rephrasing

What you need to know is…
I'll say this again…
So again, let me repeat…
The most important point is…

Signaling Additional Examples or Ideas	Signaling to Stop Taking Notes
Not only…but,	*You don't need this for the test.*
Besides…	*This information is in your books/on your handout/on the website.*
Not only do…, but also	*You don't have to write all this down.*
Identifying a Side Track	**Returning to a Previous Topic**
This is off-topic,…	*Getting back to our previous discussion,…*
On a different subject,…	*To return to our earlier topic…*
As an aside, …	*OK, getting back on topic…*
That reminds me…	*So to return to what we were saying,…*
Signaling a Definition	**Talking about Visuals**
Which means…	*This graph/infographic/diagram shows/explains…*
What that means is…	*The line/box/image represents…*
Or…	*The main point of this visual is…*
In other words,…	*You can see…*
Another way to say that is…	*From this we can see…*
That is…	
That is to say…	

Conclusion	
Concluding	*To sum up,*
Well/So, that's how I see it.	*As you can see,…*
In conclusion,	*At the end,…*
In summary,	*To review, (+ restatement of main points)*

PRESENTATION STRATEGIES

You will often have to give individual or group presentations in your class. The strategies below will help you to prepare, present, and reflect on your presentations.

Prepare

As you prepare your presentation:

Consider Your Topic

- **Choose a topic you feel passionate about.** If you are passionate about your topic, your audience will be more interested and excited about your topic, too. Focus on one major idea that you can bring to life. The best ideas are the ones your audience wants to experience.

Consider Your Purpose

- **Have a strong start.** Use an effective hook, such as a quote, an interesting example, a rhetorical question, or a powerful image to get your audience's attention. Include one sentence that explains what you will do in your presentation and why.
- **Stay focused.** Make sure your details and examples support your main points. Avoid sidetracks or unnecessary information that takes you away from your topic.
- **Use visuals that relate to your ideas.** Drawings, photos, video clips, infographics, charts, maps, slides, and physical objects can get your audience's attention and explain ideas effectively. For example, a photo or map of a location you mention can help your audience picture a place they have never been. Slides with only key words and phrases can help emphasize your main points. Visuals should be bright, clear, and simple.
- **Have a strong conclusion.** A strong conclusion should serve the same purpose as a strong start—to get your audience's attention and make them think. Good conclusions often refer back to the introduction, or beginning of the presentation. For example, if you ask a question in the beginning, you can answer it in the conclusion. Remember to restate your main points, and add a conclusion device such as a question, a call to action, or a quote.

Consider your Audience

- **Use familiar concepts.** Think about the people in your audience. Ask yourself these questions: Where are they from? How old are they? What is their background? What do they already know about my topic? What information do I need to explain? Use language and concepts they will understand.
- **Share a personal story.** Consider presenting information that will get an emotional reaction; for example, information that will make your audience feel surprised, curious, worried, or upset. This will help your audience relate to you and your topic.
- **Be authentic (be yourself!).** Write your presentation yourself. Use words that you know and are comfortable using.

Rehearse

- **Make an outline** to help you organize your ideas.
- **Write notes on notecards.** Do not write full sentences, just key words and phrases to help you remember important ideas. Mark the words you should stress and places to pause.
- **Review pronunciation.** Check the pronunciation of words you are uncertain about with a classmate, a teacher, or in a dictionary. Note and practice the pronunciation of difficult words.
- **Memorize the introduction and conclusion.** Rehearse your presentation several times. Practice saying it out loud to yourself (perhaps in front of a mirror or video recorder) and in front of others.
- **Ask for feedback.** Note and revise information that doesn't flow smoothly based on feedback and on your own performance in rehearsal. If specific words or phrases are still a problem, rephrase them.

Present

As you present:

- **Pay attention to your pacing** (how fast or slow you speak). Remember to speak slowly and clearly. Pause to allow your audience to process information.
- **Speak at a volume loud enough to be heard** by everyone in the audience, but not too loud. Ask the audience if your volume is OK at the beginning of your talk.

- **Vary your intonation.** Don't speak in the same tone throughout the talk. Your audience will be more interested if your voice rises and falls, speeds up and slows down to match the ideas you are talking about.
- **Be friendly and relaxed with your audience**—remember to smile!
- **Show enthusiasm for your topic.** Use humor if appropriate.
- **Have a relaxed body posture.** Don't stand with your arms folded, or look down at your notes. Use gestures when helpful to emphasize your points.
- **Don't read directly from your notes.** Use them to help you remember ideas.
- **Don't look at or read from your visuals too much.** Use them to support your ideas.
- **Make frequent eye contact** with the entire audience.

Reflect

As you reflect on your presentation:

- **Consider what you think went well** during your presentation and what areas you can improve upon.
- **Get feedback** from your classmates and teacher. How do their comments relate to your own thoughts about your presentation? Did they notice things you didn't? How can you use their feedback in your next presentation?

PRESENTATION OUTLINE

When you are planning a presentation, you may find it helpful to use an outline. If it is a group presentation, the outline can provide an easy way to divide the content. For example, one student can do the introduction, another student the first idea in the body, and so on.

1. Introduction

    Topic: _____

    Hook: _____

    Statement of main idea: _____

2. Body

    First step/example/reason: _____

      Supporting details: _____ _____ _____

    Second step/example/reason: _____

      Supporting details: _____ _____ _____

    Third step/example/reason: _____

      Supporting details: _____ _____ _____

3. Conclusion

    Main points to summarize: _____ _____

    Suggestions/Predictions: _____ _____

    Closing comments/summary: _____ _____

PRONUNCIATION GUIDE

Sounds and Symbols

Vowels

Symbol	Key Words
/ɑ/	hot, stop
/æ/	cat, ran
/aɪ/	fine, nice
/i/	eat, need
/ɪ/	sit, him
/eɪ/	name, say
/ɛ/	get, bed
/ʌ/	cup, what
/ə/	about, lesson
/u/	boot, new
/ʊ/	book, could
/oʊ/	go, road
/ɔ/	law, walk
/aʊ/	house, now
/ɔɪ/	toy, coin

Consonants

Symbol	Key Word	Symbol	Key Word
/b/	boy	/t/	tea
/d/	day	/tʃ/	cheap
/dʒ/	job, bridge	/v/	vote
/f/	face	/w/	we
/g/	go	/y/	yes
/h/	hat	/z/	zoo
/k/	key, car		
/l/	love	/ð/	they
/m/	my	/θ/	think
/n/	nine	/ʃ/	shoe
/ŋ/	sing	/ʒ/	measure
/p/	pen		
/r/	right		
/s/	see		

Source: *The Newbury House Dictionary plus Grammar Reference,* Fifth Edition, National Geographic Learning/ Cengage Learning, 2014.

Rhythm

The rhythm of English involves stress and pausing.

Stress

• English words are based on syllables—units of sound that include one vowel sound.

• In every word in English, one syllable has the primary stress.

• In English, speakers group words that go together based on the meaning and context of the sentence. These groups of words are called *thought groups*. In each thought group, one word is stressed more than the others—the stress is placed on the syllable with the primary stress in this word.

• In general, new ideas and information are stressed.

Pausing

• Pauses in English can be divided into two groups: long and short pauses.

• English speakers use long pauses to mark the conclusion of a thought, items in a list, or choices given.

• Short pauses are used in between thought groups to break up the ideas in sentences into smaller, more manageable chunks of information.

English speakers use intonation, or pitch (the rise and fall of their voice), to help express meaning. For example, speakers usually use a rising intonation at the end of *yes/no* questions, and a falling intonation at the end of *wh-* questions and statements.

VOCABULARY BUILDING STRATEGIES

Vocabulary learning is an on-going process. The strategies below will help you learn and remember new vocabulary words.

Guessing Meaning from Context

You can often guess the meaning of an unfamiliar word by looking at or listening to the words and sentences around it. Speakers usually know when a word is unfamiliar to the audience, or is essential to understanding the main ideas, and often provide clues to its meaning.

- Repetition: A speaker may use the same key word or phrase, or use another form of the same word.
- Restatement or synonym: A speaker may give a synonym to explain the meaning of a word, using phrases such as, *in other words, also called, or…, also known as.*
- Antonyms: A speaker may define a word by explaining what it is NOT. The speaker may say *Unlike A/In contrast to A, B is…*
- Definition: Listen for signals such as *which means* or *is defined as.* Definitions can also be signaled by a pause.
- Examples: A speaker may provide examples that can help you figure out what something is. For example, ***Mascots*** *are a very popular marketing tool. You've seen them on commercials and in ads on social media –* **cute, brightly colored creatures that help sell a product**.

Understanding Word Families: Stems, Prefixes, and Suffixes

Use your understanding of stems, prefixes, and suffixes to recognize unfamiliar words and to expand your vocabulary. The stem is the root part of the word, which provides the main meaning. A prefix comes before the stem and usually modifies meaning (e.g., adding *re-* to a word means "again" or "back"). A suffix comes after the stem and usually changes the part of speech (e.g., adding *-ion*, *-tion*, or *-ation* to a verb changes it to a noun). Words that share the same stem or root belong to the same word family (e.g., *event, eventful, uneventful, uneventfully*).

Word Stem	Meaning	Example
ann, enn	year	anniversary, millennium
chron(o)	time	chronological, synchronize
flex, flect	bend	flexible, reflection
graph	draw, write	graphics, paragraph
lab	work	labor, collaborate
mob, mot, mov	move	automobile, motivate, mover
port	carry	transport, import
sect	cut	sector, bisect

Prefix	Meaning	Example
dis-	not, opposite of	disappear, disadvantages
in-, im-, il-, ir-	not	inconsistent, immature, illegal, irresponsible
inter-	between	Internet, international
mis-	bad, badly, incorrectly	misunderstand, misjudge
pre-	before	prehistoric, preheat
re-	again; back	repeat; return
trans-	across, beyond	transfer, translate
un-	not	uncooked, unfair

Suffix	Meaning	Example
-able, -ible	worth, ability	believable, impossible
-en	to cause to become; made of	lengthen, strengthen; golden
-er, -or	one who	teacher, director
-ful	full of	beautiful, successful
-ify, -fy	to make or become	simplify, satisfy
-ion, -tion, -ation	condition, action	occasion, education, foundation
-ize	cause	modernize, summarize
-ly	in the manner of	carefully, happily
-ment	condition or result	assignment, statement
-ness	state of being	happiness, sadness

Using a Dictionary

Here are some tips for using a dictionary:

- When you see or hear a new word, try to guess its part of speech (noun, verb, adjective, etc.) and meaning, then look it up in a dictionary.

- Some words have multiple meanings. Look up a new word in the dictionary and try choose the correct meaning for the context. Then see if it makes sense within the context.

- When you look up a word, look at all the definitions to see if there is a basic core meaning. This will help you understand the word when it is used in a different context. Also look at all the related words, or words in the same family. This can help you expand your vocabulary. For example, the core meaning of *structure* involves something built or put together.

> **structure** / ˈstrʌktʃər/ *n.* **1** [C] a building of any kind: *A new structure is being built on the corner.* **2** [C] any architectural object of any kind: *The Eiffel Tower is a famous Parisian structure.* **3** [U] the way parts are put together or organized: *the structure of a song‖a business's structure*
> –*v.* [T] **-tured, -turing, -tures** to put together or organize parts of s.t.: *We are structuring a plan to hire new teachers.*
> -*adj.* **structural.**

Source: *The Newbury House Dictionary plus Grammar Reference*, Fifth Edition, National Geographic Learning/Cengage Learning, 2014

Multi-Word Units

You can improve your fluency if you learn and use vocabulary as multi-word units: idioms (*go the extra mile*), collocations (*wide range*), and fixed expressions (*in other words*). Some multi-word units can only be understood as a chunk – the individual words do not add up to the same overall meaning. Keep track of multi-word units in a notebook or on notecards.

Vocabulary Note Cards

You can expand your vocabulary by using vocabulary note cards or a vocabulary building app. Write the word, expression, or sentence that you want to learn on one side. On the other, draw a four-square grid and write the following information in the squares: definition; translation (in your first language); sample sentence; synonyms. Choose words that are high frequency or on the academic word list. If you have looked a word up a few times, you should make a card for it.

definition:	first language translation:
sample sentence:	synonyms:

Organize the cards in review sets so you can practice them. Don't put words that are similar in spelling or meaning in the same review set as you may get them mixed up. Go through the cards and test yourself on the words or expressions. You can also practice with a partner.

VOCABULARY INDEX

Word	Page	CEFR† Level	Word	Page	CEFR† Level	Word	Page	CEFR† Level
protein	104	C1	royal	144	B2	stress*	4	B1
provide	4	B1	ruins	144	B1	structure*	84	B2
psychological*	94	B2	rule	154	B1	substance	174	B2
recognition	194	C2	sample	174	B2	summarize /	54	C1
recommend	104	B1	scarce	74	C1	summarise*		
reduce	74	B1	security*	94	B1	supply	64	B2
region*	44	B1	select*	54	B1	survive	124	B2
regional*	104	B2	sequence	174	C1	target*	114	B2
reinforce	124	C1	serving	104	A2	technique	174	B1
relevant*	114	B2	shake	124	B1	theory*	14	B2
reliable	24	B1	short-term	94	B2	tiny	84	B1
remains	154	B1	signal	84	B2	tomb	144	B2
replace*	24	B1	significant*	64	B2	traditional*	44	B1
report	154	B1	similar*	94	B1	trait	164	C2
reproduce	164	C1	soil	134	B2	treasure	154	B2
require*	64	B2	source*	104	B2	uncertainty	184	C1
research*	14	B1	species	164	B2	urgent	74	B1
resource*	64	B2	specific*	104	B2	variation	174	B2
respond*	14	B2	speed	84	B1	varied*	104	B2
reveal	144	B2	still	44	A2	worldwide	34	B2
rhythm	54	B2	stimulate	114	B2	zone	124	B1
risk	64	B2	strategy*	114	B2			
romantic	94	B1	strength	114	B2			

†The Common European Framework of Reference for Languages (CEFR) is an international standard for describing language proficiency. Pathways Level 2 is intended for students at CEFR levels B1-B2. The target vocabulary is at the following CEFR levels: A1: 0%; A2: 3%; B1: 32.5%; B2: 50.5 %; C1: 9%; C2: 3.5%; off list: 1.5%.

*These words are on the Academic Word List (AWL). The AWL is a list of the 570 highest-frequency academic word families that regularly appear in academic texts. The AWL was compiled by researcher Averil Coxhead based on her analysis of a 3.5-million-word corpus (Coxhead, 2000).

RUBRICS

UNIT 1   Lesson A Lesson Task

Check (✓) if the presenter did the following:

	Name		
	_____	_____	_____
1. included an introduction	☐	☐	☐
2. talked about his/her personal health and exercise habits	☐	☐	☐
3. talked about his/her plans for staying healthy in the future	☐	☐	☐
4. included a conclusion and thanked the audience	☐	☐	☐
OVERALL RATING Note: 1 = lowest; 5 = highest	1 2 3 4 5	1 2 3 4 5	1 2 3 4 5
Notes:			

UNIT 2   Lesson B Final Task

Check (✓) if the presenters did the following:

	Name		
	_____	_____	_____
1. discussed a problem	☐	☐	☐
2. gave an overview of their product and how it would solve the problem	☐	☐	☐
3. explained the target market for their product	☐	☐	☐
4. provided other important details about their product	☐	☐	☐
5. included a conclusion	☐	☐	☐
OVERALL RATING Note: 1 = lowest; 5 = highest	1 2 3 4 5	1 2 3 4 5	1 2 3 4 5
Notes:			

UNIT 3　　Lesson B Final Task

Check (✓) if the presenter did the following:

	Name		
	_____	_____	_____
1. told the class about the type of music that he or she chose and why	☐	☐	☐
2. described the music and explained where it is from, what instruments it uses, and what it sounds like	☐	☐	☐
3. played a sample of the music	☐	☐	☐
4. compared and contrasted it with another kind of music	☐	☐	☐
5. summarized the most important information from his or her presentation and answered any questions from the class	☐	☐	☐
OVERALL RATING Note: 1 = lowest; 5 = highest	1　2　3　4　5	1　2　3　4　5	1　2　3　4　5
Notes:			

UNIT 4　　Lesson A Lesson Task

Check (✓) if the presenters did the following:

	Name		
	_____	_____	_____
1. explained which device they chose and how it works	☐	☐	☐
2. explained who the device will help and how	☐	☐	☐
3. explained why they think the device is the best	☐	☐	☐
4. used the passive voice	☐	☐	☐
5. spoke at the right volume	☐	☐	☐
OVERALL RATING Note: 1 = lowest; 5 = highest	1　2　3　4　5	1　2　3　4　5	1　2　3　4　5
Notes:			

UNIT 5 Lesson B Final Task

Check (✓) if the presenters did the following:

	Name		
	_____	_____	_____
1. answered the question they chose	☐	☐	☐
2. paused to check for understanding	☐	☐	☐
3. had each member of the group present some information	☐	☐	☐
4. gave a well-organized presentation about their ideas	☐	☐	☐
OVERALL RATING Note: 1 = lowest; 5 = highest	1 2 3 4 5	1 2 3 4 5	1 2 3 4 5
Notes:			

UNIT 6 Lesson B Final Task

Check (✓) if the presenters did the following:

	Name		
	_____	_____	_____
1. had a strong introduction	☐	☐	☐
2. described the foods and drinks they will sell	☐	☐	☐
3. clearly explained their marketing plan	☐	☐	☐
4. included a conclusion and thanked the audience	☐	☐	☐
OVERALL RATING Note: 1 = lowest; 5 = highest	1 2 3 4 5	1 2 3 4 5	1 2 3 4 5
Notes:			

UNIT 7   Lesson B Final Task

Check (✓) if the presenter did the following:

	Name		
	_____	_____	_____
1. explained where and when the type of natural disaster occurs	☐	☐	☐
2. explained the causes of the natural disaster	☐	☐	☐
3. described what happens when the natural disaster occurs	☐	☐	☐
4. explained some things that people should and shouldn't do during that type natural disaster	☐	☐	☐
5. spoke at the right pace	☐	☐	☐
OVERALL RATING Note: 1 = lowest; 5 = highest	1 2 3 4 5	1 2 3 4 5	1 2 3 4 5
Notes:			

UNIT 8   Lesson B Final Task

Check (✓) if the presenter did the following:

	Name		
	_____	_____	_____
1. described a historical site	☐	☐	☐
2. included the most important facts and some interesting details about the site	☐	☐	☐
3. looked at his or her notes occasionally, but did not read from them	☐	☐	☐
4. made eye contact with the audience	☐	☐	☐
5. asked the audience if they had questions	☐	☐	☐
OVERALL RATING Note: 1 = lowest; 5 = highest	1 2 3 4 5	1 2 3 4 5	1 2 3 4 5
Notes:			

UNIT 9   Lesson B Final Task

Check (✓) if the presenters did the following:

	Name		
	_____	_____	_____
1. talked about their research destination and topic	☐	☐	☐
2. explained their research topic	☐	☐	☐
3. explained their travel plans and equipment requests	☐	☐	☐
4. explained their follow-up plans	☐	☐	☐
5. met the time requirement	☐	☐	☐
OVERALL RATING Note: 1 = lowest; 5 = highest	1 2 3 4 5	1 2 3 4 5	1 2 3 4 5
Notes:			

UNIT 10   Lesson B Final Task

Check (✓) if the presenters did the following:

	Name		
	_____	_____	_____
1. explained the purpose of their product or service	☐	☐	☐
2. provided the cost of their product or service	☐	☐	☐
3. explained who will buy/use the product or service and why	☐	☐	☐
4. explained how they will market their product or service	☐	☐	☐
5. provided the right kind of information for their audience	☐	☐	☐
OVERALL RATING Note: 1 = lowest; 5 = highest	1 2 3 4 5	1 2 3 4 5	1 2 3 4 5
Notes:			

ACKNOWLEDGEMENTS

The Authors and Publisher would like to acknowledge the teachers around the world who participated in the development of the second edition of *Pathways*.

A special thanks to our Advisory Board for their valuable input during the development of this series.

ADVISORY BOARD

Mahmoud Al Hosni, Modern College of Business and Science, Muscat; **Safaa Al-Salim**, Kuwait University, Kuwait City; **Laila AlQadhi**, Kuwait University, Kuwait City; **Julie Bird**, RMIT University Vietnam, Ho Chi Minh City; **Elizabeth Bowles**, Virginia Tech Language and Culture Institute, Blacksburg, VA; **Rachel Bricker**, Arizona State University, Tempe, AZ; **James Broadbridge**, J.F. Oberlin University, Tokyo; **Marina Broeder**, Mission College, Santa Clara, CA; **Shawn Campbell**, Hangzhou High School, Hangzhou; **Trevor Carty**, James Cook University, Singapore; **Jindarat De Vleeschauwer**, Chiang Mai University, Chiang Mai; **Wai-Si El Hassan**, Prince Mohammad Bin Fahd University, Dhahran; **Jennifer Farnell**, University of Bridgeport, Bridgeport, CT; **Rasha Gazzaz**, King Abdulaziz University, Jeddah; **Keith Graziadei**, Santa Monica College, Santa Monica, CA; **Janet Harclerode**, Santa Monica Community College, Santa Monica, CA; **Anna Hasper**, TeacherTrain, Dubai; **Phoebe Kamel Yacob Hindi**, Abu Dhabi Vocational Education and Training Institute, Abu Dhabi; **Kuei-ping Hsu**, National Tsing Hua University, Hsinchu; **Greg Jewell**, Drexel University, Philadelphia, PA; **Adisra Katib**, Chulalongkorn University Language Institute, Bangkok; **Wayne Kennedy**, LaGuardia Community College, Long Island City, NY; **Beth Koo**, Central Piedmont Community College, Charlotte, NC; **Denise Kray**, Bridge School, Denver, CO; **Chantal Kruger**, ILA Vietnam, Ho Chi Minh City; **William P. Kyzner**, Fuyang AP Center, Fuyang; **Becky Lawrence**, Massachusetts International Academy, Marlborough, MA; **Deborah McGraw**, Syracuse University, Syracuse, NY; **Mary Moore**, University of Puerto Rico, San Juan; **Raymond Purdy**, ELS Language Centers, Princeton, NJ; **Anouchka Rachelson**, Miami Dade College, Miami, FL; **Fathimah Razman**, Universiti Utara Malaysia, Sintok; **Phil Rice**, University of Delaware ELI, Newark, DE; **Scott Rousseau**, American University of Sharjah, Sharjah; **Verna Santos-Nafrada**, King Saud University, Riyadh; **Eugene Sidwell**, American Intercon Institute, Phnom Penh; **Gemma Thorp**, Monash University English Language Centre, Melbourne; **Matt Thurston**, University of Central Lancashire, Preston; **Christine Tierney**, Houston Community College, Houston, TX; **Jet Robredillo Tonogbanua**, FPT University, Hanoi.

GLOBAL REVIEWERS

ASIA

Antonia Cavcic, Asia University, Tokyo; **Soyhan Egitim**, Tokyo University of Science, Tokyo; **Caroline Handley**, Asia University, Tokyo; **Patrizia Hayashi**, Meikai University, Urayasu; **Greg Holloway**, University of Kitakyushu, Kitakyushu; **Anne C. Ihata**, Musashino University, Tokyo; **Kathryn Mabe**, Asia University, Tokyo; **Frederick Navarro Bacala**, Yokohama City University, Yokohama; **Tyson Rode**, Meikai University, Urayasu; **Scott Shelton-Strong**, Asia University, Tokyo; **Brooks Slaybaugh**, Yokohama City University, Yokohama; **Susanto Sugiharto**, Sutomo Senior High School, Medan; **Andrew Zitzmann**, University of Kitakyushu, Kitakyushu

LATIN AMERICA AND THE CARIBBEAN

Raul Bilini, ProLingua, Dominican Republic; **Alejandro Garcia**, Collegio Marcelina, Mexico; **Humberto Guevara**, Tec de Monterrey, Campus Monterrey, Mexico; **Romina Olga Planas**, Centro Cultural Paraguayo Americano, Paraguay; **Carlos Rico-Troncoso**, Pontificia Universidad Javeriana, Colombia; **Ialê Schetty**, Enjoy English, Brazil; **Aline Simoes**, Way To Go Private English, Brazil; **Paulo Cezar Lira Torres**, APenglish, Brazil; **Rosa Enilda Vasquez**, Swisher Dominicana, Dominican Republic; **Terry Whitty**, LDN Language School, Brazil.

MIDDLE EAST AND NORTH AFRICA

Susan Daniels, Kuwait University, Kuwait; **Mahmoud Mohammadi Khomeini**, Sokhane Ashna Language School, Iran; **Müge Lenbet**, Koç University, Turkey; **Robert Anthony Lowman**, Prince Mohammad bin Fahd University, Saudi Arabia; **Simon Mackay**, Prince Mohammad bin Fahd University, Saudi Arabia.

USA AND CANADA

Frank Abbot, Houston Community College, Houston, TX; **Hossein Aksari**, Bilingual Education Institute and Houston Community College, Houston, TX; **Sudie Allen-Henn**, North Seattle College, Seattle, WA; **Sharon Allie**, Santa Monica Community College, Santa Monica, CA; **Jerry Archer**, Oregon State University, Corvallis, OR; **Nicole Ashton**, Central Piedmont Community College, Charlotte, NC; **Barbara Barrett**, University of Miami, Coral Gables, FL; **Maria Bazan-Myrick**, Houston Community College, Houston, TX; **Rebecca Beal**, Colleges of Marin, Kentfield, CA; **Marlene Beck**, Eastern Michigan University, Ypsilanti, MI; **Michelle Bell**, University of Southern California, Los Angeles, CA; **Linda Bolet**, Houston Community College, Houston, TX; **Jenna Bollinger**, Eastern Michigan University, Ypsilanti, MI; **Monica Boney**, Houston Community College, Houston, TX; **Nanette Bouvier**, Rutgers University – Newark, Newark, NJ; **Nancy Boyer**, Golden West College, Huntington Beach, CA; **Lia Brenneman**, University of Florida English Language Institute, Gainesville, FL; **Colleen Brice**, Grand Valley State University, Allendale, MI; **Kristen Brown**, Massachusetts International Academy, Marlborough, MA; **Philip Brown**, Houston Community

College, Houston, TX; **Dongmei Cao**, San Jose City College, San Jose, CA; **Molly Cheney**, University of Washington, Seattle, WA; **Emily Clark**, The University of Kansas, Lawrence, KS; **Luke Coffelt**, International English Center, Boulder, CO; **William C Cole-French**, MCPHS University, Boston, MA; **Charles Colson**, English Language Institute at Sam Houston State University, Huntsville, TX; **Lucy Condon**, Bilingual Education Institute, Houston, TX; **Janice Crouch**, Internexus Indiana, Indianapolis, IN; **Charlene Dandrow**, Virginia Tech Language and Culture Institute, Blacksburg, VA; **Loretta Davis**, Coastline Community College, Westminster, CA; **Marta Dmytrenko-Ahrabian**, Wayne State University, Detroit, MI; **Bonnie Duhart**, Houston Community College, Houston, TX; **Karen Eichhorn**, International English Center, Boulder, CO; **Tracey Ellis**, Santa Monica Community College, Santa Monica, CA; **Jennifer Evans**, University of Washington, Seattle, WA; **Marla Ewart**, Bilingual Education Institute, Houston, TX; **Rhoda Fagerland**, St. Cloud State University, St. Cloud, MN; **Kelly Montijo Fink**, Kirkwood Community College, Cedar Rapids, IA; **Celeste Flowers**, University of Central Arkansas, Conway, AR; **Kurtis Foster**, Missouri State University, Springfield, MO; **Rachel Garcia**, Bilingual Education Institute, Houston, TX; **Thomas Germain**, University of Colorado Boulder, Boulder, CO; **Claire Gimble**, Virginia International University, Fairfax, VA; **Marilyn Glazer-Weisner**, Middlesex Community College, Lowell, MA; **Amber Goodall**, South Piedmont Community College, Charlotte, NC; **Katya Goussakova**, Seminole State College of Florida, Sanford, FL; **Jane Granado**, Texas State University, San Marcos, TX; **Therea Hampton**, Mercer County Community College, West Windsor Township, NJ; **Jane Hanson**, University of Nebraska – Lincoln, Lincoln, NE; **Lauren Heather**, University of Texas at San Antonio, San Antonio, TX; **Jannette Hermina**, Saginaw Valley State University, Saginaw, MI; **Gail Hernandez**, College of Staten Island, Staten Island, NY; **Beverly Hobbs**, Clark University, Worcester, MA; **Kristin Homuth**, Language Center International, Southfield, MI; **Tim Hooker**, Campbellsville University, Campbellsville, KY; **Raylene Houck**, Idaho State University, Pocatello, ID; **Karen L. Howling**, University of Bridgeport, Bridgeport, CT; **Sharon Jaffe**, Santa Monica Community College, Santa Monica, CA; **Andrea Kahn**, Santa Monica Community College, Santa Monica, CA; **Eden Bradshaw Kaiser**, Massachusetts International Academy, Marlborough, MA; **Mandy Kama**, Georgetown University, Washington, D.C.; **Andrea Kaminski**, University of Michigan – Dearborn, Dearborn, MI; **Phoebe Kang**, Brock University, Ontario; **Eileen Kramer**, Boston University CELOP, Brookline, MA; **Rachel Lachance**, University of New Hampshire, Durham, NH; **Janet Langon**, Glendale Community College, Glendale, CA; **Frances Le Grand**, University of Houston, Houston, TX; **Esther Lee**, California State University, Fullerton, CA; **Helen S. Mays Lefal**, American Learning Institute, Dallas, TX; **Oranit Limmaneeprasert**, American River College, Sacramento, CA; **Dhammika Liyanage**, Bilingual Education Institute, Houston, TX; **Emily Lodmer**, Santa Monica Community College, Santa Monica Community College, CA; **Ari Lopez**, American Learning Institute Dallas, TX; **Nichole Lukas**, University of Dayton, Dayton, OH; **Undarmaa Maamuujav**, California State University, Los Angeles, CA; **Diane Mahin**, University of Miami, Coral Gables, FL; **Melanie Majeski**, Naugatuck Valley Community College, Waterbury, CT; **Judy Marasco**, Santa Monica Community College, Santa Monica, CA; **Murray McMahan**, University of Alberta, Alberta; **Deirdre McMurtry**, University of Nebraska Omaha, Omaha, NE; **Suzanne Meyer**, University of Pittsburgh, Pittsburgh, PA; **Cynthia Miller**, Richland College, Dallas, TX; **Sara Miller**, Houston Community College, Houston, TX; **Gwendolyn Miraglia**, Houston Community College, Houston, TX; **Katie Mitchell**, International English Center, Boulder, CO; **Ruth Williams Moore**, University of Colorado Boulder, Boulder, CO; **Kathy Najafi**, Houston Community College, Houston, TX; **Sandra Navarro**, Glendale Community College, Glendale, CA; **Stephanie Ngom**, Boston University, Boston MA; **Barbara Niemczyk**, University of Bridgeport, Bridgeport, CT; **Melody Nightingale**, Santa Monica Community College, Santa Monica, CA; **Alissa Olgun**, California Language Academy, Los Angeles, CA; **Kimberly Oliver**, Austin Community College, Austin, TX; **Steven Olson**, International English Center, Boulder, CO; **Fernanda Ortiz**, University of Arizona, Tucson, AZ; **Joel Ozretich**, University of Washington, Seattle, WA; **Erin Pak**, Schoolcraft College, Livonia, MI; **Geri Pappas**, University of Michigan – Dearborn, Dearborn, MI; **Eleanor Paterson**, Erie Community College, Buffalo, NY; **Sumeeta Patnaik**, Marshall University, Huntington, WV; **Mary Peacock**, Richland College, Dallas, TX; **Kathryn Porter**, University of Houston, Houston, TX; **Eileen Prince**, Prince Language Associates, Newton Highlands, MA; **Marina Ramirez**, Houston Community College, Houston, TX; **Laura Ramm**, Michigan State University, East Lansing, MI; **Chi Rehg**, University of South Florida, Tampa, FL; **Cyndy Reimer**, Douglas College, New Westminster, British Columbia; **Sydney Rice**, Imperial Valley College, Imperial, CA; **Lynnette Robson**, Mercer University, Macon, GA; **Helen E. Roland**, Miami Dade College, Miami, FL; **Maria Paula Carreira Rolim**, Southeast Missouri State University, Cape Girardeau, MO; **Jill Rolston-Yates**, Texas State University, San Marcos, TX; **David Ross**, Houston Community College, Houston, TX; **Rachel Scheiner**, Seattle Central College, Seattle, WA; **John Schmidt**, Texas Intensive English Program, Austin, TX; **Mariah Schueman**, University of Miami, Coral Gables, FL; **Erika Shadburne**, Austin Community College, Austin, TX; **Mahdi Shamsi**, Houston Community College, Houston, TX; **Osha Sky**, Highline College, Des Moines, WA; **William Slade**, University of Texas, Austin, TX; **Takako Smith**, University of Nebraska – Lincoln, Lincoln, NE; **Barbara Smith-Palinkas**, Hillsborough Community College, Tampa, FL; **Paula Snyder**, University of Missouri, Columbia, MO; **Mary; Evelyn Sorrell**, Bilingual Education Institute, Houston TX; **Kristen Stauffer**, International English Center, Boulder, CO; **Christina Stefanik**, The Language Company, Toledo, OH; **Cory Stewart**, University of Houston, Houston, TX; **Laurie Stusser-McNeill**, Highline College, Des Moines, WA; **Tom Sugawara**, University of Washington, Seattle, WA; **Sara Sulko**, University of Missouri, Columbia, MO; **Mark Sullivan**, University of Colorado Boulder, Boulder, CO; **Olivia Szabo**, Boston University, Boston, MA; **Amber Tallent**, University of Nebraska Omaha, Omaha, NE; **Amy Tate**, Rice University, Houston, USA; **Aya C. Tiacoh**, Bilingual Education Institute, Houston, TX; **Troy Tucker**, Florida SouthWestern State College, Fort Myers, FL; **Anne Tyoan**, Savannah College of Art and Design, Savannah, GA; **Michael Vallee**, International English Center, Boulder, CO; **Andrea Vasquez**, University of Southern Maine, Portland, ME; **Jose Vasquez**, University of Texas Rio Grande Valley, Edinburg, TX; **Maureen Vendeville**, Savannah Technical College, Savannah, GA; **Melissa Vervinck**, Oakland University, Rochester, MI; **Adriana Villarreal**, Universided Nacional Autonoma de Mexico, San Antonio, TX; **Summer Webb**, International English Center, Boulder, CO; **Mercedes Wilson-Everett**, Houston Community College, Houston, TX; **Lora Yasen**, Tokyo International University of America, Salem, OR; **Dennis Yommer**, Youngstown State University, Youngstown, OH; **Melojeane (Jolene) Zawilinski**, University of Michigan – Flint, Flint, MI.

CREDITS

PHOTOS

Cover ©Angiolo Manetti. **iv** ©Angiolo Manetti, **iv** Peathegee Inc/Getty Images, **iv** CAPMAN Vincent/Getty Images, **iv** ©SAM ABELL/National Geographic Creative, **iv** ©Gerd Ludwig/National Geographic Creative, **iv** CARY WOLINSKY/National Geographic Creative, **vi** VCG/Getty Images, **vi** ©Alberto Garcia, **vi** RANDALL J. OLSON/National Geographic, **vi** ©Mattias Klum/National Geographic Creative, **viii** ©Michael Hanson/Aurora Photos, **viii** ©Stefano Politi Markovina/AWL Images/Aurora Photos, **viii** Oleksiy Maksymenko Photography/Alamy stock photo, **001** (c) Peathegee Inc/Getty Images, **002** (c) GIANLUCA COLLA/National Geographic Creative, **003** (c) Cengage Learning, Inc., **003** (bc) GIANLUCA COLLA/National Geographic Creative, **003** (tr) GIANLUCA COLLA/National Geographic Creative, **003** (tl) ©Claudine Doury/Agence VU/Redux, **004** (t) ©Helene Bamberger/Cosmos/Redux, **007** (bc) ©Pete McBride/National Geographic Creative, **009** (c) AP Images/Michael Conroy, **010** (t) Bill Hatcher/National Geographic Stock, **011** (bc) Pep Roig/Alamy stock photo, **012** (t) ©Anand Varma/National Geographic Creative, **015** (bc) Stanton j Stephens/Getty Images, **019** (bc) PSU Entomology/Science Source, **020** (t) ©Dorothea Schmid/laif/Redux, **021** (c) CAPMAN Vincent/Getty Images, **022-023** (c) The Washington Post/Getty Images, **023** (br) ©Fototeca Gilardi/akg images, **023** (cr) Photo 12/Alamy stock photo, **23** (tr) BART MAAT/Getty Images, **024** (tr) Edwin Levick/Getty Images, **024** (cr) ©Jeff Christensen/REUTERS, **024** (br) Ben Hider/Getty Images, **26** (b) The Asahi Shimbun/Getty Images, **029** (t) ©Konstantin Trubavin/Aurora Photos, **31** (t) Bloomberg/Getty Images, **032** (t) ©David Mdir/REUTERS, **34** (bc) ©RUBEN SALGADO ESCUDERO/National Geographic Creative, **38** (bc) STEVE RAYMER/National Geographic, **041** (c) ©SAM ABELL/National Geographic Creative, **042-043** (c) Maggie Steber/National Geographic Creative, **043** (tr) Ethan Miller/Getty Images, **043** (br) Barcroft Media/Getty Images, **045** (br) ©Dirk Eisermann/laif/Redux, **046** (bl) Robb Kendrick /National Geographic, **046** (br) Robb Kendrick/National Geographic, **047** (t) Gabriel Perez/Getty Images, **051** (bc) Joel Sartore/National Geographic Creative, **052** (t) ©Steve McCurry/Magnum Photos, **055** (t) JONATHAN NACKSTRAND/Getty Images, **056** (c) ©Jean-Baptiste Rabouan/laif/Redux, **058** (bc) VisitBritain/Britain on View/Getty Images, **059** (c) ZipporahG/Shutterstock.com, **061** (c) ©Gerd Ludwig/National Geographic Creative, **065** (t) ©HagePhoto/Aurora Photos, **066** (tr) Cengage Learning, Inc., **066** (t) ©Christian Heeb/laif/Redux, **69** (t) ©Peter McBride/National Geographic Creative, **070** (c) CB2/ZOB/Newscom/WENN/, **070** (br) ©Kickstart International, **071** (t) ©LifeStraw, **072** (t) ©Peter McBride/National Geographic Creative, **074** (c) ©NGM Maps, **076** (bc) ©Randy Olson/National Geographic Creative, **077** (t) ©Randy Olson/National Geographic Creative, **081** (c) CARY WOLINSKY/National Geographic Creative, **082** (t) JAMES P. BLAIR/National Geographic Creative, **082** (br) ©MELISSA FARLOW/National Geographic Creative, **083** (tr) JGI/Tom Grill/Getty Images, **083** (br) Rock and Wasp/Shutterstock.com, **085** (bl) Mike Powell/Getty Images, **087** (t) ©Woods Wheatcroft/Aurora Photos, **091** (c) ©Markus Kirchgessner/laif/Redux, **092** (t) Oleksiy Maksymenko Photography/Alamy stock photo, **094** (b) MELISSA FARLOW/National Geographic Stock , **097** (b) ©CATHERINE KARNOW/National Geographic Creative, **101** (c) VCG/Getty Images, **102-103** (c) ©Michael Hanson/Aurora Photos, **103** (br) ©Stefano Politi Markovina/AWL Images/Aurora Photos, **104** (bc) ©Christian Jungeblodt/laif/Redux, **106** (bc) ©Toby Binder/Anzenberger/Vault/Redux, **109** (bc) Liba Taylor/Alamy stock photo, **111** (bc) Keren Su/Getty Images, **112** (t) ©Rodrigo Cruz/New York Times/Redux, **113** (b) Gonzalo Azumendi/Getty Images, **114** (tr) Africa Studio/Shutterstock.com, **116** (tc) Rafael Ben-Ari/Alamy stock photo, **118** (tc) ©Gerd Ludwig/National Geographic Creative, **121** (c) ©Alberto Garcia, **122-123** (c) Tom Bean/Alamy stock photo, **126** (t) Cengage Learning, Inc., **129** (t) ©JOHN STANMEYER/National Geographic Creative, **130** (b) ©ALEJANDRO CHASKIELBERG/National Geographic Creative, **132** (t) CARSTEN PETER/National Geographic Creative, **134** (c) Auscape/UIG/Getty Images, **136** (bc) CARSTEN PETER/National Geographic Creative, **139** (h) Roy I ANGSTAFF/Alamy stock photo, **141** (c) RANDALL J. OLSON/National Geographic, **142-143** (c) Werner Forman/Getty Images, **143** (br) ©Victor R. Boswell, Jr/National Geographic Creative, **143** (t) ©James L. Stanfield/National Geographic Creative, **144** (cl) Kenneth Garrett /National Geographic Creative, **144** (bl) Kenneth Garrett /National Geographic, **146** (bc) Tuul and Bruno Morandi/Alamy stock photo, **147** (t) ©Macduff Everton/National Geographic Creative, **149** (bc) RICHARD NOWITZ/National Geographic, **150** (bc) Ira Block/National Geographic, **151** (tl) KENNETH GARRETT/National Geographic Image Collection, **151** (tr) OTIS IMBODEN/National Geographic Image Collection, **152** (t) ©National Geographic Learning, **154** (b) Kenneth Garrett/National Geographic Image Collection, **157** (bc) Dong Bui/Shutterstock.com, **159** (bc) ©Raymond Gehman/National Geographic Creative, **161** (c) ©Mattias Klum/National Geographic Creative, **162** (t) Alfredo Maiquez/Shutterstock.com, **162-163** (bc) ©Michael and Patricia Fogden/Minden Pictures, **163** (br) ©Frans Lanting/National Geographic Creative, **163** (tr) Tim Laman/National Geographic Creative, **166** (bc) iliuta goean/Shutterstock.com, **169** (c) PAUL NICKLEN/National Geographic Creative, **170** (tl) blickwinkel/Alamy stock photo, **170** (bl) tomgigabite/Shutterstock.com, **170** (tr) Derrick Hamrick / Rolfnp/Alamy stock photo, **170** (br) Sari ONeal/Shutterstock.com, **172** (t) ©Pete Oxford/NPL/Minden Pictures, **174** (bc) ©Joel Sartore/National Geographic Creative, **176** (bc) ©Joel Sartore/National Geographic Creative, **177** (t) ©Joel Sartore/National Geographic Creative, **179** (t) ©Tim Laman/National Geographic Creative, **181** (c) ©Ko Sasaki/The New York Times/Redux, **182** (c) ©Giovanni Troilo/LUZ/Redux, **183** (bc) ©Conor Beary/The New York Times/Redux, **183** (t) ©Dan Regan/Rex Features, **184** (cl) ©Catherine Karnow/National Geographic Creative, **187** (tl) Bloomberg/Getty Images, **189** (t) ©Nicolas TAVERNIER/REA/Redux, **190** (b) ©Melissa Farlow/National Geographic Creative, **192** (t) KAT KEENE HOGUE/National Geographic Creative, **192** (cr) Cengage Learning, Inc., **194** (cl) Cengage Learning, Inc., **194** (tr) ©Neela Kapadia/Shrujan Trust, **195** (t) Dinodia Photos/Alamy stock photo, **196** (bc) Alexandra Verville/National Geographic Creative, **199** (bc) BORIS HORVAT/Getty Images, **201** ©Alberto Garcia.

Maps

52 Mapping Specialists; **66** Mapping Specialists; **123** (t) NGM Maps/National Geographic Creative, **126** "The Geography of Transport Systems" https://people.hofstra.edu/geotrans/eng/ch9en/conc9en/plate_tectonics.html; **164** (tr) Cengage Learning, Inc., **165** (tr) NG Maps/National Geographic Creative, **165** Map source/credit info: SUSAN ANTÓN, NEW YORK UNIVERSITY; ALISON BROOKS, GEORGE WASHINGTON UNIVERSITY; PETER FORSTER, UNIVERSITY OF CAMBRIDGE; JAMES F. O'CONNELL, UNIVERSITY OF UTAH; STEPHEN OPPENHEIMER, OXFORD UNIVERSITY; SPENCER WELLS, NATIONAL GEOGRAPHY SOCIETY; OFER BAR-YOSEF, HARVARD UNIVERSITY NGM MAPS; **192** Mapping Specialists; **194** Mapping Specialists

Illustrations, Graphics, and Infographics

2-3 Sources: 5W; The Blue Zones: Lesson For Living Longer From the People Who've Lived The Longest, by Dan Buettner: Published by the National Geographic Society © 2008, Dan Buettner; The Blue Zones Solution: Eating and Living Like the World's Healthiest People, by Dan Buettner: Published by the National Geographic Society, ©2015 Dan Buettner; World Economic Forum, 9 Lessons from the Blue Zones, by Dan Buettner; Jill Michaels "Top 10 Ways to Stay Healthy" by Cynthis Meyers; American Academy of Family Physicians familydoctor.org "What You Can Do To Maintain Your Health"; Forbes "7 Ways to Stay Healthy" by Sveta Basroan; **14** (c) NGM ART/National Geographic Image Collection, **36** (bc) ©Bruce Morser/National Geographic Creative, **062-063** (c) ©Sean McNaughton/5W Infographics. Art: Jason Lee Photography: Rebecca Hale Sources: Globalization of Water, Water Footprint Network, Waterfootprint.org, **124** (cl) ©Bryan Christie Design, **124** (cr) ©Bryan Christie Design, **124** (bl) ©Bryan Christie Design, **124** (br) ©Bryan Christie Design, **132** (br) ©Bob Kayganich/Illustration Online, **144** (tl) Dumitrascu, Vlad/National Geographic Creative, **103** Adapted from National Geographic Magazine, 2014. The data was sourced from FAOSTAT. Values reflect domestic utilization for food consumption in each country or region from 1961 to 2011. Food groupings and units of measure vary slightly from those depicted on the FAOSTAT site.; 5W **175** Dictionary definitions for *substance and sample: The Newbury House Dictionary Plus Grammar Reference, Fifth Edition*, National Geographic Learning/Cengage Learning, 2014;

Listening And Text Sources

4 Sources: "New Wrinkles on Aging", by Dan Buettner: NGM Nov 2005, "The Secrets of Long Life" by David McLain and Dan Buettner: NGM Nov. 2005; **15** Source: "Misery for All Seasons" by Judith Newman: NGM May 2006; **16** Sources: FARE Food Allergy Research and Statistics https://www.foodallergy.org/facts-and-stats; NPR Children's Health "The Doctor Trying To Solve The Mystery of Food Allergies" Heard on Fresh Air April 15, 2013; **24** Source: Live Science, History of A.I: Artificial Intelligence (Infographic) by Karl Tate and Tanya Lewis http://www.livescience.com/47544-history-of-a-i-artificial-intelligence-infographic.html; **26–27** Source: "How Artificial Intelligence Will Revolutionize Our Lives" by Simon Worrall Oct. 2015 http://news.nationalgeographic.com/2015/10/151007-computers-artificial-intelligence-ai-robots-data-ngbooktalk/; **30** Source: Business Insider Tech Insider, "10 million self-driving cars will be on the road by 2020", by BI Intelligence http://www.businessinsider.com/report-10-million-self-driving-cars-will-be-on-the-road-by-2020-2015-5-6; **33** National Geographic Explorers Bio "Chad Jenkins, Computer Scientist and Roboticist" http://www.nationalgeographic.com/explorers/bios/chad-jenkins/; **34** Sources: "Power to the People" by Michael Edison Hayden: NGM Nov. 2015, "The Will to Change" by Robert Kunzig: NGM 2015; **36–37** "As the Trash Turns" by Eve Conant: NGM April 2016, **46–47** Source: "21st Century Cowboys: Why the Spirit Endures" by Robert Draper: NGM Dec. 2007; **51** Source: HawaiiHistory.org, "Introduction of Cattle" by Grafik http://www.hawaiihistory.org/index.cfm?fuseaction=ig.page&CategoryID=254; **52** Sources: The Villager, "Steve McCurry Sees India, in spectacular color" by Norman Borden March 2016 http://thevillager.com/2016/03/09/steve-mccurry-sees-india-in-spectacular-color/; National Geographic "Steve McCurry" http://www.nationalgeographic.com/contributors/m/photographer-steve-mccurry; **64** Source: PBS Thirteen Nova Next "The Undamming of America" by Anna Lieb April 12, 2016; http://www.pbs.org/wgbh/nova/next/earth/dam-removals/ **66–67** Sources: PBS Thirteen WGBH Education Foundation, Wonders of the World Databank "Itaipu Dam"; Encyclopædia Britannica "Itaipú Dam, Dam Brazil-Paraguay" by The Editors of Encyclopædia Britannica https://www.britannica.com/topic/Itaipu-Dam; https://www.itaipu.gov.br/en/energy/energy; **76–77** Source "To the Last Drop" by Laura Parker and Randy Olson: NGM Aug. 2016; **78** "Typical Water Used in Normal Home Activities" http://www.pittsfield-mi.gov/DocumentCenter/View/285; USGS, THE USGS Water Science School, "Water Questions and Answers How much water does the average person use at home per day?" https://water.usgs.gov/edu/qa-home-percapita.html **82–83** HealthFitnessRevolution "Top 10 Health Benefits of Chess" April 6, 2015 http://www.healthfitnessrevolution.com/top-10-health-benefits-chess/; Chessity "The Benefits of Chess" by Laimonas Sept. 12, 2014 https://www.chessity.com/en/blog/431/ The Benefits of Chess; HealthFitnessRevolution, Top 10 Health Benefits of Pottery May 22, 2015 http://www.healthfitnessrevolution.com/top-10-health-benefits-pottery/ by Health Fitness Revolution; CBS News "Which hobbies help an aging brain?", by Jessica Firger CBS News April 8, 2015; http://www.cbsnews.com/news/which-hobbies-help-an-aging-brain; **84** Sources: National Geographic Kids, "Your Amazing Brain" http://kids.nationalgeographic.com/explore/science/your-amazing-brain/; **86–87** Sources: National Geographic Kids, "Your Amazing Brain" http://kids.nationalgeographic.com/explore/science/your-amazing-brain/;Harvard Health Publication Harvard Health Review "Regular Exercises changes the brain to improve memory, thinking skills by Heidi Godman, Executive Editor, *Harvard Health Letter*; **92** Source: "The New Science of the Brain" by Carl Zimmer and Robert Clark: NGM Feb. 2014; **94** Adapted from "Love" by Lauren Slater: NGM Feb. 2006; **106–107** Sources: *The American Journal of Clinical* "The Nutrition Transition in South Korea by Soowon Kim, Soojae Moon, and Barry M Popkin: *Nutrition* http://www.ajcn.org/cgi/reprint/71/1/44.pdf American Journal of Clinical Nutrition; The New York Times "South Korea Stretches Standards for Success" by Choe Sang-Hun Dec. 2009 http://www.nytimes.com/2009/12/23/world/asia/23seoul.html; **114** Sources: NPR "Mind Over Milkshake: How your Thoughts Fool Your Stomach" by Alix Spiegel http://www.npr.org/sections/healthshots/2014/04/14/299179468/mind-over-milkshake-how-your-thoughts-fool-your-stomach; PubMed.gov. Health Psychol. 2011 Jul;30(4):424-9; discussion 430-1. doi: 10.1037/a0023467. "Mind over milkshakes: mindsets, not just nutrients, determine ghrelin response."Crum AJ1, Corbin WR, Brownell KD, Salovey P. https://www.ncbi.nlm.nih.gov/pubmed/?term=crum+ghrelin **118** Source: "On a Roll: Food Trucks" by David Brindley: NGM July 2015; **124** Adapted from "Safe Houses" by Chris Carroll: NGM June 2010; **126–127** Sources: "Safe Houses" by Chris Carroll: NGM June 2010; "Active Earth" by Beth Geiger: National Geographic Explorer: Pioneer Jan.-Feb. 2010 Encyclopædia Britannica " Chile earthquake of 2010" by Richard Pallardy and John P. Raffery https://www.britannica.com/event/Chile-earthquake-of-2010; Encyclopædia Britannica "Nepal earthquake of 2015 by John P. Rafferty https://www.britannica.com/topic/Nepal-earthquake-of-2015; "Active Earth" by Beth Geiger National Geographic Explorer: Pioneer 2009; **130–131** Sources: "Tsunami Memories Berlin" by Jeremy and Alejandro Chaskielberg: NGM March 2016; http://www.chaskielberg.com/; **134** "The Gods Must Be Restless: Living in The Shadow of Indonesia's Volcanoes", by Andrew Marshall: NGM 2008; **139** "Natural Disasters Quiz: http://environment.nationalgeographic.com/environment/natural-disasters/quiz-natural-disasters/ **144** Source: "The Dawn of the Maya Kings" by William Saturno: NGM: Jan. 2006; **146–147** Sources: UNESCO "Pre-Hispanic Town of Uxmal" http://whc.unesco.org/en/list/791; Ancient™ History Encyclopedia "Uxmal" http://www.ancient.eu/Uxmal/; Ancient Origins " The Spectacular Ancient City of Uxmal" http://www.ancient-origins.net/ancient-places-americasy/spectacular-ancient-maya-city-uxmal-003768; "A historical overview of recording architectural at the ancient Maya city of Uxmal, Yucatan, Mexico 1834-2007" by Lawrence G. Desmond, Ph.D. http://maya.csueastbay.edu/archaeoplanet/Uxmal%20History/Uxmal%20History.html, **152** Sources: National Geographic Society "Sarah Parcak: Space Archaeologist and Egyptologist: http://www.nationalgeographic.org/media/sarah-parcak/; National Geographic "Pioneer in Space Archaeology Wins Million-Dollar Prize" by Tom Clynes: National Geographic Nov. 8, 2015 http://news.nationalgeographic.com/2015/11/151108-TED-prize-Sarah-Parcak-satellite-archaeology/; "Space archaeologist Sarah Parcak launches TED prize wish: GlobalXplorer", by Erin Allweiss: ALABAMA NEWSCENTER January 30, 2017 http://alabamanewscenter.com/2017/01/30/space-archaeologist-sarah-parcak-launches-ted-prize-wish-globalxplorer/ **154** "Modern Technology Reopens the Ancient Case of King Tut" by Williams, A.R. et al.: NGM June 2005; **156–158** Source: "Geographica: Vietnam Unearths its Royal Past" by Dana Sachs and Le Quang Vu: NGM June 2005; **164** "Darwin's First Clues" by David Quammen: NGM Feb. 2009; **165** "Massive Genetic Study Supports "Out of Africa Theory" by John Roach : National Geographic News http://news.nationalgeographic.com/news/2008/02/080221-human-genetics.html; **166–167** Sources: Goldfinch (Carduelis carduelis); http://www.arkive.org/goldfinch/carduelis-carduelis; Birds of the World European Goldfinch Carduelis chloris; Belfast Telegraph Digital "What's that bird?" www.belfasttelegraph.co.uk/news/environment/whats-that-bird-28520287.html; EOL Encyclopedia of Life "Carduelis carduelis European Goldfinch" http://eol.org/pages/1051079/details; **174** "Scanning Life" by Robert Kunzig: NGM May 2010; **176–177** "Every Last One" by Rachel Hartigan Shea: NGM April 2016; **178** Source: "Discovery in the Foja Mountains" by Mel White: NGM June 2010; **184** Source: Entrepreneur "The 7 Traits of Successful Entrepreneurs" by Joe Robinson https://www.entrepreneur.com/article/230350; **186–187** Entrepreneur Magazine "Starbucks Coffee Is All About Culture...For A Reason" by GG van Rooyen http://www.entrepreneurmag.co.za/advice/success-stories/case-studies/starbucks-coffee-is-all-about-culture-for-a-reason/ , "What is the Role and Responsibility of a For-Profit Public Company?" https://www.starbucks.com/responsibility/global-report; **190** Source: "Taking Back Detroit" by Susan Ager and Wayne Lawrence: NGM May 2015; **192** Source: National Geographic Explorers Bio "Sanga Moses Social Entrepreneur; 2014 Emerging Explorer" http://www.nationalgeographic.com/explorers/bios/sanga-moses/; **193** Sources: Index Mundi "Uganda Literacy" http://www.indexmundi.com/uganda/literacy.html; Uganda Bureau of Statistics Census 2014 Final Results http://www.ubos.org/2016/03/24/census-2014-final-results/; **194–195** Sources: National Geographic Explorer Moments "Turning an Ancient Form of Art Into New Income" , http://news.nationalgeographic.com/2016/12/chanda-schroff-explorer-moments-reviving-hand-embroidery-sustainable-income-women/,http://www.shrujan.org/about,shrujan.html; **196–197** Sources: National Geographic Explorers Bio "Jack Andraka Inventor"; 2014 Emerging Explorer http://www.nationalgeographic.com/explorers/bios/jack-andraka, https://www.jackandraka.com/about

Definitions for glossed words and vocabulary exercises: *The Newbury House Dictionary Plus Grammar Reference, Fifth Edition*, National Geographic Learning/Cengage Learning, 2014

NGM=National Geographic Magazine

INDEX OF EXAM SKILLS AND TASKS

Pathways Listening, Speaking, and Critical Thinking 2nd Edition is designed to provide practice for standardized exams, such as IELTS and TOEFL. Many activities in this book practice or focus on **key exam skills** needed for test success. Here is an index of activities in Level 2 that are similar to common questions types found in these tests.

Listening

Key Exam Skills	IELTS	TOEFL	Page(s) / Exercise(s)
Activating prior knowledge	X	X	26 A, 46 CTB, 46 A, 96 A, 106 A, 112 A, 146 A, 166 A, 176 A, 186 A
Distinguishing facts and opinions	X	X	186 LSB, 187 D
Identifying main ideas	X	X	6 LSB, 7 D, 16 B, 26 B, 46 B, 66 B, 76 B, 86 B, 106 B, 126 B, 136 B, 146 B, 166 B, 176 B
Listening actively (by predicting)	X	X	6 B, 57 LSB, 57 C, 72 B, 86 A, 112 B, 136 A
Listening for causes and effects	X	X	169 E
Listening for key details	X	X	6 A, 7 E, 27 LSB, 37 D, 87 C, 96 C, 136 C, 147 C, 177 C, 187 C
Listening for numbers and statistics	X	X	107 LSB, 107 D
Listening for problems and solutions	X	X	77 LSB, 77 C
Listening for repeated information	X	X	166 LSB, 166 B
Listening for supporting examples	X	X	157 LSB, 157 NTB, 157 C
Listening for reasons and explanations	X	X	86 LSB, 87 C
Making inferences	X	X	47 D, 133 D, 152 C
Organizing the notes you take	X	X	56 NTB, 66 NTB, 116 NTB, 117 B, 127 NTB, 127 C
Recognizing steps in a process	X	X	96 NTB, 97 D
Recognizing transitions	X	X	137 LSB, 137 D
Taking notes on key words and phrases	X	X	16 NTB
Using abbreviations when taking notes	X	X	27 NTB, 27 C

Common Question Types for Listening	IELTS	TOEFL	Page(s) / Exercise(s)
Connecting content		X	177 C, 186 B
Multiple response		X	16 B, 136 B
Matching	X		87 C
Multiple choice	X	X	76 B, 146 B, 156 B
Multiple response		X	16 B, 136 B
Note completion	X		47 C, 57 B, 67 C, 117 B, 127 C, 167 C, 197 B
Sentence completion	X		96 B, 136 C, 187 C
Short answer	X		31 C, 126 B, 147 C, 158 A
Table completion	X		107 D

INDEX OF EXAM SKILLS AND TASKS

Speaking

Key Exam Skills	IELTS	TOEFL	Page(s) / Exercise(s)
Brainstorming ideas	X	X	39 A, 60 A, 98 C, 111 A, 119 A, 159 A, 180 A, 199 A
Chunking and thought groups	X	X	189 PRON, 189 D
Comparing and contrasting	X	X	60 C
Discussing causes and effects	X	X	169 SSB, 169 F, 171 I
Discussing problems and solutions	X	X	77 D, 90 G, 91 C, 98 CTB, 99 D
Discussing pros and cons	X	X	30 B, 118 A
Expressing agreement or disagreement	X	X	39 C, 75 D, 97 F, 111 C, 191 A
Expressing frequency	X	X	8 GFS, 9 C, 10 E, 10 F
Expressing opinions	X	X	17 E, 78 SSB, 78 A, 78 B, 98 A, 111 C, 111 D, 119 C, 191 A
Expressing purpose	X	X	198 GFS, 198 A, 198 B
Giving advice		X	38 ELB
Giving reasons for an opinion	X	X	29 SSB, 29 C, 39 C, 75 D
Interpreting visuals	X		17 CTB, 17 D, 31 C
Linking	X	X	89 PRON
Making predictions	X	X	86 A
Making suggestions		X	89 SSB, 90 G
Pronouncing the ends of words clearly	X	X	8 PRON, 8 A
Speaking about familiar, everyday topics	X	X	18 B, 30 A
Speaking about habits	X	X	11 D, 26 A
Speaking at an appropriate volume	X	X	71 PSB
Speaking at the right speed	X	X	140 PSB
Summarizing what you have heard		X	158 SSB, 158 C, 159 D
Talking about abstract concepts	X		5 E, 27 E, 29 B, 33 F, 35 D, 57 E, 60 C, 65 F, 105 D, 117 F, 131 B, 150 E, 177 D, 187 E
Talking about conditional situations	X	X	108 GFS, 108 B, 109 C
Talking about likes and dislikes	X	X	130 D, 130 E
Talking about personal experiences	X	X	131 C, 167 F, 185 C
Talking about yourself, your life, or your job	X		88 C, 97 E
Using correct stress	X	X	39 PRON, 39 E, 59 PRON, 59 E, 69 PRON, 69 E, 69 F, 138 PRON, 138 A, 138 B, 168 PRON, 168 B, 168 C
Using natural intonation	X	X	110 PRON, 110 F, 148 PRON, 148 B, 148 C
Using transitions	X	X	128 SSB

Common Question Types for Speaking	IELTS	TOEFL	Page(s) / Exercise(s)
Part 2: Individual long turn	X		171 B, 171 C

Pathways	CEFR	IELTS Band	TOEFL Score
Level 4	C1	6.5–7.0	81–100
Level 3	B2	5.5–6.0	51–80
Level 2	**B1–B2**	**4.5–5.0**	**31–50**
Level 1	A2–B1	0–4.0	0–30
Foundations	A1–A2		

KEY

CT	Critical Thinking
EL	Everyday Language
GFS	Grammar for Speaking
LS	Listening Skill
NT	Note-Taking Skill
PRON	Pronunciation
PS	Presentation Skill
SS	Speaking Skill